Precocious Children & Childish Adults

Precocious Children & Childish Adults

Age Inversion in Victorian Literature

Claudia Nelson

The Johns Hopkins University Press
Baltimore

© 2012 The Johns Hopkins University Press
All rights reserved. Published 2012
Printed in the United States of America on acid-free paper
2 4 6 8 9 7 5 3 1

The Johns Hopkins University Press
2715 North Charles Street
Baltimore, Maryland 21218-4363
www.press.jhu.edu

Library of Congress Cataloging-in-Publication Data

Nelson, Claudia.
    Precocious children and childish adults : age inversion in Victorian literature / Claudia
Nelson.
        p. cm.
    Includes bibliographical references and index.
    ISBN-13: 978-1-4214-0534-6 (hdbk. : acid-free paper)
    ISBN-13: 978-1-4214-0612-1 (electronic)
    ISBN-10: 1-4214-0534-2 (hdbk. : acid-free paper)
    ISBN-10: 1-4214-0612-8 (electronic)
    1. English literature—19th century—History and criticism.   2. Children's stories,
English—History and criticism.   3. Children in literature.   4. Adulthood in
literature.   5. Books and reading —Great Britain—History—19th century.   I. Title.
    PR468.C5N45 2012
    820.9'354—dc23

                                                                            2011042884

A catalog record for this book is available from the British Library.

*Special discounts are available for bulk purchases of this book. For more information,
please contact Special Sales at 410-516-6936 or specialsales@press.jhu.edu.*

The Johns Hopkins University Press uses environmentally friendly book materials,
including recycled text paper that is composed of at least 30 percent
post-consumer waste, whenever possible.

To my father, David A. Nelson
In Memoriam

Contents

Acknowledgments

I am grateful to Texas A&M University and to the many people within and beyond its boundaries who helped to make this book possible. I benefited from a Cornerstone Faculty Fellowship from the TAMU College of Liberal Arts and from a Faculty Development Leave, without which the publication of this work would have been delayed by several years. The Melbern G. Glasscock Center for Humanities Research provided a forum for discussion of my project within a supportive community of scholars who offered helpful guidance, including (but by no means limited to) my English Department colleagues David McWhirter, Mary Ann O'Farrell, Margaret Ezell, and Sara Day.

I also profited from suggestions and encouragement offered by Dennis Denisoff, Matthew Grenby, Kimberley Reynolds, and in particular Teresa Mangum, who reviewed the manuscript for the Johns Hopkins University Press and gave invaluable feedback. Joanne Allen improved the text by skillful copyediting. Portions of this work have been presented, and useful criticism received, at the University of Newcastle, the British Women Writers conference, the North American Conference on British Studies, the Children's Literature Association conference, the CUNY Graduate Center Victorian Symposium, and the 2005 meeting of the Nineteenth Century Studies Association, which invited me to give the address from which this book emerged.

Material originally published in my article "The Child-Woman in Victorian Literature," in *Nineteenth Century Studies* 20 (2006), has been reworked in the introduction and chapters 3 and 4 of the present book. An earlier version of my conclusion appeared as "Adult Children's Literature in Victorian Britain" in *The Nineteenth-Century Child and Consumer Culture*, ed. Dennis Denisoff (Farnham, etc: Ashgate, 2008), 137–49, copyright © 2008, and is used by permission of the Publishers.

Finally, as is often the case for me, I owe an enormous debt to my favorite first reader, Anne Morey, who pored over the manuscript in its various stages and provided invaluable advice.

Precocious Children & Childish Adults

Introduction

It is a truism that, to an extent not shared by any previous culture, the Victorians were fascinated by childhood. On a social level, this fascination was manifested in child-labor laws, mandatory education (with the designated minimum gradually increasing over the late Victorian and Edwardian years), innovations in the treatment of juvenile offenders and other dependent minors, and other initiatives targeting the children of the working classes. For the middle and upper classes in particular, the changing landscape of youth was punctuated by such landmarks as public-school reforms and the kindergarten movement, an explosion of texts designed for the instruction and/or entertainment of the young, the establishment of pediatrics as a medical specialty and child psychology as matter for scientific inquiry, and the commodification of childhood in visual media from mass art (advertisements and greeting cards) to Royal Academy offerings. There are of course numerous additional manifestations of the interest childhood held for legislators, consumers, writers, reformers, scientists, and private individuals; one such manifestation is our own inheritance of the conviction that childhood is an appropriate preoccupation for a mature culture. (Consider the proportion of today's newspaper and magazine articles, commercial entertainments, public policy initiatives, and overall household spending for which minors are subjects and/or audience.) In the nineteenth and early twentieth centuries as today, childhood was an object of simultaneous adulation and obsessive anxiety. Although we may not express these feelings in precisely the same way as our predecessors, we continue to participate in them.

This fascination with childhood was echoed during the Victorian era by a corresponding interest in old age, often represented as an allied but possibly inferior state. Indeed, the use of the phrase *second childhood* to refer to extreme old age, while dated to circa 1900 by such reference works as the *American Heritage Dictionary of Idioms*, was a familiar term in earlier nineteenth-century usage. For instance, it shows up in the entry on Dr. Edward Young (appropriately enough) in the 1823 edition of the *Encyclopaedia Britannica*,[1] as well as in the entry on age in the 1875–89 edition, which lists the stages of life as "infancy, childhood, boyhood or girlhood, adolescence, manhood or womanhood, age, and old age or second childhood"; in an August 1848 article in the *North British Review*, "Ghosts and Ghost-Seers," attributed to Samuel Brown, which refers to excessive skepticism about the existence of ghosts as a rejection of "the views of our fathers. . . . nothing less than a kind of dotage or second childhood of the human mind; a second childhood wanting the beauty, innocence and boundless promise of the first" (395); in an 1858 speech by Charles Dickens pointing to "that so miscalled second childhood when the child's graces are gone and nothing but its helplessness remains" (Speech 47); and in an 1861 poem by Richard Monckton Milnes, Lord Houghton, entitled "Second Childhood," which complains, "What can Childhood—made to deck/Time with early flowers—/Have in common with the wreck/Of uncounted hours?/ . . . /Nothing but the froward will,/Now without controul,/Self-absorbed, for good or ill/Of body and of soul" (lines 4–16).

As Karen Chase has noted, old age was the object of its own barrage of legislation and other mechanisms for social control or amelioration, from the governance of workhouses to the establishment of pension schemes, and "cross-generational relationships [were] an abiding preoccupation of imaginative life" (6). Thus literary pairings such as that of Little Nell and her senile grandfather in *The Old Curiosity Shop* (1840–41) sometimes showed youth and age as interdependent allies against a more powerful mainstream. At other times, or even simultaneously, however, the aged might be perceived as preying on, exploiting, or projecting their own weaknesses onto children. The ambivalent relationship between different life stages is encapsulated by an assortment of Victorian fantasies, such as *Dr. Jekyll and Mr. Hyde* (1886), *The Picture of Dorian*

Gray (1890), and *Vice Versâ* (1882), that figure the relationship between an adult consciousness and an unnaturally youthful body as at once possessive and hostile.

This book focuses on one aspect of the Victorian and immediate post-Victorian envisioning of childhood and adulthood or old age: the rhetorical tendency of that era, especially evident in fiction, to liken adults to children and children to adults. I refer here not to subtleties of characterization that may prompt isolated readers to perceive an adult character as childish or a child character as unusually mature but rather to comments within a narrative that make the parallel explicit and inescapable, such as Becky Sharp's remark in *Vanity Fair* (1847–48) that "she never had been a girl . . . she had been a woman since she was eight years old" (Thackeray 21), or H. G. Wells's Time Traveler's 1895 description of Weena as "exactly like a child. . . . [a] little doll of a creature" (44), or the plot of *Vice Versâ*, by F. Anstey (Thomas Anstey Guthrie), in which a boy and his father inadvertently trade bodies, to comically disastrous effect. The discrepancies of genre and tone evident in these three examples go some distance toward illustrating the breadth of uses to which texts of this period put this figure of speech. Although far from ubiquitous, the terms *child-woman*, *child-man*, and *old-fashioned child*, and lengthier descriptions that evoke these terms, appear frequently enough to pique the interest of the cultural critic as to the possible motivations and meanings of such generational border crossings.

The present study rests on a number of observations whose implications will be examined in detail in subsequent chapters:

1. As widespread literary phenomena used in a sense usually more anxious than admiring,[2] child-women and child-men emerge several decades into the nineteenth century, although one might point to a few isolated instances, such as the monster in *Frankenstein* (1818), before that moment.

2. Although the same term was used to describe both childlike adults and adultlike children, in function and connotation these figures are by no means interchangeable. In order to distinguish between the two at points when confusion might arise, I refer to "precocious" or "arrested" child-men and child-women. Even within these subcategories, moreover, the emotional valences of what, following Arthur Adrian, I call "age inversion" vary, although they tend to occupy one side or the other of the emotional continuum rather than clustering neutrally in the middle; whether positive or negative, some audience reaction is sought.

3. The terms *child-man* and *child-woman* are strongly inflected by race, gender, and social class. Among many aspects of working-class life that worried Victorian social observers was that poverty had the effect of shortening childhood. Thus both *child-man* and *child-woman*, when applied to a member of the lower orders of native-born British society, typically refer to precocity rather than to prolonged immaturity,[3] while conversely, the rhetoric of ethnic otherness frequently stresses the childlike nature of adult members of cultures deemed less civilized than Britain's. Similarly, the child-woman tends to be a less disturbing and more prominent figure overall than the child-man, although this is not to say that she was regarded with equanimity.

4. The numbers do not move in lockstep. In the mid-Victorian years, for instance, arrested child-men form a relatively small literary population relative to their female counterparts; at the turn of the century the situation may seem to have reversed itself. The frequency with which any of the subcategories appears at any given moment may indicate the extent of particular cultural preoccupations at that time.

5. While the chronological age of childlike adults in the literature of this era often exists outside both childhood and "second childhood," hovering somewhere between twenty-five and fifty, the adultlike child, particularly what the Victorians referred to as the "old-fashioned" child, is frequently described in terms of extreme old age. Such rhetoric highlights the general instability of age categories in the Victorian era. Chase describes "the indeterminacy of old age," the "radically ambiguous and radically theatrical" modes of being adopted by Victorian literary elders (6, 33); Helen Small points out that "the age we feel is not necessarily the same as our calendrical age, nor is it the same as how we are perceived, or how we register ourselves being perceived by others" (3). As is apparent from many of the texts examined here, the dismantling of chronological age is frequently a way of tracking power or its loss, as child-men and child-women escape or are expelled from their assigned social categories.

In her provocative study *Men in Wonderland: The Lost Girlhood of the Victorian Gentleman*, Catherine Robson argues that for mid-nineteenth-century male authors, the figure of the female child was a means for connecting with an "ideal . . . lost childhood" (179), a feminine stage considered essential to a man's extreme youth and forbidden thereafter. Some child-women and child-men clearly tap into this phenomenon, appealing through their exploitation of the nostalgic longing for innocence. Consider, for instance, Adrian's description of how Bella Wilfer shows her love for her father in *Our Mutual Friend* (1864–65):

"Bella chides him for his grubby hands. She carves his meat, she pours his drink. 'We must keep his little clothes clean,' she warns as she ties a napkin under his chin at dinner. In short, she makes a plaything of him. And if her behaviour strikes the reader as ludicrous at times, or even repellent, this is obviously not the author's intention" ("Parenthood" 10). Bella and Dickens are both aware here of the man's wish to set responsibility aside and be coddled, and since in Mr. Wilfer's case this vacation from adulthood is purely temporary, Dickens does not think the worse of him for accepting his part in Bella's game. It was not until Freud's advent, Robert Hemmings points out, that "the nostalgic becomes the neurotic" with the theory of regression (55).

Thus not a few child-women, in particular, are offered to the reader as illustrations of the idea that one can go home again—or, better, never leave home in the first place—holding fast to the winsomeness of childhood despite the press of years. But certainly this is not the only purpose to which child-women and child-men are put. Frequently their presence permits an author to critique falseness, vanity, the shallowness of immaturity, and what Small (discussing *The Old Curiosity Shop*) describes as "the 'immeasurable sadness' attached to old age, and the homicidal impulse implicit in its treatment of childhood" (194). In yet other cases, child-women and child-men may have no overtly nostalgic side, serving rather as vehicles for the indictment of a social system that can result in the contravention of natural order, or for the exploration of the uncanny and the horrific, or for the exploding of false assumptions about the triviality of children's emotions. There can be no one representative child-man any more than there can be only one representative Victorian author; age inversion is turned to different purposes by different pens, or even at different points within a single narrative.

Adrian suggests that the many "unforgettable parent-child inversions" in Dickens's works have biographical roots in "the boyhood sense of injury and rejection, the struggles and disappointments, the later frustrations of his own household," even while they simultaneously provide a metaphor by which Dickens is enabled to critique the England of his day "as one vast family with incompetent and indifferent leadership" ("Parenthood" 11). In contrast, Malcolm Andrews argues that "Dickens's lifelong preoccupation with childhood and its unresolved relation to the adult world is due quite as much to the complicated cultural status of childhood in nineteenth-century England as to the private experiences of Dickens's early life" (1). Andrews sees Dickens's handling of childhood not merely as a perennial reworking of his youth but, more, as a "confront[ing of] the cultural values forming and solidifying over the period of his own life" (4).

The present study takes a similar approach to Andrews's, first and foremost by moving beyond Dickens to some of the many other authors who employed age inversion in their writings. While Dickens is the originator of a disproportionate number of narratives of this type, and while his influence on Victorian tastes and Victorian literature is enormous, I am reluctant to ascribe the entire body of fictional child-women and child-men in the nineteenth and early twentieth centuries to the personal traumas of a single author. Age inversion's textual usefulness in this period and its pertinence to Victorian anxieties are too great to make this explanation do duty for all. It is certainly striking that from the 1850s through at least 1878 it seemed a profitable proposition for various American firms to publish a dozen abridged volumes packaging an assortment of Dickens's child-men and child-women with a minimum of adultist interruption.[4] Nevertheless, my point in raising this bibliographical specter is not only to highlight a distinctive aspect of Dickens's literary imagination but, still more, to emphasize Victorian culture's fascination with the concept.

Within the middle-class ideal from the mid-nineteenth century on, two experiences in particular were expected to differentiate adulthood from childhood: paid employment and sexual intercourse. But within the lived experience of many Victorians, of course, either or both could well occur during one's minority. Despite the sustained and earnest efforts of reformers, child labor continued to be a fact of life; if legislation curbed the numbers of children working as chimney sweeps, miners, factory hands, and so on, plenty of their peers remained in fields such as piecework, vending, domestic service, message-taking and delivery-making, and agriculture.[5] Meanwhile, until 1875 the legal age of consent for girls was twelve, and from 1875 to 1885 it was thirteen. While reformers publicized the sexual vulnerability of girls more often than that of boys, the newspapers and reform literature of the day nonetheless made plain that the young of both sexes could be found among the ranks of prostitutes and victims of sexual assaults, including incest.

Age inversion, in short, was already readily apparent to the Victorian observer, who had ample opportunity to note that traffic between the supposedly separate spheres inhabited by children and adults was an everyday matter. So, of course, was traffic between other spheres whose separateness the dominant ideology labeled natural and desirable. The consciousness was acute that practice diverged from the ideal where the divisions between masculine and feminine, public and private, were concerned, and this awareness led variously to policing—for instance, in the prosecution of male homosexuality, which was perceived as an offense against nature in transgressing gender, or of prostitution, which turned sexual intercourse from a private matter into a public commodity—and to exploration and analysis in literature and medicine. In other words, as many critics have noted, the question of the degree to which masculinity might resemble femininity recurs again and again in Victorian texts, and this recurrence helps to identify gender roles and their fluctuations as contested ground within Victorian society. A parallel, equally revealing but less thoroughly examined question is the degree to which childhood might resemble adulthood or the end-of-life years: age roles too were unstable and anxiety-ridden.

One response to the nineteenth-century consciousness that the pace of social change in the industrial era was rapidly increasing was a proliferation of advice manuals and social commentary by public sages, of whom Thomas Carlyle and John Ruskin are today two of the best-known examples. At midcentury the dominant note of such texts was to urge the salvific potential of the adult gender roles expected within the middle classes: career and parenthood, the outgrowths of those experiences that were inaccurately designated adult-only within the ideal. As Robert Newsom shrewdly points out, "The development of a new conception of the child is necessarily accompanied by a new conception of the grownup," and the Victorian grownup was accordingly pressed to embrace "responsibility, respectability, earnestness, stability, seriousness," while the child was associated with imagination, charm, and playfulness (102). In their different ways Carlyle and Ruskin—together with Samuel Smiles, Dinah Mulock Craik, Charlotte Yonge, and a host of other popular writers—preached the gospel of work, whether in the marketplace or in the home, as the cure for depression, feelings of uselessness, and fears of helplessness. Both men's work and women's work, readers were told, could reclaim not only the individual but also the family and indeed the nation from anomie and powerlessness. Similarly, society placed substantial pressure on women in particular to marry and reproduce; the drive toward maternity, women were told, was not to be thwarted, and women who failed to fulfill their "natural" function would surely be doomed to unhappiness unless they could divert their energies into some sort of substitute.

Yet partly because of the enormous cultural authority bestowed upon the concept of being an adult, which in practice often fell far short of the ideal, many writers also dwelt upon the dark side of work and family. The era gave considerable publicity to domestic abuse, divorce, institutionalized elder abuse via workhouses, and the soul-destroying qualities of working in both the marketplace and the home. Thus adults might perceive childhood as a refuge from the trap represented by the web of expectations surrounding adulthood. From the larger cultural emphasis on the need to improve the lot of children and on the spiritual refreshment that children could furnish adults, it is only a short step to the attempt on the part of some fictional adults to *be* children. Meanwhile, the awareness that children could and did—but should not have to—perform a number of adult roles, from parental figure to romantic object to financial provider, furnished cultural critics with an unexpected but effective means of discussing adulthood's negative aspects. As Paul Goetsch has pointed out, the figure of the precocious, or old-fashioned, child in mid- and late Victorian literature is often the figure of a victim. Goetsch sees the precocious child's purpose as "dramatiz[ing] the plight of children" (45), but arguably, such children also suggested to readers that perhaps the problem was not merely that children were out of place in the adult world. Perhaps the adult world was also inimical to adults.

In what follows I expand upon the ideas outlined in this brief introduction. Chapter 1 begins with a discussion of the old-fashioned child in domestic fiction, using five representative works written between the 1840s and the first decade of the twentieth century to explore this figure's relationship to a range of social phenomena. The hallmark of the old-fashioned child is the uncanny, a modality that authors often use to foreground the contradictions inherent within Victorian and Edwardian culture. As a primarily middle-class figure, the old-fashioned child exists not on the margins of society but at what authors (themselves typically members of the bourgeoisie writing for other members of the bourgeoisie) considered to be its heart. Such children are thus ideally situated to function as indicators of stress points affecting the dominant society; instead of illustrating problems comfortably elsewhere, they bring those problems home.

In chapter 2 I survey the ambivalence with which writers during the period under discussion approached the figure of the arrested child-man, and through him childhood itself. Here the distinction between good and bad, semantically expressed via the distinction between *childlike* and *childish*, depends upon altruism and purity on the one hand and egotism and criminality, particularly sexual criminality, on the other. Even so, childlike men do not command wholehearted admiration even when they are the moral superiors of the mature men around them, while childish men of the late nineteenth century, at least, are often credited with both considerable power and an enviable freedom. That the arrested child-man of the *fin de siècle* tends to differ in force and range from his early and mid-Victorian predecessor may be attributed in some measure to a post-Darwinian scientific and parascientific discourse that was passionately interested in the past's connection to the present, modern humankind's relationship to the primitive and to the not quite human.

Chapter 3 examines the stasis associated with the arrested child-woman. Early and mid-Victorian texts in particular often engage this stasis in visual terms, emphasizing the child-woman's status as art object; she is the subject of portraits, the central figure in tableaux, the object of her own gaze in the mirror. While she may be genuinely reluctant to change and mature, her inability to grow is frequently also encouraged by the paradigms of Victorian romance, since society, especially male society, may reward the child-woman with admiration and protection, a circumstance that some authors see as less than ideal. As the century progressed, female stasis, like its masculine counterpart, became a matter for speculation within the new discipline of anthropology. Whereas Victorian anthropologists and human biologists tended to be dismayed by evidence of the enduring presence of the primitive within the male, evidence that aspects of the female had changed little over time might be read as demonstrating that women retained vestiges of prelapsarian perfection. Men, much more than women, were seen as having a responsibility to grow and change, so that female stasis was deemed more natural than male atavism, rendering the arrested child-woman potentially less disturbing than her male counterpart. But when, near the end of the century, the arrested child-woman took on a political coloration with the advent of the New Woman, many commentators saw new cause for anxiety in the figure.

Chapter 4 deals with girls who take on adult roles in the marketplace and/or the home. To a significant extent, this discussion breaks along class lines: working-class girls are more likely to display economic precocity, serving as the principal wage earners within their beleaguered families, while it is typically more affluent girls who are cast as forming early and lasting romantic attachments. While we might expect both versions of precocity to be represented in negative terms, the economically precocious child-woman is frequently cast as a heroine, an exemplar of family values that the adults around her may be failing to uphold. Meanwhile, the sexually precocious child-woman is often praised for the very prematurity of her passion, which demonstrates for the Victorian observer a womanliness that is ipso facto virtuous. Instead of clinging, as Dora Copperfield does, to the separate sphere represented by childhood, the precocious child-woman embraces an adultlike agency, at least in the domestic arena. And she generally uses her power to good effect. While some precocious child-women (*Vanity Fair*'s Becky Sharp is a familiar example) threaten other families' stability through their cavalier attitudes toward maternity and the marital tie, most step into an empty space in their own families and work to preserve the domestic union, or they take an active part romantically because their instinct for love is too powerful to be repressed. Although writers may lament the necessity that brings such girls to premature womanhood, they do not condemn the girls themselves. Significantly, however, the denouements of fictions about precocious child-women often alleviate the perceived unnaturalness of the situation by removing some measure of these girls' hard-won authority.

In chapter 5 I discuss the precocious child-man. Examples of this type range from the criminal, such as the Artful Dodger in *Oliver Twist* (1837–39); to the heroic or mock-heroic, after the pattern of Jim Hawkins in *Treasure Island* (1881–82); to the comic, instanced by the shape-swapping Paul Bultitude in *Vice Versâ*; to the tragic, most notably Little Father Time in *Jude the Obscure* (1894–95) but also including briefly glimpsed figures such as the syphilitic infant in Sarah Grand's *The Heavenly Twins* (1893). Like their female counterparts, precocious child-men are often created by a family's financial hardship. In Arnold Bennett's *Clayhanger* (1910), for example, the child Darius is required to perform strenuous physical labor at age seven. Yet while the economically precocious child-woman typically succeeds in keeping her family together, Darius, Tom Gradgrind, and others may serve as the harbingers of family fragmentation, the embodiments of the failure of the father and the obsession of the son with money matters. Little Time's account of his motivation for fratricide and suicide, "*Done because we are too meny*" (Hardy 355, emphasis in original), testifies to his sense of his parents' inability to provide and his belief that it is up to him to find a solution. Meanwhile, that there are few male versions of the sexually precocious child-woman speaks to the divergence of gender roles during this period. Precocity in boys is more likely to be figured by their engaging in adult behaviors, from smoking to adventure, and particularly by their connection to financial concerns, than by their display of mature emotion.

The study ends with "The Adult Reader as Child," a brief account of what Lynne Rosenthal has termed the "Victorian children's book for adults": literary narratives that seem to urge age inversion upon the adult reader as a resocializing mechanism, a way of molding characters that might appear already set. Florence Montgomery's bestselling *Misunderstood* (1869), Smiles's *Self-Help* (1859), and a fantasy by George MacDonald serve here as the type specimens of this largely mid-Victorian textual phenomenon. While narrative representations of child-women and child-men often manifest anxiety about these conditions, then, associating them with the unnatural and sometimes with the socially destructive, authors who ask readers to adopt a childlike mind-set clearly see the process as beneficial. Of course, a distinction to be made between the fictional characters in the texts examined in the body of this study and the implied readers of the "children's book for adults" is that the readers are not being asked to regress to childhood and stay there, but to take on childlike characteristics (such as malleability) for the duration of the reading experience and then to return, improved, to their adult lives. Ultimately, such readers are not prey to the alarming stasis of the arrested child-woman; rather, they are stasis's masters.

Victorian uses of age inversion have received substantially less critical attention than the same era's uses of gender and sexual inversion. Yet the queering of age has much in common with the queering of gender and sexuality. Arguably, since age constantly changes, while gender was presumed to be fixed and deviant sexuality to be a matter of criminality, illness, or innate difference, age might seem either inherently queer from the outset or so universally fluid as to be unqueerable. Yet, as we shall see, because the identities expressed by the terms *child* and *adult*, however inflected by intersecting identities of gender and class, remain stable over the course of all but long social interactions, they too could be turned inside out to interrogate pressing questions having to do with work and family life, responsibility and desire, faith and doubt, masculinity and femininity, the primitive and the civilized, and more. The doubt and social questioning necessarily involved in any inversion of a norm, not least the age norm, provide fertile ground for insight into Victorian uncertainties.

one

The Old-Fashioned Child and the Uncanny Double

When Frederic Adye contributed "Old-Fashioned Children" to *Macmillan's* in 1893,[1] he was referring not to children who evoked a bygone era but to children who seemed like pocket versions of adults. The *Oxford English Dictionary Online* defines the term in this sense as "having the characteristics of a grown-up person; precocious, intelligent, knowing, cunning," but this definition misses some of the emotional valences with which some Victorian and post-Victorian users invested the quality. For Adye, if not always for his contemporaries, these valences are positive; delineating the concept, he writes of "that gravity of mien which, combined with natural sweetness of disposition, and brightened by the sense of humour such children almost invariably possess, makes up that delightful attribute" (287). Adye's old-fashioned child is born with "the faculty of feeling [poetry]" (290); he or she is "the most charming of comrades, the truest of friends" (290), a creature of "bright and holy innocence" (291). This is the Romantic child par excellence.

Yet Adye also notes that the old-fashioned child is often associated with death, perhaps the death of a parent, when "consequent deprivation of that sympathy which is to such children as the breath of life" results in a child "introspective and reflective beyond its years" (287), or perhaps the impending death of the child itself. "They do so often die," writes Adye, for "there is somewhat in them which is not of this world" (286). That his tone is more admiring than melancholy signals what Paul Goetsch sees as Adye's tendency to "simplify and sentimentalize the character type and do justice neither to its mid-Victorian modifications nor to its late-Victorian transformations" (46). Although his criticism is on target, in this chapter I propose a refining of Goetsch's definition as well as of Adye's. Goetsch uses the term *old-fashioned children* to refer to all precocious Victorian child-men and child-women; he instances figures from *Oliver Twist*'s Artful Dodger to *Jane Eyre*'s Helen Burns to the magically transformed Paul Bultitude of *Vice Versâ*. I suggest that the old-fashioned child represents a distinct subset of the breed and that by limiting our examination to a representative sample of children explicitly termed *old-fashioned* within the texts in which they appear, we may reach a more precise sense of the nineteenth- and early twentieth-century uses of this concept, in particular of how the concept functioned to express anxiety about various aspects of the era. Through the ambiguity associated with the old-fashioned child, writers draw attention to the dark as well as the brilliant side of progress.

The Uncanny Old-Fashioned in *Dombey and Son*

While Adye's *Macmillan's* piece also mentions Juliana Ewing, Frances Hodgson Burnett, and Lewis Carroll,[2] he cites Charles Dickens as the creator of a disproportionate number of fictional old-fashioned children. Of all Dickens's novels, *Dombey and Son* (1846–48) reiterates the term most frequently, as in the title of chapter 14, "Paul Grows More and More Old-Fashioned, and Goes Home for the Holidays." If Cornelia Blimber's school report on little Paul finds old-fashionedness a hard quality to pin down—"he is singular (what is usually termed old-fashioned) in his character and conduct, and . . . without presenting anything in either which distinctly calls for reprobation, he is often very unlike other young gentlemen of his age and social position" (155)—the reader is to understand that to "grow old-fashioned" has a deeper meaning. Dickens's working notes for chapter 8 indicate that Paul's status as an "old child" (738, emphasis in original) was always inextricable in his creator's mind from his fate: "The old, old fashion—Death!" and "that older fashion yet, of Immortality" (191; see also 740, notes for chapter 16). "Home," for Paul, refers not to the Dombeys' London mansion but to heaven.

Paul's decline and death, like Nell's in *The Old Curiosity Shop* (1840–41), are one of Dickens's great sentimental set pieces, designed to counter what Dickens sees as the businessman's ghastly ethic of hardness by eliciting tears from its audience. This effort succeeded. David Lee Miller observes that Dickens "executed [his self-appointed task of child sacrifice] with such flamboyance that England responded to the death of little Paul Dombey with 'a national period of mourning'" ("Dickens" 131).[3] But as Miller and Malcolm Andrews both point out, Dickens's real innovation was not to stir up sentiment but rather to reproduce "the child's point of view—Paul being the first child in a major English novel to offer his consciousness directly as an angle on the world" (Miller, "Dickens" 131).[4] If Paul's death is at least partly caused by Dombey's "impatient failure to acknowledge his son *as a child*" (Miller, "Dickens" 148, emphasis in original), the reader is not permitted to share this failure but must look at the world through Paul's eyes, temporarily entering into the strangeness of his perceptions; Andrews, indeed, suggests that the adult narrator's "close partnership [with Paul] is another version of the grown-up child" (114).

For Paul, then, and (as I argue in this chapter) for his later counterparts as well, old-fashionedness is located at the intersection of principles whose fundamental incompatibility is made clear even as we are asked to participate in both. In Paul's case, these mismatched principles are his identity as child and his father's insistence on his indistinguishability from his progenitor and from the family firm, Son to his father's relentless enactment of Dombeydom. Innocence and industry, both prized by Victorian society, are here shown to be at odds, so that Paul is "fashioned old" less by congenital frailty than by the requirement that he occupy the place of a miniature adult, even a miniature old man, from infancy on. As the reader learns, "some sensitive part of his nature . . . could not recover itself in the cold shade of his father," who from the son's earliest childhood imagines him "not so much as an infant, or as a boy, but as a grown man" (Dickens, *Dombey* 75, 76). This pathetic juxtaposition of childish sensitivity and adult coldness recalls one of Dickens's favored techniques, diagnosed by Henry James (writing of Dickens's child-woman Jenny Wren) as the layering of the abnormal with the sentimental: "Like all Mr. Dickens's pathetic characters, she is a little monster; she is deformed, unhealthy, unnatural; she belongs to the troop of hunchbacks, imbeciles, and precocious children who have carried on the sentimental business in all Mr. Dickens's novels; the little Nells, the Smikes, the Paul Dombeys" (qtd. in Newsom 97). The ensuing social discomfort, which enables authors to point out the inconsistency and multiplicity of significant cultural strands, is heightened in *Dombey and Son* inasmuch as the old-fashioned child, like the presumed reader, is figured as middle-class.

The narrator reinforces the overlaying of incompatible ages in one childish body. While, as Miller notes, this omniscient eye sometimes reports on Paul's mental processes in a way that compels sympathy (e.g., "But there seemed to be something the matter with the floor, for he couldn't stand upon it steadily; and with the walls too, for they were inclined to turn round and round, and could only be stopped by being looked at very hard indeed" [*Dombey* 159]), sometimes, contrariwise, he distances us from Paul by stressing the alien qualities of the old-fashioned child: for all that Paul's death wrings the reader's heart, there is in life something innately disturbing about him. Our introduction to Paul as a personality, which occurs shortly before his fifth birthday, begins the cycle. Here we are asked to focus first on traits that we might associate as much with childhood as with the Dombey heritage. If he gives "abundant promise of being imperious in after life" and has "an apprehension of his own importance," so do many four-year-olds, and like them he is "a pretty little fellow" who is "childish and sportive enough at times." Immediately thereafter, however, we are asked to focus on the strangeness in his "old-fashioned, thoughtful way . . . when he looked (and talked) like one of those terrible little Beings in the Fairy tales, who, at a hundred and fifty or two hundred years of age, fantastically represent the children for whom they have been substituted" (76). In his father's presence, Paul is "like an old man or a young goblin"; in Florence's, tellingly, he is "so much brighter, so much younger, and so much more child-like altogether" (79). This duality, like the references to the world of faëry, recurs throughout the narrative's handling of Paul. Only after his death can he become a fixed and fully sentimentalized quantity, defined (to the imagined reader's satisfaction if not initially to Mr. Dombey's) by his love for figures whom we too are expected to esteem.

In his chapter on *Dombey and Son*, Andrews emphasizes the shifting meanings of *old-fashioned* in Dickens's novel, where the term also carries the sense of "out of date." He contends that Paul inverts his "new-fashioned" father (118) and that "the rise to prominence of this type of child is closely related to the rise of the adult type represented in Mr. Dombey" (128), which it critiques and which makes childhood "an endangered culture" (134). Although Andrews's point is well taken, I want to focus instead on how Dickens's handling of the old-fashioned child intersects with the quality that Freud would later term *uncanniness*, since the uncanny, along with the embodiment of dueling but socially valued principles, comes to be a hallmark of old-fashioned children throughout the period. In his 1919 essay "The 'Uncanny'" Freud defines his subject as "that class of the frightening which leads back to what is known of old and long familiar" (620), much as John Forster in his *Life of Charles Dickens* quotes the author as reporting, in a passage written during the writing of *Dombey and Son*, that "I often forget in my dreams that I have a dear wife and children; even that I am a man; and wander desolately back to that time of my life [the traumatic sojourn in the blacking warehouse at age twelve]" (53).[5]

Connecting the uncanny to "something repressed which *recurs*" ("'Uncanny'" 634, emphasis in original), Freud finds that "animism, magic and sorcery, the omnipotence of thoughts, man's attitude to death, involuntary repetition and the castration complex comprise practically all the factors which turn something frightening into something uncanny" (635). It is suggestive, however, that his conclusion that "an uncanny experience occurs either when infantile complexes which have been repressed are once more revived by some impression, or when primitive beliefs which have been surmounted seem once more to be confirmed" (639) is one of more than two dozen times within the essay when Freud mentions children, childhood, or the infantile without ever fully developing the connection of childhood to the uncanny. Phillip McCaffrey, indeed, contends that behind Freud's overt discussion lurk two archetypes, "the Urgent Child and the Archaic Father" (373). McCaffrey's description of Freud's use (and misquoting or eliding) of these figures both in "The 'Uncanny'" and in his work on dreams suggests not only that both had qualities of the child-man for Freud but also that these qualities rendered the figures sufficiently uncanny to require repression by the psychoanalyst himself.[6]

Particularly pertinent in "The 'Uncanny'" to treatments of the old-fashioned child in *Dombey* and elsewhere is Freud's discussion of the double as a source of uncanniness. Doubles, Freud notes, may look alike or think so similarly that they communicate telepathically, but it may also be the case that "the subject . . . is in doubt as to which his self is, or substitutes the extraneous self for his own. In other words, there is a doubling, dividing and interchanging of the self. And finally there is the constant recurrence of the same thing—the repetition of the same features or character-traits or vicissitudes, of the same crimes, or even the same names through several consecutive generations" (629–30). Compare here the remark of *Dombey*'s narrator that at no time did [Paul] fall into [old-fashionedness] so surely, as when, his little chair being carried down into his father's room, he sat there with him after dinner, by the fire. They were the strangest pair at such a time that ever firelight shone upon. Mr. Dombey so erect and solemn, gazing at the blaze; his little image, with an old, old, face, peering into the red perspective with the fixed and rapt attention of a sage. Mr. Dombey entertaining complicated worldly schemes and plans; the little image entertaining Heaven knows what wild fancies, half-formed thoughts, and wandering speculations. Mr. Dombey stiff with starch and arrogance; the little image by inheritance, and in unconscious imitation. The two so very much alike, and yet so monstrously contrasted. (77)

Throughout, it is specifically association with his father that renders Paul an eerie figure. As Paul later explains his father to his schoolmate Toots, "He's Dombey and Son" (130), a locution that asserts Dombey's lack of proper borders not only vis-à-vis his business but also vis-à-vis his heir apparent. Drawing on the work of Otto Rank, Freud remarks that historically, a culture's desire to construct a double springs "from the soil of unbounded self-love, from the primary narcissism which dominates the mind of the child and of primitive man. But when this stage has been surmounted, the 'double' reverses its aspect. From having been an assurance of immortality, it becomes the uncanny harbinger of death" (630). *Dombey and Son* transfers this process from society to the individual, but with a twist: far from giving way to another outlook (a consummation that will not occur until the end of the novel), Dombey's narcissism in effect creates little Paul as the "uncanny harbinger" of the child's demise, the destruction of the family firm, and the father's enforced re-formation as grandfather to yet another set of doubles, Paul the third and Florence the second. The "monstrous" old-fashionedness of the original little Paul Dombey marks the excessive presence of Dombey himself.[7]

In *Strange and Secret Peoples: Fairies and Victorian Consciousness*, Carole Silver examines the Victorian preoccupation with changelings, which, she argues, functioned on a folk level to explain phenomena otherwise baffling to nineteenth-century medicine (such as certain metabolic disorders, progeria, and homocystinuria) and gave folklorists and other scholars a lens for the discussion of regression, reversion, and humankind's less evolved past (59–87). Paul Dombey, the "old child" identified as a changeling in the narrator's comment (quoted above) about "those terrible little Beings in the Fairy tales," does not share the mental incapacity characteristic of many Victorian changelings. Even so, writes Silver, he and other "sympathetically depicted" changelings "are still perceived as outsiders and aliens, threatening the established order and social norms by their very difference" and highlighting "an almost innate Victorian fear of the 'other'" (80). I would suggest that Paul's uncanny otherness is a threat not so much to the larger social order (that which incorporates everyone from the Blimbers to Miss Tox to Captain Cuttle to Polly Toodle) as to the specific order represented by Dombey, by Dickens's youthful experience in the blacking warehouse, and even by the author's own conspicuous failures as a father to sons who found it hard to mature in his shadow: the childhood-stealing order, the identity-usurping order, associated in *Dombey* with commerce but in other novels with phenomena such as imperialism, education, and more. If Paul is described as sly and goblinlike, he is also a figure of innocence—an innocence so imbricated with its own opposite that its possessor cannot live.

In other words, Paul is doomed less because he is an outsider, to use Silver's term, than because he must exist simultaneously as outsider (innocent child) and insider (son and heir to the thriving business concern of Dombey and Son). Consider the emblematic moment at which he "begin[s] to be Dombey and Son" by furnishing money to Walter's uncle, "turn[ing] up the old face for a moment" and "a young and childish face immediately afterwards" (112). On the one hand, Sol Gills stands in desperate need of the loan, while on the other, the transaction puts the Wooden Midshipman in the power of the larger business and relegates Walter to the position of inferior. As Dombey notes, we see here "how powerful money is" (112), and like most Victorians, Dickens is keenly aware that the power in question may be used for good or for ill, and even for both at once. The double, of course, is a likeness with a difference, the same and yet not the same, and those who encounter it are typically invited to experience a doubled affect as well, responding one way toward one avatar and another toward its uncanny likeness. The texts examined in this chapter recognize and indeed help to create such feelings of ambiguity. Like imperialism, education, and other issues around which (as we shall see) Dickens's successors constructed old-fashioned children, the great commercial advances of Victorian Britain are a source simultaneously of national pride and national anxiety.

Silver's discussion is particularly useful in that it places little Paul in the context of explorations of the Victorian mind-set by authors other than Dickens, since changeling references appear in texts from horror stories to news reportage. Not all changelings are old-fashioned children, and not all old-fashioned children are changelings; indeed, there is perhaps less overlap between the categories than we might expect, since changelings are likely to populate works of fantasy, while old-fashioned children are more commonly found in works in the realist mode.[8] What, then, distinguishes old-fashioned children from other forms of the precocious child-man or child-woman? I propose that at least within the tale of family life, the hallmark of the breed is the frisson of abnormality—represented sometimes as attractive, sometimes as repellent—arising from circumstances that may differ in their particulars and varying in the degree of their uncanniness, but typically involving both doubling and mismatching, as these figures are required to embody principles that are at once incompatible with one another and central to Victorian society.

Kathleen Woodward sees a similar association between the aged, decrepit body and the uncanny double (56). Writing of Freud's encounter, in a sleeping compartment on a train, with an intrusive elderly man whom he perceived as eerie and unpleasant before realizing that he was seeing himself in a mirrored door, Woodward notes that the image "is uncanny because it is something familiar that has been repressed—Freud's own old age," a moment that reveals another significant, repression-born lacuna in Freudian theory: "By interpreting everything in terms of infantile psychology and the primitive stage of the development of the human species, Freud was unable to even formulate the possibility that there could be a psychoanalytic stage of development and conflict associated with old age" (57). Woodward sees in the uncanny elderly double a prefiguration, for more than one writer, of suffering, loss of ability, and gradual and tragic estrangement of the self. Although little Paul Dombey is young, the illness and death of this old-fashioned child function in much the same way for his father, for whom the loss of Paul is merely one important episode in a protracted process that involves Paul senior's own movement from independent middle age to a humbled second childhood spent playing with his grandchildren. In the two Paul Dombeys, the old-fashioned child stretches from childhood to maturity to old age, his uncanny voluminousness suggesting an indeterminacy that is anathema to the category-loving Dombey whom we originally encounter and illustrating more generally how the erasure of the "child" under the pressures of powerful age may destabilize the latter as well as the former.

Mary's Meadow and the Anxiety of Territory

Silver sees a frequent link in Victorian texts between changeling imagery and mental retardation. By contrast, old-fashioned children are more likely to be figured as intellectually precocious, part of what David Grylls identifies as a lengthy tradition of child prodigies (36), than as developmentally delayed. One of the few exceptions, Christopher in *Mary's Meadow* (1883–84), a novella by the successful writer for children Juliana Ewing, has a head "rather large for his body, with some water having got into his brain when he was very little, so that we have to take great care of him"; even so, notes the narrator (his oldest sister, Mary), "though he does say very odd things, very slowly, I do not think any one of us tries harder to be good" (10). Yet Chris's virtue has its limits: Mary continues that he "is very simple, but sometimes we think he is also a little sly" (11–12). Slyness, a characteristic we have already seen noted in little Paul Dombey, marks a disjuncture between what is said or done and what is felt. This disjuncture is thematically connected to the novella's use of doubling and mismatching, which extends beyond Chris to the other children in the family but is especially prone to involve him.

Mary's Meadow recounts the efforts of Mary, herself a child-woman in that she is her siblings' "Little Mother" (13), to entertain the other children through imaginative play centering on the title piece of property. The meadow, which belongs to the curmudgeonly local squire, is a point of contention between its owner and the children's hot-tempered father, who claims a right-of-way through it to one of his own fields. For both men, the meadow's primary use is as a symbol of their own territorial prerogatives. For the children, however, the meadow is a place to cultivate for its own sake. Mary in particular sows it with flowers, and ultimately the Squire makes the title over to her as atonement for having wrongfully accused her of theft. As Marah Gubar notes, the meadow is symbolic not merely for the adult male characters but also for Ewing: "Here and elsewhere in Golden Age children's literature, gardening provides a rich metaphor for creativity and the development of selfhood" (*Dodgers* 56). The garden, then, doubles all the children, foremost among them Mary as its chief caretaker and eventual owner.

Yet this doubling is prefigured by earlier doublings centered not on Mary but on Chris. These begin when Chris, his mother, and Aunt Catherine go abroad for his health and the children are visited by the Squire's dog, Saxon. Mary reports that "we told [Saxon] all about it, and he looked very sorry. Then we said that he should be our brother in Christopher's stead, whilst Chris was away; and he looked very much pleased, and wagged his tail, and licked our faces all round" (13). In the Squire's view, Saxon is a fierce guard dog devoted to protecting his master's interests; in that of the children, he is their playmate and the originator of the role of the Dwarf (later given to Chris) in their game; in that of the Squire's gardener, he is an annoying invader of spaces that he has no right to occupy. At one point the gardener kicks the dog for walking on Mary's garden plot. Later he says of the children's father's library, "It's a rare privilege, the free entry of a book chamber like this. I'm hoping, young gentleman, that you're not insensible of it?" And then, noticing that Saxon has illicitly joined the group, he "beat[s] him out of the room with his hat" (20). The "young gentleman" in question is not Chris but his oldest brother, for Chris, like Saxon, cannot read.

Gubar and Donald Hall separately discuss the relationship of *Mary's Meadow* to imperialist ideology. While they reach different conclusions, both see "the Squire and his bulldog . . . [as] complacent actors in the colonial game" (Hall 53) and Chris's question about whether, if Mary "could dig through to the other side of the world, [there could] be a field the same size in Australia that would be hers" (Ewing 90) as the articulation of a selfish and masculinist imperialism. "If Chris goes on as he has begun," Gubar remarks, "he runs the risk of turning into another Squire," unlike Mary, whom Gubar sees as the voice for a feminine, anti-imperialist sensibility (*Dodgers* 63). Yet it is worth noting that just as Saxon is not, in fact, the ferocious guardian of property that his owner desires—at story's end, the Squire talks about replacing him with a more reliably vicious mastiff, while his forays into others' territory, which the children recognize as friendly rather than warlike, are repeatedly punished by the gardener—Chris is not well equipped for colonizing or for landholding. Rather, as a hydrocephalic child in an era that lacked effective treatment for this condition, he is more likely to regress to infancy than to become a soldier, settler, or squire.[9] His association with the Dwarf, which implies thwarted development and its ties to Victorian notions of primitive survivals (discussed in chapter 2), suggests that he is better cast as the victim than as the villain of aggressive enterprises of expansion.

Chris thus embodies key contradictions: he is at once human and animal, "large-headed" (11) and intellectually impaired, akin to the Squire in his assertive expansionism and to the servant Bessy's aunt in his self-identification with the double cowslips that she donates to the meadow. In his multiple roles, he plays an especially active part in moving forward the action of the story. Because he lacks the social inhibitions that characterize the other children— "Chris is never afraid of [father]" (58); "[Lady Catherine] likes him far better than any one of us, and he is very fond of her; and they say quite rude things to each other all along" (12)—it is he who recruits the redoubtable Aunt Catherine into their game and thus demonstrates that it can extend beyond a single household, and he who ventures forth to find that the double cowslips have taken root in the meadow and thus brings about the denouement in the conversion of the Squire. Mary's virtue lies in part in her feminine readiness to resist asserting herself, which enables the development of the cooperative game along lines that she has not initially envisioned and that ultimately lead to her being endowed with the land but which also threatens to end the game forever when she permits the angry Squire to chase her off the property. Christopher's "Christ-bearing" virtue, the necessary complement to Mary's, resides in his unselfconscious extension into otherness—of which, as an old-fashioned child, he is the natural representative.

If we accept the argument that the novella is a comment on imperialism, we are faced with the question whether this comment is positive or negative. Yet this question is not readily settled. Hall sees Ewing's text as "a very effective mechanism through which cultural ideology is transmitted; the young reader is invited to participate in and identify with an imperial project" in part because the project promises "stability" (53). Gubar disagrees, classifying *Mary's Meadow* with Ewing's *A Great Emergency* and *We and the World* as works that "characterize imperialism as a morally suspect form of masculine overreaching" (*Dodgers* 63). The evident difficulty of reaching consensus on Ewing's meaning highlights the ambiguity on display here. I propose that this ambiguity is situated primarily in Chris, that "sly" but "simple" child whose expressions of desire for emoluments ranging from a hedgehog to multiple titles within the game are balanced by gestures of renunciation. His reiterated muttering as he prepares to end a quarrel with one of his brothers by surrendering a favored toy, *"Dos first and feels afterwards"* (11, emphasis in original), acknowledges the possibility of a discrepancy between action and sentiment. That a similar discrepancy might manifest itself in an imperialist enterprise motivated at once by self-interest and by idealism was no secret to thoughtful Victorians in an era in which empire was both a matter for celebration and a source of deep anxiety. In combination with a disability that renders healthy maturity unlikely, Chris's assertions of masculine privilege (e.g., " 'But you and Adela are girls,' said Chris complacently. 'The boys have two names'" [57]) have a pathetic ring. Although his old-fashionedness enables him to assert himself with adult confidence in social situations that intimidate his siblings, it also presages that confidence's end.

Elf and the Anxiety of Patriarchy

That Chris's old-fashionedness results from a medical problem beyond his family's control deviates from the general pattern in domestic tales involving old-fashioned children, which usually suggest that a strong environmental factor has helped to create this condition. Such fictions proliferated during and after the 1880s, perhaps partly in response to changes in the social construction of childhood. Grylls notes that "the big child-parent issue of the eighties was institutionalised prevention of cruelty" (65); and Monica Flegel observes in her study of the London (later National) Society for the Prevention of Cruelty to Children, founded in 1884 in emulation of similar organizations in New York and Liverpool, that the organization found it important to represent "cruelty to children . . . [as] a classless crime," affecting "children and families from a variety of backgrounds, from the poorest of the poor to the very wealthy" (*Cruelty* 21). Once sacrosanct, parental—and specifically paternal—authority was under attack throughout the Victorian and Edwardian years, but particularly from the 1870s on, as men's custody and decision-making rights over their children were first challenged and then limited by the courts (see Nelson, *Men* 109–37). What Grylls terms "the 'soft' school" of child management had come to dominate over more authoritarian approaches in the 1850s (54), and the concept of the callous, brutal, or simply misguided parent was receiving extensive publicity. Over the Victorian period, writers developed many ways of discussing parental absence or failure, from criminal case histories to temperance tracts. The fascination with precocious child-men and child-women, including old-fashioned children, may be more oblique than many but often manifests the same anxiety.

The father in *Mary's Meadow*, though somewhat intimidating because of his hot temper, receives little narrative attention and cannot be held responsible for his son's hydrocephaly. Fathers in other domestic or quasi-domestic texts involving old-fashioned children are more culpable. As we shall see, the overbearing nature of Dickens's Dombey is recapitulated in *The Mighty Atom*'s Mr. Valliscourt, just as the reclamation of Professor Cadman-Gore in the same novel recalls Dombey's eventual salvation through sentiment. Conversely, the absence of Captain Crewe in *A Little Princess*, initially treated as natural and indeed motivated by a desire for his daughter's well-being, in due course brings Sara to misery and even danger. Captain Crewe dies, leaving his paternal responsibilities to another man, and the latter is doomed to invalidism mental and physical until he can take the Captain's place at Sara's side. In both cases, the child's old-fashionedness is exacerbated or even created by the father's error.

Jeanie Hering's *Elf* (1887) conforms to this pattern as well—with the minor variation that a custodial grandfather is substituted for the father, thus permitting direct parallels to be drawn between youth and old age—but offers comfort by suggesting that although certainly undesirable, old-fashionedness is a reversible condition, treatable by transferring child-rearing decisions into feminine hands.[10] The name by which the title character is known nods, à la Dickens, to the world of faëry. Elf is introduced to us as a neurotic problem child

> whose age it would have been impossible to guess—she might have been any age between five and ten. She was a slender, fragile little thing, with small, pointed, sensitive features, too delicate-looking to be exactly pretty, with a fair skin like a lily, too perfectly colourless, in spite of all the breezes which blew round the desolate old house where she lived. Her quick, intelligent eyes travelled restlessly and ceaselessly in every direction, and there was a nervous, quivering, twitching movement of her face; even her fingers shared the restless disquiet which seemed to have possession of her. (14–15)

The child's nervousness may derive in part from trauma in infancy. She is the only grandchild of a Scots laird, Murray of Auchinvellan, whose ten children are all dead. Late in the novel we learn that Elf's parents were the laird's third son and his immoral wife, who was responsible for the deaths of her two older brothers-in-law. One day, Auchinvellan visits his estranged son only to find "him lying dead, and a frail wee lassie of two years old asleep, with her head on her dead father's face, and her mother away with her relations, having fled away from sorrow and darkness. Auchinvellan took away his own, his dead son and his grandchild, and sent her word never to approach him or his again; and she married again almost directly" (131–32).

But despite this background of female frailty and outraged male virtue, Elf's fundamental problem is her closeness to her grandfather. As an elderly servant, David, chides Auchinvellan, "She shouldna be a companion to you, but have young companions of her own age; it's easy seen she's different to other children, in being so old-fashioned and cute, and I am sorry to see it. People have enough to bear through life, without looking serious when they are babies" (80). Like little Paul Dombey, Elf doubles the patriarch to uncanny effect, even down to wearing a scaled-down version of his favorite Balmoral cap and reading unused volumes of works that he is studying. David remarks, "Chips from the same block, she's as like you as two peas; but they [observers] turn away with a sigh, because the child is not as a child" (81). Auchinvellan, "who had ruled his own children with a rod of iron," is described as insufficiently masterful where Elf is concerned (33). Yet her practice of imitating his actions, habits, and outlook suggests that he merely accomplishes mastery in a different way. His reluctance to discipline Elf for fear of once again "turn[ing] a loved child from me with sternness and hardness" (70), his position as her caregiver and companion, and the powerful influence that he has over her all hint that he has expunged her mother by providing his own version of maternity.

Inflicted disproportionately by Elf's mother, Auchinvellan's family losses have prompted him to fear the incursions of the female world, in particular, as heralds of a mortality and diminution of power that he is initially unable to face. As the narrative begins, he has sought to locate all authority in himself, effectively colonizing his granddaughter in order to hold other threats at bay. For instance, he has taken on the role, unusual in a man of his rank, of Elf's teacher instead of employing a governess or sending Elf to school. While ostensibly this decision results from a fear that Elf, a difficult and temperamental child, might otherwise reject education altogether, and she is happy to be so close to her grandfather, onlookers perceive something disturbing and unhealthy manifested in the girl as a result. Thus when Bluebell Nicol, the embodiment of ideal femininity within the novel, initially encounters Elf, whom she immediately identifies as "a weird, uncanny bit thing" (14),

> the first thing that impressed itself on Bluebell's mind was, "That child is being brought up without any woman around her."
>
> And Bluebell was now so much of a woman herself, that the thought haunted her; she scarce knew why; she instinctively felt something was wrong. (15–16)

The "something wrong" may be set right via a reorganization of Elf's life, however. Misguided, Auchinvellan is nonetheless easier to redeem than Dombey. He can listen to others' concerns, and having done so, "a shadow of a doubt came over him. He and the child were all-in-all to one another, sharing the same pursuits and habits, and her mind had been prematurely developed; all had been happy and free from care up to the present time, but the result was the child differed from other children of her own age. Was this right?" (31–32). That this question arises at the beginning rather than the end of the novel enables its successful resolution as Auchinvellan rethinks the coopting of the maternal that prompted his adoption of his granddaughter and his banishment of her mother. In contrast to Dombey, whose tragedy is that he invariably surrenders too late his preconceived notions, the aging laird, made aware by painful experience that death is inevitable for all, can retract the projecting of himself into the child through which he evidently hoped at one time to stave off his own end.

The first step in healing Elf is to furnish her with a potential role model more suitable than her grandfather: Theo, the daughter of the local minister. Theo shares Elf's motherless state, her age, her lack of siblings, and her surname, and while at the outset their interaction is strained because Elf does not acknowledge her likeness to the other, soon a degree of camaraderie springs up. The relationship with Theo is not enough, however, possibly because Theo too is a girl overshadowed by a man. Mr. Murray's child-rearing philosophy, as expressed to Auchinvellan, is, "I tell a child what to do, and if that child fails to do it, I punish that child" (69). An attempt to transfer Elf's education from Auchinvellan to Theo's governess, Miss Gordon, ends abruptly when Miss Gordon decides that Elf is unmanageable. Yet Elf feels an attraction toward Bluebell, and when the latter's father dies and it becomes necessary for her to earn her own living, she moves into the castle as Elf's governess and the missing feminine presence.

Bluebell's makeover of Elf involves loosening her ties to her grandfather and lessening the signs of his influence over her. Overtly, the object is to consult Auchinvellan's convenience by making Elf less exigent and demanding of his time; covertly, it is to eradicate the signs of his tastes and the child's excessive interest in imitating him. The reclamation of the exterior works powerfully to change the interior. Explaining why Elf's new wardrobe has worked behavioral wonders, Bluebell notes that the old clothes "were much more expensive than these, but they made her look old-fashioned. Of course you did not understand this, dear [Auchinvellan]; but you see, Elf is a little woman, and a very sensitive one, and it made her nervous to feel she was not dressed like other children, and being so much alone with you made her still more shy of children and strangers" (172). The implication is that in Elf's case, old-fashionedness was an imposed rather than an innate condition, created by her grandfather's inability to "understand" (or permit) the feminine. This problem having been corrected via the importation of the sympathetic Bluebell, a happy ending is possible. As Auchinvellan reports to Bluebell's mother at the end of the narrative, having Bluebell in the family "is like having a daughter again; the child thrives and flourishes in her presence. Elf and I are happier than ever together. You see, we all wanted a womanly influence in the house, and nothing could have been a greater success, and it was the child's own idea" (186).

Thus despite the implication that the unnaturalness that dominates before Bluebell arrives has to do with Elf's excessive power over her grandfather, the solution turns out to be to follow "the child's own idea" by importing another young woman and giving her a free hand in decision making, thus further reducing Auchinvellan's domestic power. That is, Elf's uncanniness is shown to have resulted not from her excessive power but from his. The contradictions inherent in this way of formulating the situation speak to the gender politics of the late nineteenth century, an era characterized by distrust both of excessive domestic authority on the part of men and of "unwomanly" attempts to usurp male prerogative. The first was manifested, among other phenomena, by the Society for the Prevention of Cruelty to Children's desire to challenge paternal rights and by anxiety about adult men's sexual comportment toward young girls, as expressed in documents such as W. T. Stead's sensational 1885 exposé *The Maiden Tribute of Modern Babylon* (see, e.g., Flegel, *Cruelty* 25, 166–69). The second is represented in *Elf* through the unsympathetic figure of Elf's mother, who in her sexual aggressiveness may stand in for other types of unacceptable female self-assertion. Bluebell, "so much of a woman herself," successfully mediates between these unpalatable extremes. On the one hand, Auchinvellan's willingness to accept her demonstrates that after all, his domestic authority knows limits and that he can be brought to appreciate, rather than to attempt unsuccessfully to usurp, the mother's role; on the other, although she is a wage earner, the emblematically named Bluebell is no New Woman, but a traditional girl committed to family and child rearing. Her ability to exert womanly influence for good heals the mismatch between male and female roles that has hitherto held sway, thus restoring nature to an unnatural situation. Once the genders are no longer in conflict, Elf's old-fashionedness is at an end.

The Mighty Atom and the Anxiety of Eschatology

In *The Mighty Atom* (1896), by Marie Corelli (Mary Mackay), the masculinist adult confidence that comes in for condemnation in *Dombey and Son*, for questioning in *Mary's Meadow*, and for reform in *Elf* is a source of horror. This novel by the most popular writer of her day enjoyed a first printing of twenty thousand copies; the average Corelli novel, reports Annette Federico, "sold 100,000 copies a year" (2). Like Dickens, Corelli was understood by at least some of her turn-of-the-century contemporaries as a didactic writer whose works effectively mixed sensation and improvement. Thus, noting that "Marie Corelli never writes without a purpose," her 1903 biographers, T. F. G. Coates and R. S. Warren Bell, discuss how *The Mighty Atom* illuminates "the criminally mistaken up-bringing of children" (192, 193). More recent Corelli scholars, however, have focused instead on the elements of her aesthetic: her connection to the "feminine sublime" (Kuehn), her reliance on melodrama and sentimentality (Kershner) and on the gothic (Hartnell), her "conflicting views of womanhood" and her complicated position on feminism (Casey 164; see also Federico 12), and in particular what Nickianne Moody terms the "polysemic" nature of her novels, which "can be read from many and contrasting subject positions" (191). To today's critics, in other words, Corelli defies certainty, while her contemporaries were more concerned with how she offered it. Both modes are on display in *The Mighty Atom*.

The novel tells the story of Lionel Valliscourt, whom we first see studying his lessons

> with an air of methodical patience and resignation strange to see in one so young. He might have been a bank clerk, or an experienced accountant in a London merchant's office, from his serious old-fashioned manner, instead of a child barely eleven years of age; indeed, as a matter of fact, there was an almost appalling expression of premature wisdom on his pale wistful features;—the "thinking furrow" already marked his forehead,—and what should still have been the babyish upper curve of his sensitive little mouth, was almost though not quite obliterated by a severe line of constantly practised self-restraint. (8–9)

Lionel is the only child of a militant atheist and his disaffected wife, who elopes with a dissolute baronet midway through the novel. Rarely in the company of either parent and unable to attend a public school because such institutions encourage a Christian sensibility in their pupils, Lionel is a solitary boy whose interactions with others over the course of the novel are largely limited to those with his tutors, the servants, and the sexton and his young daughter; the latter, several years Lionel's junior, appears to be the only child friend he has ever had. When little Jessamine dies of diphtheria and Lionel comes upon her father, Reuben Dale, digging her grave, the boy's religious confusion (he is pulled between training and instinctual faith) reaches a crisis, and he hangs himself in order to find out whether an afterlife exists. As the culmination of a pattern that places pathos alongside righteous indignation, the narrative concludes by juxtaposing an affecting account of the funeral with a confrontation between his callous father and his tutor Professor Cadman-Gore, whose curmudgeonly heart has been touched by his relationship with the child.

The aura of the "almost appalling" that hangs about Lionel—worthy Reuben, the novel's most admirable adult figure, thinks of him as "uncanny" (67), and the Professor, a man of limited perception, expresses his sense of the boy's abnormality on their first meeting by describing him as "a little puny-faced ass" (142)—is evidently discernable only by adults and results from his old-fashionedness. An extraordinarily bright boy, he has been too rapidly advanced intellectually at his father's orders, learning "more facts of science and history, than [Professor Cadman-Gore], in his time, had known when he was twenty." As the narrator notes, "This is often the fate of brilliant and intelligent children,—the more quickly they learn, the more cruelly they are 'crammed,' till both heart and brain give way under the unnatural effort and forced impetus, and disaster follows disaster, ending in the wreck of the whole intellectual and physical organization" (148). Lionel, who is likened several times over the course of the narrative to a dead child and who repeatedly expresses his desire for rest, is clearly on the verge of tragedy throughout the tale, although the reader may initially be uncertain about whether his fate will be mental breakdown, meningitis, pining away over the loss of his mother and Jessamine, or self-murder.

The references to generic dead children suggest one use of doubling in this novel: to foreshadow the denouement and create a sense of the inevitability of Lionel's fate. In discussing other fictions by this author, Moody finds a "sustained interest in the representation of death" (202), a topic linked both to Corelli's often unorthodox religious beliefs and to her fascination with the transcendent. Building upon this point, one might argue that the ultimate purpose of *The Mighty Atom* is the extended depiction of Lionel's death and that all that leads up to the boy's end—his parents' flaws, the encounter with a suicide's body while on holiday, Jessamine's fatal illness, the borderline mental and physical condition that here marks old-fashionedness—is in a sense immaterial beside the emotionalism, shocking even to Victorian readers, of Lionel's end. Corelli heightens the horror by juxtaposing, à la James's insight about Dickens, the disturbingly precocious with the pathetic: the composition of the multiple suicide notes; the mature philosophical discourse of Lionel's lengthy extemporized prayer, followed by "the dawning angel-smile" that "transfigure[s]" him into a figure of childish innocence as he recites Jessamine's favorite verse, "Gentle Jesus, meek and mild"; the selection of the instrument of death, a silken sash embroidered for him in his infancy by his mother; and the details provided about his mental processes and their aftermath:

> Pausing here, he stared fixedly upward, and hesitated a moment,—then went to the door which was slightly ajar, and with careful noiselessness, shut it fast, locked and bolted it. Safe now from any chance of interruption, and all alone except for the unseen "cloud of witnesses" encompassing us all, this mere child, nerved to sternest resolution, calmly confronted the vast Infinite, and went forth on his voyage of discovery to find the God denied him by the cruelty and arrogance of man! And not another sound disturbed the quietude of the house, save the quick, dull "thud" of a chair overturned and thrown down. After that came a heavy stillness . . . and a sudden sense of cold in the air, as of the swift passing of the Shadow of Death. (309–10)

Unlike *Dombey and Son*, where Paul's death occurs comparatively early in the narrative, *The Mighty Atom* certainly presents the boy's death scene as the novel's climax. Yet the foreshadowing and ultimate portrayal of death is not Corelli's only use of doubling. Through the invoking of the myth of Psyche, who is "just like me, and you, and everybody" (255), Lionel is given an allegorical meaning as the eternally questing soul, desperate to see God yet doomed to frustration. As he writes to Professor Cadman-Gore in the lengthiest of his suicide notes, "I've been trying, as Psyche did, to see with my little light,—but I've got it into my head that if I put out my lamp altogether I shall see much better" (321). According to Lionel's own explication of the Psyche story, the soul herself may never know the ultimate truth: "All at once the thunder comes and the darkness,—and we die!—our lamps go out! But we don't hear the rush of wings, do we? If we only heard that,—just the rush of wings—we should feel that Someone had gone—Somewhere!—and we should try to follow—I'm sure we should try. Perhaps we shall hear it when we die—that rush of wings,—

and we shall know what we can't know now, because our lamps go out so quickly" (255–56). Whether or not Lionel hears the "rush of wings" as he hangs himself, the reader is privy in the death scene to the ineffable "sudden sense of cold in the air"; however, while this moment clearly has supernatural overtones, we cannot tell whether they are benign or malevolent, an uncertainty that heightens the uncanniness of the moment. Lionel's death has a meaning, but it is not for the reader to know what it is. Faith and doubt, those twin poles of Victorian spiritual striving, are left in equilibrium.

Just as Lionel's death scene specifically associates the close relationship between the sentimental and the uncanny with the feminine, Lionel's self-identification with a female mythological figure points to a final dimension of doubling in this novel, the linking of the boy to his transgressive mother, Helen. She too is a leaver of final messages before acting in a way that, we are to recognize, is as final and tragic as suicide. Before her departure, she makes a late-night visit to her son, whom she knows she will never see again, to assure him of her love and to ask his forgiveness for an action whose nature the reader understands but Lionel cannot. The visit shares the uncanniness of Lionel's approaching end. Helen laughs "a little cold, mirthless laugh which somehow chilled Lionel's blood" (214), invokes the French Revolution and speaks of having heard "the wheels of my death-cart" on the gravel outside (215), and departs, leaving Lionel calling after her while "a door swung to with a creaking groan and rattle,—a rising wind [surely akin to the "sudden sense of cold in the air" at Lionel's passing] sighed through the crevices" (217). Meanwhile, the note that she has left for her estranged husband, accusing him of having "robbed [her] of God" (244), contains certain phrases that Valliscourt reads as "threats" and that are invoked twice more after Lionel's death: "My spirit is in the boy's blood, and already he rebels against your petty tyranny. Sooner or later he will escape you" (245).

Helen's identification of herself with Lionel through the claim that "my spirit is in the boy's blood" gives us another way to read the child's death and, since Valliscourt strongly rejects not only Helen's claim but also the realms of the supernatural and of emotion, the uncanny and the sentimental as well: they constitute a revolutionary rejection of the authority of the socially dominant male. Immediately after her flight, the narrator contrasts Helen with the sympathetic servant Lucy, who, untainted by modern thought as represented by Ibsen and Grant Allen, "had 'barbaric' notions of motherhood,—she believed in its sacredness in quite an obstinate, prejudiced and old-fashioned way.

She was nothing but a 'child of nature,' poor, simple Ibsen-less housemaid Lucy!—and throughout all creation, nature makes mother-love a law, and mother's duty paramount" (236).[11] In other words, the narrator makes clear that Helen's action is wrong and unnatural and that in some measure it leads to her child's suicide. Yet at the same time, in contrast to Hering's representation of Elf's mother and typifying what Federico identifies as Corelli's oscillation between "antifeminism and pro-woman feeling" (12), we are led to sympathize with Helen's ferocious anger at her husband's insistence upon total possession of their son and the destructive "arrogance" (Corelli 244) of his assumption that his outlook on life represents the only possible reality. The passion that drives her to elopement is not love for her paramour (whom in fact she despises) but hatred of her husband. In this context, Corelli hints that Lionel's suicide is in one sense a feminist statement, a misguided but understandable response to the real social problem of upper-class male dominance. While there is hope for Professor Cadman-Gore, who accuses his employer of murder and declares his love for his lost pupil, there is none for Valliscourt, who, noting that the newly dead boy "is the image of his mother" (323), dismisses him as insane and announces his intention of remarrying and replacing him with more satisfactory children: "Losses can always be remedied" (337).

Hartnell holds that "Angela Carter's description of the *function* of the Gothic . . . provides the most fruitful starting point in our attempt to understand Corelli's novels. For if, as Carter suggests, Gothic literature 'retains a singular moral function—that of provoking unease,' then Corelli's novels fulfil this function admirably" (285, emphasis in original). *The Mighty Atom* is no exception. Corelli asks her Victorian readers to feel unease about any number of matters that they suspect might in a simpler and more ideal world be sources of certainty: the infallibility of parents' child-rearing decisions, the supremacy of the mothering instinct, the existence of an afterlife, the authority of the educated landowner. All these are questioned through the figure of the old-fashioned child, himself a challenge to another supposed certainty, the childishness of the child.

As Corelli makes clear, Lionel, the representative at once of Victorian scientific modernity, with its sophisticated scorn for the "semi-barbari[sm of belief] . . . in anything divine or super-natural" (73), and of Victorian longing for religious faith, is the victim of the war between two incompatible principles. Complicating the problem, as with the other contradictions that we have seen embodied in old-fashioned children, is that it is not a simple matter of evil versus good; although Reuben's simple faith is dignified and appealing, the novel suggests that it may lack intellectual satisfaction, and while science is presented as emotionally unsatisfying, Lionel demonstrates that the desire to *know* is passionate and legitimate. Such is the significance of the conflict between incompatibilities that even the novel's title becomes ambiguous: the "mighty Atom" is simultaneously the chance-begotten "First Cause of the universe . . . productive of other atoms which moved in circles of fortuitous regularity, shaping worlds indifferently, and without any Mind-force whatever behind the visible Matter" (Corelli 73), and Lionel himself, small but dauntless challenger of the Unknown. If indeed certainty is an impossibility, his challenge becomes at once more heroic and more disturbing. And in placing certainty beyond our reach, Corelli offers her own disturbing challenge to the literary and social conventions into which her generation was born.

A Little Princess and the Anxiety of Identity

Like Corelli, Frances Hodgson Burnett had "the Midas touch" (Thwaite 86). Of her best-selling novel, *Little Lord Fauntleroy* (1885–86), there were forty-three thousand copies in print by October 1887, and the book earned its author "at least a hundred thousand dollars in her lifetime [she died in 1924]" (94). *Fauntleroy* outsold both *A Little Princess* (1905) and *The Secret Garden* (1911), the other two Burnett productions that retain the status of children's classics today, but all three successfully incorporate the figure of the old-fashioned child into an adaptation of the Cinderella story. Of the three, however, *A Little Princess* offers the most developed treatment of old-fashionedness, here focused particularly on the relationship between changing economic circumstances and identity.

A longer version of a story published in *St. Nicholas* in 1888 as "Sara Crewe, or What Happened at Miss Minchin's," *A Little Princess* traces the fall and rise of its title character, born in India and brought at age seven to London to be reared in a climate supposedly more salubrious to British children. Sara's fabulously wealthy young father, a widower, lavishes expensive gifts upon his daughter before leaving her in the school run by Miss Minchin and her sister, Miss Amelia. The "odd-looking little girl" with the "queer old-fashioned thoughtfulness in her big eyes" (7) excites dislike in a few of the pupils and in Miss Minchin herself, who resents Sara's perfect adult manners, exquisite French, and luxury-filled upbringing, but creates disciples out of Lottie, the youngest pupil in the school; Ermengarde, the stupidest; and Becky, the abused teenaged maid-of-all-work. On Sara's eleventh birthday, Miss Minchin learns that Captain Crewe has died of brain fever brought on by what is thought to have been a disastrous speculation in a friend's diamond mines. The orphaned and penniless Sara is cast upon Miss Minchin's charity and becomes an unpaid and half-starved errand girl, living next to Becky in one of the school's unheated garret rooms. After about two years, a secret benefactor begins to provide comforts to Sara, who shares them with the loyal Becky. Finally it turns out that the benefactor is the school's next-door neighbor Tom Carrisford, who befriended Sara, via his Indian servant Ram Dass, without knowing that she was the daughter of his dead business partner, the child he has been vainly seeking across Europe so that he might restore her enormous fortune. Once all is revealed, Carrisford adopts Sara and employs Becky as her maid, leaving Miss Minchin chagrined and humiliated.

Sara's old-fashionedness may begin as mere precocity. Like some of the child-women to be discussed in chapter 4, she has taken her dead mother's place as her father's companion and chief emotional interest. Victorian narratives sometimes, though not always, represent such relationships as conferring old-fashionedness. Thus Polly in Charlotte Brontë's *Villette* (1853) responds to her separation from her adored father "with an old-fashioned calm most unchildlike" (5), whereas the similarly positioned child-woman Mary Marchmont in Mary Elizabeth Braddon's *John Marchmont's Legacy* (1862–63) lacks the quality that *Villette*'s Lucy Snowe sees as making Polly "most strange," "very unique" (27). In Sara's case, the uncanniness that marks the old-fashioned child seems to increase with age, and particularly with the dramatic change in her circumstances at the time of her father's death. What begin as mere predictions, born of jealousy, that "she will grow up eccentric" (37) enter the present tense on her eleventh birthday, when, newly clad in an outgrown black frock, she is transformed into "a strange, desolate, almost grotesque little figure" (86). Her affect changes along with her appearance, and the adjective repeatedly applied to her, both by her detractors within the novel and by the narrator, is *queer*. As Anita Levy writes of Brontë's Polly, she "is an unsettling figure combining features both of the child and the adult, the paradox of the both/and, belonging to neither category, disrupting both" (395). That such disruptions are disturbing to the representatives of ordinariness is apparent from the comment of an older pupil, Jessie, that Sara is "different from other people. . . . Sometimes I'm a bit frightened of her" (199).

Others' varied and changing responses to Sara signal an important trope within this novel, namely, multiplicity of identity. Not only Sara but many of the other sympathetic characters as well maintain alternate personae; such is the potency of storytelling as a means of creating other realities that everyone is narrativized. As Sara tells Ermengarde, "*Everything's* a story. You are a story— I am a story. Miss Minchin is a story" (116, emphasis in original). Thus Becky is both herself and, in the saga inspired by Sara's reading of Carlyle's *The French Revolution*, "the prisoner in the next cell"; the children of Carrisford's lawyer, Mr. Carmichael, in reality Donald, Nora, Janet, and so on, gain in Sara's fancy romantic names such as Ethelberta Beauchamp Montmorency, Violet Cholmondeley Montmorency, and Claude Harold Hector Montmorency; and Carrisford appears variously as the Indian Gentleman, Sara's "friend" and "Uncle Tom," and Crewe's business partner, who may be either dishonest, misguided, or pitiable. The archetypes featured within the story of the moment condition not only others' response to the narrativized subject but also that subject's response to the self and the world.

Moreover, as Mavis Reimer notes, Burnett's play with narrative point of view is such that the reader's vantage point repeatedly shifts; we are asked to see through the eyes of adults, children, unknown passers-by, and even a rat in moments that threaten to make Sara "the subject of the wrong story" (121) and that call our own identity into question. But while it is Sara herself who has the largest number of parts to play, this proliferation of selves paradoxically functions in part to assure us of the consistency of her Sara-ness. Initially she is her father's "little Missus," Miss Minchin's "show pupil," Lottie's adoptive "mamma," and the seminary's "princess." After her father's death she is known to the Carmichael children in one guise as "the-little-girl-who-is-not-a-beggar" and in another as "the little un-fairy princess," while Carrisford addresses her as "the Little Girl in the right-hand attic." In the stories that she constructs for herself, she plays starring roles ranging from Marie Antoinette to the chatelaine of a medieval castle to a beneficiary of Magic. Yet as Sara is always aware, her trials, the stories imposed on her from outside, are a means by which she and the reader may know "whether I am really a nice child or a horrid one" (36), or put another way, whether her inner self will shift in tandem with the outward markers of her position in society.

Unsurprisingly, then, Sara acquires a number of doubles over the course of the story, including her doll Emily, who shares her bed and wardrobe; Lottie, who shares her initial status as the indulged pet of a wealthy father; an unseen orphan named Emily Carew, who was similarly left penniless in a boarding school upon her father's death and whom Carmichael traces from Paris to Moscow thinking that she may be Sara; and the beggar girl Anne, who shares Sara's hunger and destitution and who, in a working-class mirroring of Sara's happy ending, is eventually given a home by a better-off adult.[12] Yet in part the point of all these doubles is not to shake but to confirm the stability of Sara's identity, which, thanks to her old-fashioned qualities, has remained unchanged from the first page of the novel, despite the vicissitudes of her shifting financial status, appearance, and effect upon others. If Sara's situation is potentially that not only of many "wretched little servant girls" in other attics in the square but also of others in "all the attics in all the other squares and streets" (Burnett 143–44), she herself is unique and may be neither confused nor replaced with Becky, Emily Carew, or any of her other simulacra. Carrisford becomes a "new man" upon his discovery of Sara (235), but Sara remains the same child she always was,[13] successfully warding off what U. C. Knoepflmacher terms "self-fragmentation" by walking the tightrope stretched over the abyss of "not-self" (xiv, xv).

As many critics have pointed out, *A Little Princess* is on one level a narrative about imperialism and class, a Cinderella story in which social elevation goes hand in hand with class origins. Soon after her bereavement, Sara speculates that if she should forget the information that she has stored up from her reading and become "a scullery maid who knows nothing, I shall be like poor Becky. I wonder if I could *quite* forget and begin to drop my *h*'s and not remember that Henry the Eighth had six wives" (94–95). Reassuringly for the Georgian middle-class reader, the answer is no. Sara's aitches are sacrosanct, her education indelible, and while Becky's and Anne's lots are materially improved, neither they nor Ram Dass will "*quite* forget" their place at the end; rather, they will rejoice that Sara is restored to hers. Yet if we accept Sara's terms, the class position of some of her schoolmates may not be so secure. Surely Ermengarde, for one, would be as ready to forget the number of Henry the Eighth's wives as she is to forget any other piece of academic information, while Lottie is too young to be troubled with much learning. The comforting fixity of Sara's class identity is partly a function of her old-fashionedness; the fixity of Ermengarde's and Lottie's seems rather a function of the fact that they have not sustained the kind of upheaval that has afflicted Sara.

Particularly against the backdrop of her schoolmates, then, Sara paradoxically embodies both the appropriateness of the class system (rich or poor, we are to acknowledge her as a "princess") and its injustice (at a moment's notice, she may be moved from one end of the social scale to the other). Her first conversation with Becky illuminates the novel's simultaneous egalitarianism and elitism:

> She put her hand against Becky's cheek.
>
> "Why," she said, "we are just the same—I am only a little girl like you. It's just an accident that I am not you, and you are not me!"
>
> Becky did not understand in the least. Her mind could not grasp such amazing thoughts, and "an accident" meant to her a calamity in which someone was run over or fell off a ladder and was carried to "the 'orspital." (53)

Here, on the one hand Sara's sense of their kinship is ironic evidence of the superiority of her perceptions to Becky's, while on the other the narrative insists that even if Becky is not altogether "like" Sara, she is at least deserving of the same amount of readerly respect as Ermengarde, say. Similarly, it is no coincidence that the ultimate identification of Sara as the lost daughter of Captain Crewe is brought about by Sara's own ability to identify Ram Dass as a "Lascar," which, like her ability to speak to him in Hindustani, is used to signal her Indian birth. She is simultaneously an unmistakable member of the imperialist ruling class, someone whom Ram Dass addresses "as if he were speaking to the little daughter of a rajah" (134), and a child whose innate nobility is manifested in her friendly courtesy to a figure of whom her more insular peers are inclined to be wary. In upholding dominant hierarchies of class, ethnicity, and even identity itself, the novel simultaneously asserts the importance of using the imagination to move beyond them.

Conclusions

That this chapter focuses primarily on old-fashioned children in the context of the domestic novel, or in the case of Sara Crewe its close relative the school story, is the case because the domestic tale is the genre in which most such children are to be found. Nevertheless, just as *Dombey* is more than a domestic novel, the old-fashioned child extends well beyond the domestic space. As my reference, in a note, to Braddon's ghost story "The Shadow in the Corner" will have suggested, these figures may be found in tales of the supernatural (another example is H. G. Wells's "The Door in the Wall," published in 1906); they also appear in tracts such as Margaret Scott MacRitchie's 1883 *Chick, or, Yet There Is Room*, in adventure stories such as Gordon Stables's 1888 *From*

Squire to Squatter, and in colonial examples such as the Australian author Henry Lawson's first published tale, "His Father's Mate" (1888), among other venues. As the figure moves beyond the domestic environment, narrative pre-occupations change somewhat, so that we may see less attention given to failures in parenting and more given to the flaws of society itself.

In other words, genre works to shape the conventions of the narrative of the old-fashioned child. For instance, because it is characteristic of the Victorian tract to focus on the working class, figures such as MacRitchie's Chick provide a combination of old-fashionedness and social marginality unusual in the middle-class domestic setting, while the tendency of the late-century boy's adventure to avoid complex characterization lessens the uncanniness of the old-fashioned child in novels such as Stables's.[14] Even so, we are still led to see the old-fashioned child as distinctive in some important way, so that Chick is able to bring a roomful of adults to Christ, while Rupert in *From Squire to Squatter* grows up to practice a form of colonialism that differs from that practiced by his brother (the protagonist) and the other English immigrants in the novel: he "did not turn squatter, but missionary" (381), and arguably to better effect, for "it is owing to such earnest men as Rupert that so great a change has come over the black population [of Australia], and that so many of them, even as I write, sit humbly at the feet of Jesus, clothed and in their right mind" (382). Otherness, in short, remains a factor beyond the domestic tale.

Even within the domestic tale, as the examples explored here indicate, we see substantial variation. Adye finds both Paul Dombey and Lord Fauntleroy lovable, but their affects otherwise differ to a considerable degree, just as Paul also shares important traits with Corelli's Lionel without being by any means his identical twin. The flexibility of the old-fashioned child is suggestive; while authors may employ the figure to new purpose with each use, there clearly remains a kernel of indispensable similarity that enables the term *old-fashioned* to communicate a particular meaning to its nineteenth- and early twentieth-century reader. If some parts of the package must change in order to provide scope for the individual author, others must remain the same, most fundamentally an aura of peculiarity that highlights peculiarities in the child's environment. Adye identifies this strangeness as the old-fashioned child's association with death, but it has other components as well.

One of these components is the striking tendency to locate in the old-fashioned child both excess and want.[15] The children discussed in this chapter benefit, in ways disproportionate to the general run of society, from the social principles that the authors explore in these narratives, but they also lose by them. Thus, for instance, the firm of Dombey and Son gives Paul a place and a security enjoyed by no other major character within the novel, as he alone seems immune to the reversals of fortune that form a part of the general experience, but his too-close association with his father's business kills him. Sara Crewe initially profits to a "ridiculous" extent from the Empire- and class-based venture in which "strange, dark men [dig diamonds] out with heavy picks" (58, 57), but the diamond mines deprive her of her father and apparently of her fortune as well. Ewing's Chris asserts his masculine privilege and right to dictate terms in a game invented by his sister, but his "large-headed[ness]" signals a physicality that is lacking precisely to the degree that it is excessive. Similar arguments may be made of Elf and Lionel. Like the use of doubling, this pattern places the child at the crossroads of ambiguity, presenting concepts such as industrialism and imperialism as simultaneously positive and negative, beneficial and devastating.

If the primary purpose of the strangeness (old-fashionedness) of the old-fashioned child is to illuminate inconsistencies in the surrounding society, the figure's simultaneous identity as *child* goes some way toward suggesting what kinds of issues may be of particular concern. Predictably, child rearing is taken to task here, but there is considerably less interest in matters involving the nursery regimen than there is in the ideological food offered to the young in Victorian and Edwardian society. Noticeable in the texts examined in this chapter is how frequently a working-class figure is used to represent good child-rearing sense; the voices of reason include Polly Toodle in *Dombey and Son*, David in *Elf*, Reuben Dale in *The Mighty Atom*, and even Becky in *A Little Princess*, although as she is of Sara's generation she is something of an anomaly. If *Mary's Meadow* lacks such a figure, it is presumably because the tale's most problematic adult is the Squire; the children's parents, who also appear not to contribute to Chris's old-fashionedness, are not held up for criticism. The contrast between down-to-earth working-class instinct and selfish middle-class error helps to establish the old-fashioned child as a problem specific to the privileged classes and thus associated on some level with "progress" and social dominance.[16] By and large, those in authority refuse to listen to the wise impulses of their social inferiors, thus encouraging the reader to look nostalgically back to a simpler time when children were children.

Like today's discussions of children who "grow up too early," in which preteens' clothing, sexual precocity, taste for violence in entertainment, and so on are said to signal excessive exposure to the less salubrious aspects of adult culture, nineteenth- and early twentieth-century discussions of the old-fashioned child hint at adults' inability to contain the complexities of a changing world. The social problems on display for these Victorian and Edwardian writers, in other words, are not those signaled by some of the precocious girls and boys profiled in chapters 4 and 5, such as child labor or the excessive delegation of family responsibility to the young. Rather, they are problems that bedevil adults as well: how to establish an appropriate relationship between work and family life, between territorial possessions and other people, between male and female, between reason and belief, between one's social identity and one's inner self. By situating the child as the battleground for such conflicts, narratives of the type discussed in this chapter evoke a particular set of emotions in their reader. But even while they hint at adult culpability in not providing the middle-class child with an upbringing that shields him or her from the contradictions and difficulties of the world, they also suggest the adult's own helplessness in the face of these same problems. In the old-fashioned child extremes meet, creating not only feelings of strangeness but also enhanced possibilities for identification on the part of a reader who may initially seem to have little in common with so eerie a figure. Thus it comes as no surprise that little Paul Dombey, in all his otherness, attracts love both from his fellow characters within the novel and from many Victorian readers. Ultimately, Paul's uncanny ambiguity is no bar to our affection if, entering into his consciousness and identifying with what we find there, in what Freud terms the "telepathy" in which "the one possesses knowledge, feelings and experience in common with the other" ("'Uncanny'" 629), we recognize that his truest double is ourselves.

two

The Arrested Child-Man
and Social Threat

In 1833, when he published his first volume of poetry, Hartley Coleridge
(1796–1849) was in his mid-thirties. Abnormally small of stature and prematurely gray of hair, Coleridge had been "very little of a boy in actual
childhood," as Walter Bagehot put it (3), but in adulthood struck observers as
boyish. Although he was a talented poet in his own right, Coleridge spent (or
misspent) his life in the shadow of his more famous father. His melancholy
sonnet "Long Time a Child, and Still a Child," included in *Poems*, expresses
the discomfort of being a child-man in an adult body:

> *Long time a child, and still a child, when years*
> *Had painted manhood on my cheek, was I;*
> *For yet I lived like one not born to die;*
> *A thriftless prodigal of smiles and tears,*
> *No hope I needed, and I knew no fears.*
> *But sleep, though sweet, is only sleep, and waking,*
> *I waked to sleep no more, at once o'ertaking*
> *The vanguard of my age, with all arrears*

> *Of duty on my back. Nor child, nor man,*
> *Nor youth, nor sage, I find my head is grey,*
> *For I have lost the race I never ran,*
> *A rathe December blights my lagging May;*
> *And still I am a child, tho' I be old,*
> *Time is my debtor for my years untold.*

The sonnet is something of a rarity for its day inasmuch as the psychological turmoil of the arrested child-man was explored less frequently at the dawn of the Victorian age than it was at the turn of the twentieth century, by which time childhood had been identified ever more firmly by theorists of psychology, race, social melioration, and evolution (among other discourses) as a watershed for both the individual and the species. That the child-man tends to be a less problematic figure in the 1830s than in the 1890s, say, reflects the lingering influence of Romantic writers, who were apt to celebrate "the carrying on of the freshness and feelings of childhood into the powers of manhood" as a mark of genius rather than of trouble, as Samuel Taylor Coleridge put it in 1818 (85). But the younger Coleridge's understanding—based, it would seem, on painful experience—that the child-man is tragically out of step with his world would remain a keynote of the figure for the next seventy-odd years.[1]

As I argue in chapter 3, the arrested child-woman, like her precocious sister, sometimes signals social and familial problems that are not lost upon the writers who employ her, but she may also be figured as an ideal. In the present chapter I contend that child-men—and, significantly, that hyphenated term is less common in Victorian works than is *child-woman*, although it may nonetheless be found in a variety of fiction and nonfiction texts in the mid-, late-, and immediate post-Victorian years—represent a category at once more capacious and often more disturbing to Victorian sensibilities. In Bagehot's estimation, Hartley Coleridge had "the waywardness of childhood without the innocency of its impulses . . . the passions of manhood without the repressive vigour of a man's will,—he lived as a woman lives that is lost and forsaken, who sins ever and hates herself for sinning, but who sins, perhaps, more on that very account" (16). The equivalency that Bagehot makes here between the child-man and the fallen woman, particularly interesting inasmuch as the overt subject for discussion at this point in Bagehot's essay is not sexual incontinence but tippling, is likely to have been the more distressing to the mid-nineteenth-century reader because not only sexual mores but also sex roles are being twisted. While the tendency to use sexual and gender irregularities to discuss the child-man is not universal among nineteenth- and early twentieth-century writers, it occurs frequently enough to attract our interest and to suggest a reason why this figure should be so disturbing.

Catherine Robson notes among male Victorian writers "a marked tendency . . . to reimagine the young self as feminine" (10), a phenomenon that permits "an increasingly attractive image of the innocent self of childhood, isolated from a progressively threatening world" (12). Yet the keynote of this "temporally displaced self-love" (10) is precisely that it posits a lost self, one that exists only in the past. The presumed femininity of a child-self that no longer exists need not impugn the masculinity of the present self. In contrast, the man who carries juvenile characteristics into adulthood is often perceived as posing a threat, frequently expressed in sexual terms, not only to himself (as in Coleridge's sonnet) and to his family but to those beyond his immediate circle as well. In many Victorian fictions the arrested child-woman's immaturity, like the precocious child-woman's adultlike competence, includes sexual immaturity and functions to keep an imperfect family together. Arrested child-women are commonly depicted as admirable or endearing even while they are patronized or identified as freakish. Even such undesirable specimens as Mary Elizabeth Braddon's Lady Audley ultimately manifest only a limited destructiveness. But particularly in the later years of the Victorian period, in the context of influential sociological commentary by such writers as Cesare Lombroso and Max Nordau, the arrested child-man often carries with him an aura of the pathologically damaged or damaging. The changes that take place in the figure of the child-man over time, affected as they are by debates focusing on evolution, psychology, imperialism, social purity, and other mid- and late Victorian issues, offer insight into understandings of boyhood, the masculine domestic and sexual role, and the larger society in prewar England.

Ambivalence and the Child-Man

To be sure, despite the preponderance of negative examples, even at the end of the century not all arrested child-men are presented in a sinister light. For a positive specimen who preserves the feminine child-self identified by Robson, we may turn to George Du Maurier's *Trilby* (1894), whose beautiful and infantilized hero, known as Little Billee, "was young and tender . . . he had never been to any school, and was innocent of the world and its wicked ways" (8). As

Dennis Denisoff has pointed out, not only is Little Billee's age ambivalent but so are his "sexuality, gender performance, ethnicity, genius, and artistic genre" (147). In his "almost girlish purity" (Du Maurier 10) he is more feminine than the novel's eponymous heroine. Denisoff and other critics rightly emphasize the novel's sexually transgressive side. Mary Titus, for one, places it in the tradition discussed by Eve Sedgwick in *Between Men*, insofar as "shared admiration of a woman [Trilby] provides a safe context for expressions of male affection" between Little Billee and his roommate Taffy (30). Nevertheless, it is important to note further that this transgressiveness is enabled by Little Billee's childlike persona and is in fact an unusually positive version of a trope that we will see expressed in much more threatening ways in other late Victorian works.

Victorian fiction, particularly children's fiction, frequently describes young boys in feminized terms.[2] Compare, for instance, Juliana Ewing's description of a six-year-old boy's "long, fair hair . . . pliable, nervous fingers . . . and, above all, his beautiful eyes, in which the tears now brimmed over the eyelashes as the waters of a lake well up through the reeds that fringe its banks" (*Story* 4) with Du Maurier's description of Little Billee, who is "small and slender . . . had a straight white forehead veined with blue, large dark-blue eyes, delicate, regular features, and coal-black hair. He was also very graceful and well built, with very small hands and feet, and much better dressed than his friends" (6). With a change in pronoun, both descriptions could readily apply to the heroine of a romantic novelette. As a child-man, then, Little Billee stands outside the requirements of normal late Victorian masculinity. That in Du Maurier's hands his femininity is a marker of his moral superiority to his unchildlike and sexually more aggressive antagonist, Svengali, suggests that the author is using him as an instrument for the critique of masculine norms, which *Trilby* associates with the Other by identifying Svengali as a foreigner and a Jew.

His hero's nickname continues this implicit criticism. It derives from W. M. Thackeray's comic ballad by this title, written in the winter of 1844–45 and first published in *Sand and Canvas* in 1849, which concerns three sailors—of whom "the youngest he was little Billee," a line that Du Maurier misquotes as "the third he was 'Little Billee'" (6)—who run out of food midvoyage:

> *Says gorging Jack to guzzling Jimmy,*
> *"I am extremely hungaree."*

To gorging Jack says guzzling Jimmy,
"We've nothing left, us must eat we."

Says gorging Jack to guzzling Jimmy,
"With one another we shouldn't agree!
There's little Bill, he's young and tender,
We're old and tough, so let's eat he."

(lines 9–16)

Their prospective victim, whose diction is free of the pronoun confusion that his shipmates evince and that is typical of the speech of non-English cannibals in humorous works of the nineteenth and early twentieth centuries, pleads for a few more minutes of life so that he can say the catechism that he learned at his mother's knee. Midway through his recitation of the "Twelfth Command-ment" (*sic*), he spies land and the British navy, with the result that he is re-warded with a promotion, while Jack and Jimmy are punished.

Du Maurier's invoking of Thackeray's poem functions to absolve his hero of the appetite that characterizes the passionate, controlling Svengali. Little Billee is no "guzzling" man, whereas Svengali insists (his colleague Gecko muses) that Trilby "think his thoughts and wish his wishes—and love him at his bidding with a strange unreal factitious love . . . just his own love for himself turned inside out—*à l'envers*—and reflected back on him, as from a mirror" (458). The child-man for Du Maurier, then, though not for all his contemporaries, is he who is not a consuming egotist. Yet Little Billee's premature death, caused in part by his assumption that "[no] woman who had eyes to see should ever quite condone the signs of physical weakness" that he displays (267), suggests that the lack of masculine confidence may bring problems of its own.

We can see the beginnings of this uncertainty in a much earlier example, Thomas Carlyle's Jocelin of Brakelond, the monkish chronicler in book 2 of *Past and Present* (1843), who has a "beautiful childlike character" (56), a "wise simplicity in him; a *veracity* that goes deeper than words" (372, emphasis in orig-inal). Carlyle clearly envies "Jocelin, Eadmer, and such religious men, [who] have as yet nothing of 'Methodism'; no Doubt or even root of Doubt. Religion is not a diseased self-introspection, an agonising inquiry: their duties are clear to them, the way of supreme good plain, indisputable, and they are travelling on it" (76). Yet Jocelin is presented as the ideal follower rather than as a shaper of his world. For Carlyle, one of his most praiseworthy traits is his esteem for the strong leader Abbot Samson, a regard that elicits from Jocelin no ambition to become a leader himself. He remains "a learned grown man, yet with the heart as of a good child; whose whole life indeed has been that of a child,—St. Edmundsbury Monastery [was] a larger kind of cradle for him, in which his whole prescribed duty was to *sleep* kindly and love his mother well!" (54, emphasis in original). Carlyle's definition of the hero, to him a figure of consuming interest, is not sufficiently capacious to include Jocelin, whose very lack of egotism and assertiveness elicits condescension rather than admiration.

Carlyle's stance appears to be that if Jocelin is a child, he cannot be a man in the heroic sense. Or perhaps the issue is not the presence but the prominence of childlike qualities in Jocelin, for elsewhere Carlyle demonstrates a willingness to invoke childhood in discussing heroes. In "The Hero as Poet," for instance, the "foundation" of Dante's face is "softness, tenderness, gentle affection as of a child; but all this is as if congealed into sharp contradiction, into abnegation, isolation, proud hopeless pain." By the end of the paragraph, however, no trace of the child remains in Carlyle's description, as "affection [has been] all converted into indignation: an implacable indignation; slow, equable, silent, like that of a god!" (103). Schiller too is remarkable for his "manly" and "heroic" appearance and the "fiery ardor shining through the clouds of suffering and disappointment, deep but patiently endured," while in private "he was kind-hearted, free, and gay as a little child" (*Life* 238, 239). Still another type of child-man appears in Carlyle's famous description of Thomas De Quincey as "one of the smallest man-figures I ever saw; shaped like a pair of tongs; and hardly above five feet in all: when he sat, you would have taken him, by candlelight, for the beautifullest little Child; blue-eyed, blonde-haired, sparkling face,—had there not been a something, too, which said, '*Eccovi*, this Child has been in Hell!'" (*Portraits* 25–26). In these descriptions Carlyle suggests a fundamental incompatibility between childhood and painful experience; pain both forges the hero and destroys or at least threatens the child. In contrast, Jocelin's experience has been such as to comfortably prolong his childhood, excusing him from the need to change. It is a comfort for which Carlyle has some scorn.

Other writers also appear dubious about what, exactly, a child is: innocent or solipsist? This potential ambiguity in the child-man is noted in 1871 by clergyman and littérateur Francis Jacox:

> It may, or may not, be a compliment to say of some full-grown person, Always a Child! *Cela dépend*. The import of the phrase may be, that he has never ceased to

be child-like,—in disposition, simplicity, cheery sportiveness, and artless candour,—and then it is a compliment, surely, *pure et simple*. But the import of the phrase may, on the other hand, be, that he has never ceased to be childish,— and then, as surely, it is the flat reverse. (46)

While Jacox usually aligns himself in this essay with the Romantic position by seeking the child-man within an assortment of great men from Milton to Cromwell and looking past fictional child-men with a "morbid taint" (52), exemplified for him by Nathaniel Hawthorne's Clifford Pyncheon in *The House of the Seven Gables* (1851) and George Crabbe's eponymous Edward Shore (1812), his anxiety about the "childish" marks him as a Victorian. Jacox was writing at a time when, David Grylls observes, a reaction was starting to set in against "excessive idealisation" of the child even while the "Romantic celebration of the innocence of children's ways" continued in other quarters (73). The ambivalence on display here, both in Jacox's dismissal of the "child- ish" and in a number of his descriptions of great child-men (who may be shown behaving in ways that look more childish than childlike), extends throughout discussions of the child-man from the mid-nineteenth century to the second decade of the twentieth century, complicating both positive and negative portraits.

Consider, for instance, *David Copperfield* (1849–50) and its handling of Mr. Dick, "grey-headed, laughing, and happy" (232). Although rejected by his father and brother as "almost a natural" or a madman (188), Mr. Dick is a val- ued member of Betsey Trotwood's household and a "universal favourite" among the boys in Dr. Strong's school, where, David reports, he "was as deeply inter- ested in all our sports as any one among us. How often have I seen him, intent upon a match at marbles or peg-top, looking on with a face of unutterable in- terest, and hardly breathing at the critical times!" Known for "his ingenuity in little things," Mr. Dick, apparently so ill equipped for the adult world, "could cut oranges into such devices as none of us had an idea of. He could make a boat out of anything, from a skewer upwards. He could turn crampbones into chessmen; fashion Roman chariots from old court cards; make spoked wheels out of cotton reels, and birdcages of old wire" (232). As Malcolm Andrews notes, Mr. Dick is allied to other likeable figures within the novel, such as Mr. Peggotty and Ham, whose adult bodies "conceal a childish simplicity of feeling: they are in many ways grown-up children, adults who have a particu- lar affinity with childhood" and whose difficulty functioning in the "real" world, the world scorned by Aunt Betsey as characterized by cruelty and skewed values, "is meant to be charming" (147).

Yet David's response to this child-man is equivocal from the beginning. While he will not contradict Aunt Betsey's contrary judgment, his natural tendency is to agree with Mr. Dick's male relatives that Mr. Dick is unfit. Andrews suggests that despite his affection for Mr. Dick, Mr. Peggotty, Ham, Mr. Micawber, and their ilk, and despite his anger at adults (such as the Murdstones) who hate children, David gradually moves away from his child-self, in effect privileging the side of himself that pities Mr. Dick over the side that respects him. "The adult David," Andrews points out, "asserts his maturity by distancing himself from his own childhood (and from most of his close childhood friends), as if it were in itself a manifestation of his disreputable past. In so doing he confirms that contemporary view . . . of the radically antithetical relationship between childhood and masculine adulthood" (170). As a grayheaded "child" among schoolboys, carving his oranges, Mr. Dick can be accepted as an equal when he appears at playtime. In more adult contexts he may strike David as something of an embarrassment. Mr. Dick's delusion that his scanty income as a copyist means that he is supporting Aunt Betsey—having earned his first shillings and laid them out "in the form of a heart," "'No starving now, Trotwood,' said Mr. Dick, shaking hands with me in a corner. 'I'll provide for her, Sir!' and he flourished his ten fingers in the air, as if they were ten banks" (487)—is akin to the child-woman Dora's belief that her own sporadic forays into copying enable her to assist David in his career. The shared trope of copying here hints at what they have in common: each can imitate the gender role appropriate to his or her age and sex (provider and helpmeet, respectively), but neither can internalize it.

The good child-man's very attempt to take on the archetypal patriarchal role of uniting and protecting the family may work to expose the flaws of patriarchy. In *David Copperfield*, too-confident adult masculinity is suspect. Both Mr. Murdstone and Steerforth are destroyers of domestic bliss as well as figures of masculine power. In contrast, Mr. Dick can bring Dr. Strong and his wife to a better understanding of each other, not through assertiveness but by staging a group conversation. This achievement is possible precisely because he represents another, less socially valued type of man; as he notes, "Dick's nobody!" (604). And throughout Dickens's text, being "nobody" is infinitely preferable morally to being the arrogant, phallic "somebodies" represented by Murdstone and Steerforth (and in *Trilby* by Svengali) or to feigning an "'umbleness" that is really solipsism, after the devious fashion adopted by Uriah Heep.

One source of this novel's suspicion of patriarchy is its narrator, who, Margaret Flanders Darby has suggested, is prone to "radically warped" visions of others, "self-indulgent interpretations" (156) that, in David's own phrase, make him "the hero of my own life" at others' expense (1). David, whose youth and uncertain status prevent him from qualifying as a fully successful man until the happy ending, is arguably none too welcoming of male rivals. In this reading, Murdstone and Steerforth, as the accepted suitors of women in whom David is interested (his mother in Murdstone's case, Little Em'ly in Steerforth's), must necessarily be villains and homewreckers, just as Uriah, as the pretender to Agnes's hand, must be a traitor; conversely, Mr. Dick, whose status as child-man puts him outside the competition, is eligible to become an ally who works to preserve other homes in which David has an emotional stake. But as Andrews details, even though sympathetic male characters are repeatedly shown in childlike guise, "the narrator's attitude towards such manifestations of childishness is significantly ambivalent" (148). Throughout the novel, David, fatherless even before his birth, can identify no fully acceptable male role model: Mr. Peggotty is too simple and rustic, Mr. Micawber is feckless, Dr. Strong and Mr. Wickfield are led astray by false counselors, and so on. Child-men may be preferable to men who, like Murdstone, have nothing of the child in them, but they are not what David aspires to become. That role, perhaps, is situated outside the novel in the person of Dickens himself, creator and appreciator of child-men but as an author imbued with all the control over their world that they so signally lack.

David Copperfield is reprised in 1902 by Jerome K. Jerome's semiautobiographical Künstlerroman *Paul Kelver*, an extended meditation on the connection of the child to creativity that seems strongly influenced by Dickens—who, indeed, makes a cameo appearance in it long before the title character's best friend observes that Paul reminds him of "Doady," or David Copperfield as child-man (401). Like David, Paul is the son of two adults who have themselves remained "children! poor babies they were, both of them" (4), a circumstance that has led to a somewhat tempestuous marriage but draws the young Paul particularly close to his father, "for he was the youngest thing I had met with as yet. . . . my father remained always the same. The hair about his temples was turning grey, and when you looked close you saw many crow's feet and lines, especially about the mouth. But his eyes were the eyes of a boy, his laugh the laugh of a boy, and his heart the heart of a boy. So we were very close to each other" (40–41). Paul's parents, like Jerome's, die while their son is still in his teens, leaving him torn between the desire to get on in the world and the nostalgic longing to return to childhood, which, while in many ways no very happy time for Paul in reality, is associated in his mind with innocence and the free use of his imagination.[3] Thus the awareness that childhood is escaping him (which, symbolically, comes to him as he is crossing a bridge) "troubled me for quite a spell of time, even to the point of tears. . . . I did not want to grow up; could nothing be done to stop it? Rather would I be always as I had been, playing, dreaming. The dark way frightened me. Must I go forward?" (63).

In Paul's formulation, then, the loss of control lies in maturation rather than in remaining a child-man. Child-men, like Paul's father, have discovered the secret of "remain[ing] always the same"; moreover, associated as they are with dreaming, they are already masters of the world of creativity. As Paul's friend Dan advises him, preserving one's inner child is important to the artist:

> "Don't leave him behind you," [Dan] said; "the little boy Paul—Paul the dreamer. . . . This is not his world. He is of no use to you here; won't help you to bread and cheese—no, nor kisses either. But keep him near you. Later, you will find, perhaps, that all along he has been the real Paul—the living, growing Paul; the other—the active, worldly, pushful Paul, only the stuff that dreams are made of, his fretful life a troubled night rounded by a sleep."
>
> "I have been driving him away," I said. "He is so—so impracticable."
>
> Dan shook his head gravely. "It is not his world," he repeated. "We must eat, drink—be husbands, fathers. He does not understand. Here he is the child. Take care of him." (400)

Paul's ambivalence about his child-self is profound. On the one hand, he wants to be "the active, worldly, pushful Paul" who will live up to Edwardian standards of manliness and potency by earning money, making a name for himself, and marrying, the bread and cheese and kisses to which Dan refers.[4] On the other, his history is studded with humiliating love affairs and disastrous work experiences. His first love marries for position and subsequently elopes with a contemporary of Paul's father; Paul himself inadvertently proposes marriage to a barmaid before fleeing the entanglement; Dan predicts that Norah (who will eventually marry Paul) will gravitate toward "someone who will want looking after, taking care of, managing; someone who will appeal to the mother side of her" (401). Consistently, too, Paul's employment similarly involves his exploitation and degradation. It appears, then, that it is because of, not despite, the fact that child-men do not have to provide "[m]eat, drink" or "be husbands, fathers" that they appeal to him.

Yet at the same time, Paul's child-self wields a control that has its own alarming side. Much as David Copperfield, in Andrews's reading, sees child-men as somehow shameful, Paul sees the child-man as untrustworthy, a seducer who seeks to "interfere with us" (64). It is one thing for Dan to wax protective of Paul's child-self; Dan's adulthood is not in question. Paul, who feels "instinctively . . . that in spite of years I was not yet a man" (313), feels more dubious: "I knew well his cunning. Had I let him have his way, he would have led me through the maze of streets he knew so well, past the broken railings (outside of which he would have left my body standing), along the weedy pathway, through the cracked and dented door, up the creaking staircase to the dismal little chamber where we once—he and I together—had sat dreaming foolish dreams" (385–86). That Paul's childhood home is figured as "broken," "cracked and dented," and "dismal" is allied to his sense of "finding myself two distinct individuals, contending with each other" (385). Manhood for him means that a unified self, a true return to childhood, is impossible. Moreover, that such unification is described in quasi-sexual language—"interfere with us," "have his way [with me]"—and envisioned as taking place in a bedroom indicates not only the need for resistance but also a reason for it. In contrast to those authors who, in Robson's words, see the feminized child-self as "repository of purity and moral worth" (13), Paul here puts himself not in the gender-appropriate position of the sexually aggressive male, not in the idealized position of the innocent girl, but in the powerless position of the seduced or molested female. For him there is clearly something about acknowledging oneself a child-man that is unmanning.

Conversely, much as David Copperfield finds himself persistently telling stories of betrayal—his own by Murdstone, Em'ly's by Steerforth, Wickfield's by Uriah, and so on—Paul considers that his maturing process represents a kind of self-betrayal, a desertion by childhood that he can never quite forgive. In a reprise of "that summer evening upon Barking Bridge, when, as it had seemed to me, the little childish Paul had slipped away from me, leaving me lonely and bewildered to find another Self," Paul asks, "Was my boyhood in like manner now falling from me? I found myself clinging to it with vague terror. Its thoughts, its feelings—dreams: they had grown sweet to me; must I lose them? This cold, unknown, new Self, waiting to receive me: I shrank away from it with fear" (363–64). Being unmanned is frightening, but so is being un-childed. David Copperfield's movement from self to self—down-and-out runaway, schoolboy, dandy, hard worker, child playing at marriage, man with an outgrown wife, and so on—is eased by his ability to assign blame elsewhere. Half a century later, Paul's corresponding movement is made nearly impossible by his persistent internalization of horror and guilt.

Robert Hemmings has argued that children's books of the so-called golden age, from approximately 1860 to the 1920s, "are consumed with nostalgia," a mode that "works to cover over aspects of childhood distasteful to adult sensibilities, with only partial success" (54). Citing the work of James Kincaid, Hemmings suggests that the "myth of [childhood] innocence figures children as functionaries serving the needs of the adult writer and reader for whom childhood signifies escape from the pressures of a modern, industrialized, polluted, and exploitative adult world" (56–57). In *Paul Kelver* and *David Copperfield*, which are not children's books but rather novels fundamentally concerned with childhood, Paul's and David's actual experiences of childhood seem unenviable. Paul is the product of an only intermittently functional home and finds social interaction with his peers difficult, while David is traumatized by his mother's remarriage and by his de-classing, de-childing work in the Murdstone and Grinby warehouse. In neither case does being a child permit "escape" from the pressures of the world.

Arguably, however, being an arrested child-man seems to hold out this very promise. Little Billee believes—wants to believe?—that his small size and lack of muscle render him undesirable as a husband. When it appears that a woman approved by his mother may think otherwise, he puts himself beyond the pale as a suitor for her hand by engineering a conversation on atheism with her clergyman father, first expressing to himself his awareness that the latter is unlikely to make allowances "for a poor little weak-kneed, well-meaning waif of a painter-fellow like me" (275). David dabbles with the role when courting Dora, his "child-wife," who represents the possibility of a return to his pre-Murdstone childhood, an idyll of playtime and baby talk with a partner who strongly resembles his mother. Once the marriage has been consummated, however, David rapidly turns his back on the "Doady" side of his personality and uses his function as narrator to insist upon his difference from the other child-men in the novel, his superior ability to cope with the problems of adulthood. Paul, as we have seen, both longs for and tries to repudiate his child-self. Unlike David, he has at best mixed success in the latter endeavor. While Paul's comment that his child-self "might possibly have succeeded" in taking him over but for his "vehement determination never to rest for a moment" until he has paid back a debt of two hundred pounds and his "desire—growing day by day, till it became almost a physical hunger—to feel again the pressure of Norah's strong white hand" (405) implies that maturity wins, Dan's insight that Norah wants a husband whom she can mother suggests otherwise. In all three cases, being a child-man is presented as incompatible with acting upon adult male sexuality, and the implication is that this incompatibility may be part, or even the whole, of the appeal.

Wizards of Id: The Child-Man and the Ego

But the egoless child-man represented by figures such as Jocelin and Little Billee is by no means universal. Even in the works of Dickens, child-men are frequently less admirable than the example of Mr. Dick might suggest. If Dickens offers us the kindly child-man in Mr. Dick and in Joe Gargery of *Great Expectations* (1860–61), he takes darker looks at this figure with the irresponsible "mere child" Harold Skimpole in *Bleak House* (1852–53) and Jenny Wren's "bad child" of a father in *Our Mutual Friend* (1864–65), among many others. Here we are back to the distinction between the innocent and simple childlike adult, who like Du Maurier's Little Billee is naturally virtuous, and his childish counter-part, who seeks his own gratification without thought of consequences. Whereas Mr. Dick and Joe endeavor, albeit often inadequately, to protect against a hostile world the women or children in their care, Jenny's father and Harold Skimpole acknowledge no such responsibility. Skimpole claims child status as a way of refusing to provide for his wife and daughters, and Jenny's drunken father requires her to care for him rather than vice versa. While Mr. Dick and Joe are content to be "nobody" in ways that benefit those around them, other arrested child-men in Dickens's novels are monsters of selfishness and conse-quently damage the lives of those closest to them. Although Victorian fiction contains any number of domestic tyrants who do not qualify as child-men, Dickens's creations gain a peculiar potency from their professed inability or refusal to grow up.

Moreover, the clear unreasonableness of these spoiled adult children's insis-tence that their households revolve around their needs and pleasure calls into question the justness of other men's domestic power as well. As Arthur Adrian points out, "*Bleak House* is one of Dickens's most persuasive arguments that abnormal [i.e., inverted] family relationships inevitably abound in a degenerate society" ("Parenthood" 6). Skimpole is part of a much larger pattern, and this circumstance poses a challenge to the society, and the individuals within it, that can tolerate such a pattern. Thus Skimpole's readiness to sell access to Richard, which ultimately helps to bring about Richard's end, may cause the reader to look askance at the otherwise admirable Mr. Jarndyce, who not only has introduced Richard to Skimpole but also seems incapable of fathoming Skimpole's baseness; Jarndyce's insistence on Skimpole's charm makes a bad situation worse. Jarndyce's willful blindness where Skimpole is concerned reflects his assumption that a man who refers to himself as a child must exist outside the corruption of the system, yet it exposes his own inability to weigh evidence and act in a way that will protect the young people in his charge.[5] For Alexander Welsh, Skimpole's case demonstrates that "Esther is almost immediately able to judge better than her guardian" (25). Moreover, Jarndyce's readiness to play the father to Skimpole's child enables him to "bestow freely of his charity without regard for its potentially damaging effects" (Welsh 93), a luxury that, it transpires, comes at a high cost.

Similarly, in *Our Mutual Friend*, Sara Schotland argues, Jenny's inability to "raise" her father, whom she can preserve neither from drink nor from death, is balanced by her rescue of Lizzie Hexam's beloved. She "forms the character and literally fashions the life of Eugene Wrayburn as she assists the young lawyer in the two most important decisions that he will ever make: choice of a wife and commitment to meaningful work" (n. pag.). Although it refers to literal children, Jenny's comment upon our first encounter with her, "Give me grown-ups. . . . So sensible. Sit so quiet. Don't go prancing and capering about! And I mean always to keep among none but grown-ups till I marry" (Dickens, *Friend* 224–25), nonetheless hints that even before childbirth, marriage may put women in the company of those who are not "grown-ups." Where Eugene and Lizzie are concerned, the remark may seem prophetic, for despite his superior social status, Eugene's directionlessness initially renders him as unfit a husband for Lizzie as "Mr. Dolls" (whose cognomen reminds us not only that his twelve-year-old daughter is the family breadwinner but also that he functions in this dyad primarily as the focus of Jenny's imaginative play, her "child" rather than her parent) is unfit to be a father for Jenny. With the example of Jenny's father before us, we are the more unwilling to see Eugene master of his own establishment until he becomes master of his own desires.

Dickens's contemptible child-men have at least the virtue of unimportance beyond their immediate social circles. By the end of the century, however, some social critics were identifying the selfish child-man's destructive force as potentially titanic in scope. Consider the Hungarian writer and journalist Max Nordau's influential 1892 study *Degeneration*, translated into English in 1895 and soon identified as an important, if controversial,[6] addition to the international conversation on degeneration already being conducted by the Italian criminologist Cesare Lombroso, the British psychologists Henry Maudsley and James Sully, the French neurologist Jean-Martin Charcot, the Austrian-born French psychologist Bénédict Augustin Morel, and many others. For Nordau, the degenerate's hallmark is "ego-mania," and "in the relation of his 'Ego' to his 'non-Ego,' the degenerate man remains a child all his life" (254), incapable of achieving maturity by developing altruism. This degenerate child-man and "moral lunatic" (266), who manifests the child's natural "instinct of destruction" (264), poses a clear and present danger to the social order. If he is an artist, his vision may pervert others' tastes, as witnessed, according to Nordau, by the popularity of "Swinburne's childish devilry" (96–97), the "school-boys' war" waged by the French Symbolists (137), and the "repel[lent]," "child-ish" qualities of the Pre-Raphaelites' productions (82). If he inclines rather to other modes of conquest, he will be a Napoleon, "a criminal" or "an anarchist" (266). But in all these forms he remains a warped child inhabiting a man's body, a drag on humankind's progression toward maturity.

Nordau's child-man is larger than life, frightening yet also impressive in the sheer scale of the damage that he may wreak. The conjunction of degeneracy with childishness is therefore telling. What is striking about the use of the child here is that its purpose is to illustrate the magnitude of the problem, not to arouse in the reader a spirit of amused contempt. A man who rejects the responsibilities of the masculine gender role, it seems, commits an act of violence against society. An insidious facet of this violence is that it can be combined with apparent acquiescence in the requirements of adulthood. Thus the Pre-Raphaelites, for instance, offend not by a Skimpole-like idleness but by the perversity of their approach to making a living. They paint, they sell their paintings, they make their way in the world, but they do so by commodifying a "childish" vision and inveigling the world into accepting it. They accordingly mount a Trojan Horse attack upon dominant adult culture, appearing to conform but actually subverting. That the primary victim here is masculinity is suggested by the absence of the child-woman from Nordau's calculus; the objects of his anxiety are explicitly male.

One may see in Nordau's anxiety about the corruptness of the child-man the persistence of the medieval belief that childhood is characterized by licentiousness and foolishness, what we earlier saw Bagehot describe as "the passions of manhood without the repressive vigour of a man's will." In his classic *Centuries of Childhood*, Philippe Ariès writes of the movement, which he dates to the end of the sixteenth century, to see children as innocent. The innovation represented by "the idea of childish innocence," he notes, "resulted in two kinds of attitude and behaviour towards childhood: firstly, safeguarding it against pollution by life, and particularly by the sexuality tolerated if not approved of among adults; and secondly, strengthening it by developing character and reason" (119).

Ariès's version of how and when particular attitudes toward childhood developed has been criticized by later scholars, but certainly there was substantial support in the Victorian period for the linking of innocence with youth. Even so, contrary ideas about the child's natural tendency toward sensuality remain evident in the nineteenth century. Consider, for instance, the concern about the debauching of the young evident in the warning that children should not be allowed to associate overmuch with servants, or the anxiety about (in particular) boys' masturbation. Nordau's child-man is at once corrupt and lacking in "character and reason"; he has the weakness, but not the purity, of the good child. And, indeed, for many nineteenth-century observers childish purity was a fragile and contingent matter in any case, dependent upon a privileged class status, nationality, ethnicity, and upbringing. Nordau's child-man, source rather than victim of pollution, embodies an understanding of childhood that may have been a minority view in the late nineteenth century where the offspring of the privileged were concerned but that nonetheless continued to characterize attitudes toward the young of other classes.

Nordau's work received respectful notice as well as hostile criticism, his framing of the problem evidently striking a sympathetic chord in many British readers. But other uses of the term *child-man* to denote inadequacy and arrested development proved deeply disturbing to some Victorians. In her 1894 article "The New Aspect of the Woman Question," the feminist Sarah Grand launched a scathing attack upon male privilege and masculinist assumptions. Her essay occupies seven closely printed pages, but the passage most often quoted in the various contemporaneous responses to it runs as follows: "It is the woman's place and pride and pleasure to teach the child, and man morally is in his infancy. . . . Now woman holds out a strong hand to the child-man, and insists, but with infinite tenderness and pity, upon helping him up" (273). Thus, for instance, the popular novelist Ouida scoffs at the term *child-man* as apparently embracing "Bismarck? Herbert Spencer? Edison? Gladstone? Alexander III?" (612), while Charles G. Harper complains in *Revolted Woman*, "All the toil and trouble of this work-a-day world proceed from her sex; and yet the cant of 'Woman's Mission' fills the air, and the New Woman is promised us as some sort of a pedagogue who shall teach the 'Child-Man' how to toddle in the paths of virtue and content. How absurd it all is. . . . These women writers . . . [are] margarine masquerading as 'best fresh' " (x).

In other words, Grand's suggestion that potency lay not with the child-man but with the adult (New) woman evidently represented a less palatable attack on patriarchy than those mounted by male writers who made use of the child-man.[7] If Skimpole's selfish irresponsibility and Jarndyce's refusal to see it as problematic throw Esther's virtue and good judgment into a still more favorable light, this contrast does not jeopardize masculine authority as an abstract concept in the world of *Bleak House*, since Esther goes to such lengths throughout the narrative to repudiate power. If Carlyle feels affection for Jocelin, it is partly because Jocelin is so ready to grant respect to Abbot Samson, further bolstering masculine authority in a world that in any case, like Nordau's, includes no visible women. If Paul Kelver finds navigating the adult world especially difficult because of his encounters with rapacious men who are ready to engage in any fraud that will benefit them, he encounters also his share of women who demonstrate their willingness to marry for social and financial gain; selfishness in Jerome's novel has no gender. In contrast, Grand is clearly referring to the child-man not as a pathological anomaly but as representative of his sex's "Bawling Brotherhood" of self-absorbed men who "exact all things of [women]" and give little back (271). Man, she notes, is the supreme egotist, having "set himself up as a sort of a god and required us to worship him" (272). Now that "man has shrunk to his true proportions in our estimation" (272), Grand insists upon the reassignment of power to women, to whom ruling over children comes naturally.

These writers return us to the anxiety associated with childishness. Childlike men, such as those discussed in the first section of this chapter, stand to some degree outside the activities through which adult men are normally expected to keep Victorian society functioning: production and procreation.

Tucked into the "cradle" of stasis, to draw upon Carlyle's metaphor, they resist change and experience. They ask less of life, not more, and while the narratives here surveyed suggest that this strategy has its drawbacks and discomforts—for the observer if not always for the participant—they also see its appealing side. Child*ish* men, in contrast, know no limits; even while they produce nothing, their approach to life is typified by excess. The level of attention roused by Nordau's *Degeneration* and Grand's article indicates a fear of the social consequences that may arise either from the egotistical child-man's insistence upon gratification or from others' struggle against that insistence. The solution that some late nineteenth-century feminists proposed—to reorganize the social hierarchy to define women's traditional roles of child rearing and housekeeping as giving them control not merely over the private household but also over its national counterpart—seemed to many readers of the 1890s as degenerate as any of the "moral lunacies" that Nordau identifies. It is suggestive that in the nineteenth century, arrested child-men are more likely to appear in male-authored works than in female-authored ones and that the objections that followed Grand's use of the trope did not greet its employment by male writers.

Looking Backward: The Child-Man and Atavism

Grand's contrast between man, "morally in his infancy," and the more highly developed woman draws upon a widespread nineteenth-century idea about the nature of human evolution, namely, that at any given moment the species will contain some individuals who are highly evolved and others, atavisms, in whom characteristics associated with primitive man or with other ancestral forms will resurface. But such links to an undesirable past were seen not only in isolated individuals but also in defined segments of the population. Just as the "inferior races" were frequently seen as less-evolved "survivals" showing a closer connection to the subhuman than was manifested by Anglo-Saxons, post-Darwinian science sometimes defined children and criminals (and, Nordau would add, certain kinds of artists; degeneration may be seen as a kind of backward evolution) as manifesting traits belonging to what Havelock Ellis termed "a lower and older social state than that in which [they are] actually living" (*Criminal* 206). Indeed, the more advanced humanity became, the further back some individuals or groups, including children, might appear to be situated. In Maudsley's words, "The capability of great development is the capability of great degeneration" (79–80).

Hence, as Cynthia Eagle Russett puts it, "One of the most striking instances of the rejection of early-nineteenth-century romanticism is the hard-
headed revaluation of childhood that took place among scientists of Lombro-
sian persuasion in the later part of the century" (72). Some of this revaluation
involved an apparently value-neutral tracing of young children's facial features
or other physical characteristics to the remote past, as in Louis Robinson's
series of articles with titles such as "Darwinism in the Nursery" (*Nineteenth
Century*, 1891) and "The Meaning of a Baby's Footprint" (*Nineteenth Century*,
1892); S. S. Buckman's "Babies and Monkeys" (*Nineteenth Century*, 1894), which
contends that "the actions of children when rightly interpreted tell their own
tale and may fitly be compared to ancient monuments of prehistoric times" (743);
and Alfred A. Mumford's "Survival Movements of Human Infancy" (*Brain*,
1897), which sees babies' movements as survivals of ancestral water-dwelling
forms. Other revaluations, as I discuss in chapter 3, define the child as an evolutionary form superior to the adult.

But Ernst Haeckel's precept "Ontogeny recapitulates phylogeny" was not
merely a matter of observing likenesses between human embryos and amphib-
ians. Like a number of nineteenth-century scientists, Haeckel considered the
child close kin to the savage. Thus, for instance, Maudsley asserts in an 1862
article in the *Journal of Mental Science* that "the quick passion, the vices, the
cruelties, and the other evidences of an uninformed moral sense which the
young child discovers, are invariably observable also in the infantile mind of a
barbarous people" (79), a view no more complimentary to the English child than
it is to the "barbarous" non-European adult. As "every child must at first be,
and is, eminently selfish," children, monkeys, cats, and "the lowest barbarian"
are alike, Maudsley continues, in taking pleasure in witnessing another being's
pain. This is because "there is not, by reason of the low state of mental development, any penetrating consciousness of the condition of the not-self. . . . The
ideas which correlate the feelings of compassion, sympathy, benevolence, and
other such holy states of consciousness, have not yet been developed in the
mind" (78).

A generation later, Ellis expresses a similar view, holding that delinquent or
criminal traits "are but an exaggeration of the characters which in a less degree
mark nearly all children. The child is naturally, by his organisation, nearer
to the animal, to the savage, to the criminal, than the adult. . . . Children are
naturally egoists; they will commit all enormities, sometimes, to enlarge their
egoistic satisfaction" (*Criminal* 212). Conversely, Ellis continues, "the criminal

is an individual who, to some extent, remains a child his life long—a child of larger growth and with greater capacity for evil. . . . All who have come very intimately in contact with criminals have noted their resemblance to children" (214).[8] In short, although associated particularly with the theories of Lombroso, the contention that criminality is an adult form of childhood and that both criminals and children are properly understood as atavisms had wide currency among British scientific commentators as well. Moreover, although atavism was in one sense an innate condition, like Nordau's version of degeneration it was also a kind of virus. As Lombroso warned of another type of criminal child-man, the homosexual was born, but he was also made. Such men, he said, "who manifest their evil propensities from childhood," "should be confined from their youth, for they are a source of contagion and cause a great number of occasional criminals" (qtd. in Stockton 290).

Alongside the distinction between *childlike* (good) and *childish* (bad), then, we may set that between the noble savage and the base savage. Following the lead of Jean-Jacques Rousseau, Romantics had celebrated children's freedom, simplicity, even irrationality. Later in the nineteenth century, in contrast, the primitivism sometimes associated with the young could look to post-Darwinian writers like a reminder of humankind's embarrassing membership in the animal world—this membership itself, perhaps, almost a form of criminality. As Robert Mighall writes, "Hyde is dwarfish because his moral nature is arrested or completely absent" (148). If Mr. Dick's innocent goodness hints that the child-man may be the moral superior of his fully adult counterpart, other arrested child-men seem less wholesome. In an essay cogently entitled "Between Atavism and Altruism," Jenny Bourne Taylor comments on how "the ambiguous, Janus-faced figure of the child, revealing the past of human development while representing the legacy of the present to be transmitted to future generations, came to permeate late-nineteenth-century accounts of individual and social development and to encapsulate its most profound unease" (91). The child-man in the fiction of the *fin de siècle* is in many cases similarly indebted to the new scientific literature of primitivism, to still more sinister effect.

Arthur Conan Doyle's *The Sign of Four* (1890) is one such text. In *Post-Traumatic Culture*, Kirby Farrell traces the child-man's presence in Doyle's pioneering detective story. In Farrell's persuasive reading, the villain, aptly named Jonathan Small, and his murderous pygmy double, Tonga, are part of an extensive pattern within the novel in which aggression is "associate[d] with children" (60), the infantilized racial Others of British imperial possessions are demonic and cannot be assimilated into the "family" of the homeland, and the novel at its heart is about "traumatic parent-child abuse. . . . In shooting Tonga, the masterful symbolic father Holmes is killing a renegade son" (61). The connection to late nineteenth-century discussions of atavism, racial difference, and criminality is apparent. As Farrell makes clear, however, the ambiguity that we have noticed in positive depictions of the child-man continues into this more negative version. From the standpoint of the "normal" observer, represented here by Dr. Watson, the adventure recounted in *The Sign of Four* is deeply horrific, full of unnatural and uncanny incidents and punctuated by the destruction of more than one set of family bonds. From the standpoint of Small, who turns out to be victim as well as criminal, the horror of the events is rather a matter of the covetousness, injustice, and willingness to wrong others manifested by the representatives of imperial patriarchy. If to some extent colonial adventure is most readily justified by seeing the colonized as primitive child-men in need of adult (British) guidance, Doyle's novel also permits the reader engaged by Small and Tonga to feel a certain uneasiness about how adult power may be used.

The Sign of Four has points in common with other late nineteenth-century texts, including Joseph Conrad's *Heart of Darkness* (1899) and Robert Louis Stevenson's *Strange Case of Dr. Jekyll and Mr. Hyde* (1886). Much as Jonathan Small unleashes a monstrous primitive in Tonga, whose tiny footprint causes Dr. Watson to identify him as a "child," Conrad's Kurtz and Stevenson's Dr. Jekyll conceal, release, and ultimately lose control of their own inner child-men. Kurtz, in traveling to a dark and primitive place inhabited by natives whose age "it's hard to tell" (20) but whom the colonizers term "boy[s]" (25), reverts to something latent (Marlow suspects) in all men that is normally inhibited by civilization.[9] Indeed, one of Kurtz's most frightening aspects is that his movement "beyond the bounds of permitted aspirations" (65) is not traceable to qualities unique to him, "hollow at the core" though he may be (58). To Mona Caird (writing on marriage in an 1894 *Westminster Review*) as to many other feminists, it was only too apparent that "man in any age or country is liable to revert to a state of savagery" (qtd. in Showalter, "Syphilis" 96).

Following Kurtz in what he compares to "a boyish game," Marlow finds him "crawling on all-fours" like an infant or an animal (64). To Marlow, Kurtz is both morally insane and "contemptibly childish" (67), judgments that recall the work of Lombroso and his British allies. Left behind at home, Kurtz's Intended has no place in the reversion that characterizes those who participate in the African adventure. Marlow reports that "she was not very young—I mean not girlish. She had a mature capacity for fidelity, for belief, for suffering" (73). Thus when Marlow tells her that Kurtz died with her name on his lips, whereas he has earlier testified that Kurtz's dying words were "The horror! The horror!" (68), we understand that Marlow himself has returned to civilization, to adulthood, to the land of the comforting lie about the innate goodness of the human heart.

As many readers have observed, Kurtz's journey reveals that the civilized may in fact be at least as primitive as the "backward" subjects of their imperial enterprise. Similarly, Jekyll's experiment demonstrates not that under the wrong circumstances the civilized professional man may be liable to invasion by his opposite, but that the mature exterior has always been inhabited by the dwarfish, youthful, and repellent "Master" Edward Hyde. (This honorific, applied ironically by Jekyll's lawyer, Mr. Utterson [16], is of course the title normally given to males who have not reached their majority.) Jekyll likens his double to "a schoolboy" casting off his burden of respectability and "spring[ing] headlong into the sea of liberty" (61), and while Jekyll and his friends see Jekyll as virtuous and the evil Hyde as his moral opposite, the true horror of the tale is that Jekyll in fact enjoys being Hyde, relishes "the comparative youth, the light step, leaping pulses and secret pleasures" associated with this persona (64), and repudiates the self-restraint inculcated in him during his own childhood, "when," as he puts it, "I had walked with my father's hand" (66). Hyde's attacks on patriarchy, during which he murders an elderly member of Parliament and "burn[s] the letters and destroy[s] the picture of [Jekyll's] father" (70), render him at least ostensibly horrific to Jekyll, but the child-man's rejection of order and discipline is also what motivated Jekyll to release this side of himself in the first place and what has continued to make being Hyde so disastrously desirable. Like Alan Breck Stewart in *Kidnapped* (1886) and nearly all the adults in *Treasure Island* (1881–82), Jekyll has never fully accepted the constraints of adulthood.

During the 1880s, before and after the publication of Stevenson's novella, the French psychoanalyst Pierre Janet and his uncle and mentor, the philosopher Paul Janet, published scientific discussions of dual personality. The Janets' explorations may be placed in the context of evolutionist writings on this topic produced by Sully, John Stuart Mill, Alexander Bain, and others, just as Stevenson's work may also be considered in light of what André LeBlanc calls "the many cases of 'double personality' that began appearing around 1876 and were being frequently diagnosed during the 1880s" (63). Ed Block Jr. has pointed out that Sully's findings in particular may have influenced Stevenson, since the two knew each other; for example, both were frequent contributors to the *Cornhill Magazine* in the years before the publication of *Dr. Jekyll and Mr. Hyde* (446–47).[10] Yet Ian Hacking notes that Stevenson also "corresponded with Pierre Janet while writing *Dr. Jekyll and Mr. Hyde*" (278n12), and as cited and amplified by Nordau, the Janets' writings might be considered especially apropos to the idea of Hyde as child-man: "Every person consists of two personalities, one conscious and one unconscious. . . . In the hysteric they are unequal, and out of equilibrium," writes Pierre Janet in 1886, while Nordau adds, again coupling the prehuman with the childish, "In the degenerate with disturbed equilibrium consciousness has to play the part of an ape-like mother finding excuses for the stupid and naughty tricks of a spoiled child" (111).

Stevenson's text, of course, furthers the idea that Hyde has something simian about him in Jekyll's complaints about Hyde's "ape-like spite" (71) and "the ape-like tricks that he would play me" (70) and his stress upon Hyde's hairiness and gnashing teeth. But the further stress upon the child in Nordau's citation of the Janets reminds us that the degeneracy and criminality associated with Hyde by Stevenson's text and with the hysteric by late nineteenth-century psychology were sometimes seen specifically as a manifestation of a childishness that, though delinquent and undesirable, was potentially present in any civilized being. Indeed, Charles Darwin also mentions human body hair (and its habit of bristling at moments of stress) and gnashing teeth as evidence of humanity's protosimian ancestry—again, aspects of a heritage shared by all humans rather than the stigmata of a rare pathology. As the Janets note and Stevenson's novella (like Conrad's) implies, we are all dual personalities, just as the child-man has both good and bad avatars. This insight accounts for much of Hyde's eeriness. He is not Other but Self, a horrifying incarnation of Freud's "return of the repressed" that, as detailed in chapter 1, we elsewhere see in other form as the figure of the old-fashioned child.

As *Heart of Darkness* illustrates, the association between the primitive, the degenerate, the childish, and the horrific was not limited to tales of ape-men. David Glover has pointed out that "the characters in *Dracula* are placed in relation to the conceptual field of degeneration theory" and that Dracula, in particular, may be seen as the embodiment of Nordau's "list of identifying traits" of the degenerate (253). Glover cites facial characteristics such as the Count's sharp teeth and bushy eyebrows, but within the text of Bram Stoker's 1897 novel, Van Helsing positions the battle as a conflict between the vampire-hunters' "man-brains" and Dracula's "child-brain that lie in his tomb for centuries, that grow not yet to our stature, and that do only work selfish and therefore small" (294). This emphasis on the immaturity of Dracula's all-consuming egotism is entirely in line with Nordau's and Lombroso's arguments. Indeed, Mina Harker specifically cites these figures within the novel when she realizes, "The Count is a criminal and of criminal type. Nordau and Lombroso would so classify him, and *qua* criminal he is of an imperfectly formed mind. Thus, in a difficulty he has to seek resource in habit" (296). But in invoking the child-man, Stoker simultaneously articulates an issue that had a peculiar capacity to horrify late Victorian society: that Dracula's threat is specifically against the primacy and potency of the "normal" patriarchal Victorian male. Nor is Dracula alone in his efforts.

Many critics have discussed ways in which *Dracula* hints at a demonic attack on normative Victorian understandings of gender and sexuality. Dracula's vampirized women become sexually aggressive in their approaches to potential male victims and show themselves to be callous creatures of appetite where children are concerned. Indeed, the vampire women are more stereotypically masculine than most of the novel's males, who may readily be turned into passive sexual prey by vampires and into children by women who embody "the mother spirit." For instance, in telling of comforting Arthur after the death of his fiancée, Lucy, Mina reports, "I felt this big sorrowing man's head resting on me, as though it were that of a baby that some day may lie on my bosom, and I stroked his hair as though he were my own child. I never thought at the time how strange it all was" (203). Both demonic and angelic women, in other words, have the disturbing power of transforming the normal man into a child-man, so that the novel's emphasis on Dracula's "child-brain," inferior reasoning powers, innate criminality, distinctive physiognomy, and other markers of difference helps to divert attention from another sort of masculine infantilization that affects not the pathological but the ordinary man.

Reassuringly, difference trumps similarity here, and the childlike qualities of the normal are swamped by the childlike qualities of the abnormal. Patriarchy appears to be the fulcrum. As Christopher Craft details, Dracula launches a war against patriarchy as embodied in his chief antagonist, Abraham Van Helsing (117), whose Old Testament name hints at what he represents. The weapons in this war are not only the implicit threat of homosexuality identified by Craft and other critics but also the explicit threat of humanity's extirpation by a rival form. Presently, Dracula is "only" a child-man and thus subject to defeat. Van Helsing reveals, however, that Dracula's most frightening attribute may be his ability to mature, for he will grow not into a human man but into some other, more potent type of patriarch:

> In some faculties of mind he has been, and is, only a child. But he is growing, and some things that were childish at the first are now of man's stature. He is experimenting, and doing it well. And if it had not been that we have crossed his path he would be yet, he may be yet if we fail, the father or furtherer of a new order of beings, whose road must lead through Death, not Life. . . . He has all along, since his coming, been trying his power, slowly but surely. That big child-brain of his is working. Well for us, it is as yet a child-brain. For had he dared, at the first, to attempt certain things he would long ago have been beyond our power. (263–64)

Van Helsing leaves his interlocutors in doubt as to what the "certain things" may be that would turn Dracula into the ultimately successful patriarch. The reader, however, may hypothesize that they further a strategy that Dracula has already been pursuing. Throughout, we see him forming alliances with other beings outside the conventional power structure: animals, Gypsies, madmen, and especially women, with whom the child may be thought to have a strong natural bond that potentially questions the patriarch's authority. As the Count taunts his hunters, "Your girls that you all love are mine already. And through them you and others shall yet be mine, my creatures, to do my bidding" (267).

Kurtz and his display of human heads on posts, the savage Tonga, the "troglodytic" Hyde (Stevenson, *Case* 14), the centuries-old Dracula—all speak to the potential atavism of the arrested child-man. Indeed, writing in 1913, Faith Ashford uses the term *child-man* to discuss British prehistory. Ashford's foreword to *Child-Man in Britain* seeks to enter into the state of mind of her subjects, who are "not half a step above the animals in manners and intelligence" (9). She imagines the ancient British as paranoid, confronted with a nature too vast and destructive to control: "Out of the horrors of winter, the horror of the beasts and the dark woods their home, the horrors of flood and tempest, the bewildered Child-People conceive awesome demons of evil intent towards their helplessness, and with appetites hardly to be satisfied" (10). Within a few pages of this passage, however, the focus has shifted from cave men to modern children, who, spoiled by indulgent and overprotective parents, are not at the mercy of others' appetites; rather, they are beings of unlimited appetite and demonic tendencies themselves. "The perverse despotism of the idol of the nursery" arises because "grown-ups save his weakness from the shocks of strength, his littleness from contact with bigness, and he becomes inflated with a sense of his own power" (13). This argument is identical to that made by Grand about women's relationship to men, and readers acquainted with the atavism discussions carried on over the fifty-odd years before the publication of Ashford's book will find nothing surprising in the juxtaposition of modern child and Neolithic adult.

But whereas some writers on atavism perceive the modern child as the moral equivalent of the prehistoric savage, Ashford suggests that the child is his ancestor's moral inferior. In a fashion that harmonizes with some late nineteenth-century commentators' doubts about the innate virtue of the child, and much as Kurtz turns himself into an "idol" and the focus of outré "ceremonies" (Conrad 58), Ashford's child perceives himself as the center of a universe that must bow to his will. This inability to consider others' needs or interests is also what renders Tonga, Hyde, and Dracula uncontrollable. With less threatening effects, it characterizes earlier child-men such as Dickens's Harold Skimpole and Mr. Dolls as well. Yet even while the ruthless egotism of these figures is represented as dangerous to those around them, the association with primeval freedom may excite envy.

Thus, for instance, Ashford's pampered modern child is cut off not only from the natural world but also from his own nature and so lacks the inhibitions that come with conscience. Kurtz, says Marlow, has "no restraint, no restraint" (51); the reduplication of the phrase allies it to "The horror! The horror!" but also suggests that here may be a motivation for the admiration with which the Europeans tend to regard him. Tonga's footprint is distinguished from an Englishman's by its small size but also by its lack of cramping; he has never known the confinement of shoes, just as he is also unrestrained by the codes of civilized conduct. Hyde is "younger, lighter, happier in body" than Jekyll, characterized by "a heady recklessness . . . a solution of the bonds of obligation, an unknown but not an innocent freedom of the soul" (58). Dracula is a collector of women and gold, a connoisseur of appetites that his hunters, in their bloody attacks on female vampires, seem to derive satisfaction from emulating. Arrested child-women such as Hetty Sorrel in George Eliot's *Adam Bede* (1859) and Mary Elizabeth Braddon's Lady Audley (1861–62) sometimes have their own murderous tendencies. Yet their criminality is represented as aberrant, the product of childhood neglect or mental instability. In contrast, the problem with Tonga, Hyde, Dracula, and their fellows is precisely that they are not deviant, but rather represent the free expression of qualities that, their creators hint, are commonly to be found in men but are usually more effectively repressed. The repression necessary to civilization, however, is a source of ambivalence.

The discussions of atavism that are latent (and sometimes overt) in late Victorian gothic texts such as Doyle's, Conrad's, Stevenson's, Stoker's, and indeed Nordau's identify the arrested child-man as the site of an assortment of socially undesirable traits, in particular egotism, appetite, homoeroticism, rebelliousness, and irrepressibility. Such post-Darwinian child-men remind readers of the limited extent to which humankind has evolved beyond the animal. Yet the bad child is also the energetic child, his step lighter and his being freer than is presumed to be the case for the civilized reader. Dickens's bad child-men are not objects of readerly envy, because they have essentially surrendered the authority that ought to accompany their age and gender. The pleasures they receive in return are pleasures that, to some extent, they could have had in any case. A generation later, Hyde and his brothers leave no doubt that their appetites are both more imaginative and more potent than the simple desire for drink or leisure manifested by Jenny Wren's father or Harold Skimpole. They have found what appear to be potentially viable alternatives to tame bourgeois domesticity, which is why they must be destroyed, often by representatives of patriarchal order. But before their inevitable deaths, in their alternative visions they do patriarchy a valuable service as they either displace the Angel in the House (with Hyde around, Dr. Jekyll's romance need contain no significant women), abandon her for other pleasures, or, like Dracula, vampirize her.

The Child-Man and Sexuality

As Virginia Woolf famously notes in "Professions for Women," the Angel in the House was an icon of altruism: "She was utterly unselfish. She excelled in the difficult arts of family life. She sacrificed herself daily. If there was chicken, she took the leg; if there was a draught she sat in it—in short she was so constituted that she never had a mind or a wish of her own, but preferred to sympathize always with the minds and wishes of others" (n. pag.). In this apparent self-eradication lay the Angel's domestic power, manipulated in a feminist context by New Woman writers such as Grand, who, we recall, so offended her late Victorian readers when she offered woman as the child-man's guide and teacher. Texts that, like *Dracula*, instead offer the child-man as the antagonist and thwarter of the Angel (or, in the case of *Trilby*, as the Angel's supplanter) thus performed a welcome function for beleaguered masculinity, especially since the narrative pattern invariably restores patriarchal order at tale's end.

In an American context, Kenneth Kidd has explored another link between the boy and the savage in the literature of the "feral child," which, anxious as it is about its subject's barbarism, nonetheless may celebrate the authenticity and energy of the masculinity on display. Similarly, focusing on the final two decades of the nineteenth century as an era concerned about degeneration, John Tosh discusses "the varied appeal of empire as a marker of manhood, through its association with adventure, sexual license, personal authority and violence" (202). Yet as Tosh also points out, this model of imperial manhood was most easily enacted in a frontier setting; it was not readily combined with companionate marriage in the suburbs. The association of untamed masculinity with illicit sexuality was particularly disturbing on the home front in a society eager to control epidemic venereal disease, the proliferation of prostitution, and, by the end of the century, well-publicized homosexual scandals.

Thus one way to distinguish the good child-man, such as Joe Gargery, Mr. Dick, and Little Billee, from the destructive child-man is by examining sexual continence. Throughout his marriage to Pip's sister, Joe is childless and apparently without sexual drive; Mr. Dick is devoted to Betsey Trotwood, but their cohabitation clearly does not extend to the bedroom. Little Billee may transgress gender boundaries, but the exalted terms in which the narrator describes his simultaneous transgression of age boundaries (and his professed though unconsummated love for Trilby) identifies his love for other men as pure. Paul Kelver repeatedly discusses his child-self in the context of sexuality and represents him as a seducer eager to "have his way" with him, but he also asserts that his child-self is in flight from adult urges. In contrast, Dickens's selfish child-men all father children (and refuse to provide for them); Tonga is obsessively "devoted" to Jonathan Small, who describes their relationship in terms that might also be used to describe a marriage ("He was staunch and true, was little Tonga. No man ever had a more faithful mate" [170]); Kurtz takes an African mistress; the polygamous Dracula lays alarming claim to Jonathan Harker ("This man belongs to me!" [43]); and Jekyll's friends fear that Hyde is either the good doctor's illegitimate son or his catamite. The list could be continued with other *fin-de-siècle* child-men, such as Oscar Wilde's Dorian Gray, whose sexual ambivalence—is he a seducer of child-women, a homosexual, or both?—is one with the generational ambivalence that enables the text to assert simultaneously that he is a boy and that he has left boyhood far behind.[11]

Suggestively, there is significant overlap between what Elaine Showalter identifies as the syphilis literature of the late nineteenth century, with its emphasis on the "virtually complete perversion of moral sense" ("Syphilis" 91) and its recurring "suffering, apish, shriveled, and prematurely aged . . . syphilitic children[, who] appeared to feminists as living symbols of the devolutionary force of male vice" (95), and the contemporaneous texts involving age inversion that I examine here. Showalter focuses on texts including not only *Jude the Obscure, The Heavenly Twins, The Time Machine*, and *She*, which I discuss in chapters 3 and 5, but also *Dracula, Dr. Jekyll and Mr. Hyde*, and *The Picture of Dorian Gray*. Especially where child-men are concerned, it would appear, the transgression of social norms regarding age is likely to be intimately connected to the transgression of sexual mores. Although they may sometimes become involved in illicit sexual connections, Victorian child-women do not seem designed to illustrate a domestically dangerous approach to sexuality to which all women might be liable. Victorian child-men, more disturbingly, sometimes function in the sexual realm as well as the criminal to hint at what readers might choose to see either as evil of which all men may be capable (and for which they will be duly punished) if they refuse to accept the guidance of the Angel in the House or as pleasures that might not have been forbidden but for that same minatory female figure.

Anxiety about culturally mandated altruism and the curbing of the self extends well beyond turn-of-the-century Britain. We find it analyzed in detail in Freud's *Civilization and Its Discontents* (1930), in which he comments that

> it is impossible to overlook the extent to which civilization is built up upon a renunciation of instinct, how much it presupposes precisely the non-satisfaction (by suppression, repression or some other means?) of powerful instincts. This "cultural frustration" dominates the large field of social relationships between human beings. As we already know, it is the cause of the hostility against which all civilizations have to struggle. . . . It is not easy to understand how it can become possible to deprive an instinct of satisfaction. Nor is doing so without danger. (44)

James Strachey notes in introducing *Civilization and Its Discontents* that its central idea builds upon ideas already present in Freud's work (and the surrounding intellectual culture) in the 1890s and early 1900s. For instance, Strachey comments that in *Three Essays* (1905) Freud posits an "inverse relation holding between civilization and the free development of sexuality" (Freud, *Civilization* 6). If the maturity of a culture requires "renunciation" and sexual restraint, so too does the maturity of the individual Victorian man. The suspicion that he might be losing touch with vital energies or with masculinity itself helps to explain the ambiguity that surrounds "good," sexually pure child-men such as Little Billee, Mr. Dick, and Paul Kelver, as well as the hint of envy that attaches to "bad," sexually free versions of the figure such as Hyde, Kurtz, and Dracula.

Whether hypermasculine or feminized, the arrested child-man provided an opportunity for the encoded airing of trepidation not only about parenthood (often the chief function of the precocious child-woman) but also about masculinity. When virtuous, he serves as a silent reproach to his fully mature brothers, whose good qualities seem by contrast to be ignobly motivated and whose bad qualities loom much larger. When horrific, he embodies a lack of restraint that makes his "civilized" counterparts horrific as well; he puts on display what they, by implication, only restrain with difficulty, and in the process he may suggest to the rebellious reader the potency that civilized man has surrendered. There were, of course, countless open expressions during this period of anxiety about male sexuality, selfishness, violence, and general bad behavior, of which the sexual-purity campaigns are only one example. I would argue not only that fiction and nonfiction involving arrested child-men gain narrative power by evoking the more open discourse but also that to some extent the reverse is true as well. The child-man discourse, operating extensively in the realm of the symbolic, is freed—as is the fantastic child-man himself—from the bonds of the quotidian and the plausible, liberated to enter spaces that more factually oriented complaints about male wrongdoing could not. Considering the Hyde of the child-man discourse alongside the Jekyll of realistically couched complaints about masculinity thus provides the historian of gender with a more complete picture of attitudes during this period.

three

Women as Girls

The arrested child-men discussed in chapter 2 come from many social classes, ranging from the central European aristocrat Dracula, to the British haute and petite bourgeoisie (with a working-class example in Mr. Dolls of *Our Mutual Friend*), to the apish "born criminal" of Cesare Lombroso's theorizing and the "primitive savage" represented by *The Sign of Four*'s Tonga. The dueling conditions of childlikeness and childishness, we are to understand, can characterize men of any era, nation, and condition. In contrast, the arrested child-woman in Victorian fiction is more commonly a figure of privilege. Considered as a period of leisure and protection from difficulties, childhood was a luxury, and (to adapt a concept from Thorstein Veblen) the Victorian father who was in a position to prolong it for his daughters was advertising the excellence of both his earning capacity and his domestic affections. Sons might need to be toughened up, prepared for the hard knocks of the world. Middle-class daughters, at least according to one widely accepted vision, needed sheltering.

In her most famous incarnation, as Dora in *David Copperfield*, the arrested child-woman has been sheltered to such an extent that she is usually read as an example of "infantuation" run amok.[1] Unable to mature or to function in the adult world, she signals the male protagonist's initial immaturity and naïveté, and although the narrative paints a sympathetic portrait of her charms, she must die so that her man can grow to full adulthood. As the 1878 preface to *The Child-Wife*, the much-abridged American version of *David Copperfield*, puts it, "The character of Dora in this little volume, although so lovable in its simplicity and childishness, teaches the great truth that a character so unformed, fails to satisfy the companion who has higher views of the duties and trials of life. . . . We must unite a child-like spirit with a high purpose in life, or we shall fall far short of our desire to be useful, and to be best-loved" (5).[2] But just as Margaret Flanders Darby has drawn attention to Dora's complexities—"her unyielding integrity, the strength of her weakness, and especially the persistence of her attempts to escape David's confining rhetoric" (158–59) and to cope with his "incompatible expectations" (164)—the arrested child-woman may look like a figure of simplicity without in fact being one. Indeed, just as there are multiple varieties of child-man, the arrested child-woman comes in many forms, and exploring the range of types accreting around the term in the nineteenth century helps to illuminate the complexities of Victorian conceptions of gender, age, social class, and family.

Arguably, arrested child-women often serve a substantially different cultural purpose from that of their male counterparts. Although Adam Potkay points out that the "Peter Pan syndrome" manifested in an intense adult male nostalgia for boyhood may be deemed "an eighteenth-century invention" (77), for much of the nineteenth century the child-man tended to be represented in literature as something of a freak. In their different ways, *Vice-Versâ*'s Paul and Dick Bultitude, Dickens's Harold Skimpole, Dracula, and the atavistic criminal are all depicted as disturbances to society, anomalies that will need to be removed if their narratives are to end happily. In contrast, Dora and her literary sisters not infrequently represent an ideal type, a form of womanhood demanded by those who surround them, even if their narratives may view this ideal as problematic.

We might therefore ask why *child* and *woman* appeared to belong together in a way that *child* and *man* did not. One answer, following an understanding promulgated by some Victorian feminists, would be that middle-class Victorian society was ordered in such a way as to keep its females perpetual children, sexually innocent, financially dependent, adorably helpless. While this response overlooks much in its reductiveness (including the large number of Victorian women in both fiction and fact notable for their toughness, competence, and independence), it provides us with a starting point in Dora Copperfield, brought up in such a way that she is unable to run the household or to bear children. That David finds her desirable because of, not despite, her limitations is suggestive. Catherine Robson argues that the Victorian "idealization and idolization of little girls . . . [is inextricable from] a pervasive fantasy of male development in which men become masculine only after an initial feminine stage. In this light, little girls represent not just the true essence of childhood, but an adult male's best opportunity of reconnecting with his own lost self" (3). Locating the little girl within the physically mature female body of the arrested child-woman held out the promise, appealing in theory however ill-fated it might be in practice, of a nostalgia-based marriage in which *both* participants could be children, Dora the "child-wife" returning her "dear boy" Doady to a juvenile idyll considerably happier than his actual experience.

Yet as David's eventual repudiation of Dora suggests, turning the clock back had its uncomfortable side for the middle-class Victorian man, whose culture insisted that he stand for energy and progress. The tug of war between desire and repulsion is apparent in two stories published in popular magazines in the 1870s, a few years after Eliza Lynn Linton's famous 1868 article "The Girl of the Period" had articulated, and fed, anxieties about young women's loss of innocence. Just as the ultimate force preventing Dora's further development is death, an end that both solves David's matrimonial dilemma and increases his tenderness for her, Jeffrey Graham's "Cui Bono? Or, the Story of Chloe Tenterden" (*Belgravia*, 1877) and John Richard Vernon's "Dog-Violet and Mignonette" (*Tinsleys' Magazine*, 1876) indicate that although child-women make less than ideal wives precisely because they are so innocent, death substantially augments their romantic appeal.

Both stories owe something to Dora, although in these later renditions the marriage partners are of different generations. In Graham's tale, Chloe is seventeen, while her guardian, John Hawke, is forty. Even after they marry, her immaturity prevents her from reciprocating his love in a fully adult way until she is fatally injured in a train crash, at which time love dawns. The widowed John marries one of Chloe's friends but soon dies on the battlefield, asking his comrades to bury her picture with him: "'Yes,' said he, with the joy of death in his eyes and flowing like moonlight over his face. 'Yes, we begin life anew—my girl and I'" (69). Vernon's story too features a seventeen-year-old bride, Violet. Unlike her husband, Eustace Margrave, she is no intellectual, and in the face of his scorn her health quickly deteriorates, especially after she has presented him with two children. Their marriage goes sour, Violet dies of a broken heart, and Eustace marries her cleverer cousin, only to learn both that he destroyed Violet by holding her in contempt and that she was the only woman for him.

Partly because of their brevity, these tales articulate with unusual clarity the dilemma, from a male perspective, of the arrested child-woman's sexual appeal. On the one hand, the source of her desirability is her childlike quality—even, in Vernon's rendition, her petlike quality, expressed in "the loving dog-eyes that looked up at [Eustace], content to love without understanding; the girl-wife sitting at his feet and just happy there; how happy if a caress were yielded now and then, or if a hand were spared" (62). On the other hand, as Graham indicates, her emotional inexperience is problematic. In Chloe, "the child-side of this little child-woman came uppermost. She had read many novels, and had condensed the sentiments [on romantic love] contained in them into two, command and obedience" (Graham 61), a misunderstanding that, like Violet's "pretty little petting ways that used to weary [Eustace]" (Vernon 62), leaves her husband unsatisfied. John and Eustace find, as David Copperfield does before them, that immaturity is not well suited to marriage. Nevertheless, having upgraded to more sophisticated models of wife, they pine after the lost child. That in both cases (and again following the Copperfield pattern) the replacement is associated with the original by friendship and/or by blood suggests that we might read these stories symbolically, with train crash and invalidism standing in for the normal growth process that may give the husband of a newly mature wife the sensation that he is married to a different woman. What is dead here, perhaps, is childhood itself. Significantly, John finds death a refuge for himself as well, while Eustace apparently becomes fixated on the past, "look[ing] into the years behind, remembering this as once his own; the tenderness which men cannot supply; the suppleness and sweetness, the weakness even, ay, even the somewhat of silliness, if it were so—these began to be tenderly recalled from the days that are no more" (Vernon 62).

If, as these stories imply, only the grave can be the site of a genuinely happy marriage to an arrested child-woman, the reader may wonder about the extent of her commitment to sexuality. As the next chapter details, marriages involving precocious child-women are frequently represented as successful, since readiness for intimacy is an important measure of maturity. In contrast, we shall see in this chapter, in which almost all romances involving child-women fail, that the question of arrested child-women's suitability for wifehood recurs again and again. The marital relation, after all, appears to be fatal to the Dora type;

Violet's invalidism is associated with childbearing, and Chloe's eventual understanding of "the glory of new-born love" seems to have as a prerequisite "the wanness of her face and the heaviness of her eyes" that betoken approaching death (Graham 66). Although Violet, who bears two children, appears more romantically interested in Eustace than Chloe is in John, neither marriage is entirely functional. In fact, it is arguably the unions' very dysfunctionality that excites these widowers' nostalgia and longing, even though—or, as I suggest above, because—women ostensibly better suited to marriage have been found. Much as Jerome K. Jerome's Paul Kelver desires both to move beyond and to return to childhood, the magazine stories imply that what Violet and Chloe primarily have to offer is stasis, represented by death or a fixation on the past, and that while this prospect may be less productive than some other kinds of marriages, there is a sense in which it is also more appealing.[3]

In short, the frequent (though by no means universal) desire to prolong female childhood was sometimes connected not only to the perceived needs of the girl but also to those of the adult man. If, as I argue in chapter 2, the inability or refusal to grow is both tempting and horrifying in the adult male, Victorian society was often more comfortable with a corresponding stasis where women were concerned; like Dora, the child-woman might remain immature both on her own account and on her man's. Contending that the Victorian age's "intense valorization of the little girl at the expense of mature femininity" is rooted in its "fraught constructions of masculinity" (4), Robson discusses the middle-class "male figure who constructs, in one way or another, a fantasy of his feminine childhood" (11) that functions on some level to demonstrate his innocence, since "by 1850 it is a truism that there is nothing so unlike a criminal as a little girl" (12).[4] Although, as we shall see, not all arrested child-women are devoid of criminal tendencies, even the delinquents typically enact the innocence that positions them as objects for male desire; stasis is often a response to the perceived demands of the surrounding culture. Like the Infant Phenomenon in Dickens's *Nicholas Nickleby* (1838–39), a girl in her mid-teens whose growth has been deliberately stunted by her actor parents so that she has the appearance of a ten-year-old, the arrested child-woman can play the part of a child playing the part of an adult, a back-and-forth reflection of the ways in which girlhood and womanhood both resemble and diverge from each other.

The appearance of the Infant Phenomenon, otherwise known as Ninetta Crummles, in a ballet entitled "The Indian Savage and the Maiden" is emblematic:

> Being left to himself, the savage had a dance, all alone, and just as he left off the maiden woke up, rubbed her eyes, got off the bank, and had a dance all alone too—such a dance that the savage looked on in ecstasy all the while, and when it was done, plucked from a neighbouring tree some botanical curiosity, resembling a small pickled cabbage, and offered it to the maiden, who at first wouldn't have it, but on the savage shedding tears relented. Then the savage jumped for joy; then the maiden jumped for rapture at the sweet smell of the pickled cabbage. Then the savage and the maiden danced violently together, and, finally, the savage dropped down on one knee, and the maiden stood on one leg upon his other knee; thus concluding the ballet, and leaving the spectators in a state of pleasing uncertainty, whether she would ultimately marry the savage, or return to her friends. (364)

Ninetta is at once ersatz, an actress who, by the standards applied to her social class, is classifiable as an adult yet whose small stature and frilly dresses enable her to pass as a middle-class child, and genuine, a girl whose father—like the fathers validated by middle-class domestic ideology—evidently controls not only her activities but even her size. Throughout his commentary on her, the narrator stresses her position as a commodity to be decorated, displayed, assessed, and even physically attacked "with the view of ascertaining whether she was real" (388). Any ballet in which she performs, clearly, will be conceived and directed by others—even while her one recorded line in the novel, a brief remark about the inadequate proceeds from her benefit performance, suggests a practicality and potential agency that belie her passive role as commodity.

Sardonically described by the narrator, the ballet nonetheless tells a story that Victorian audiences were eager to consume, that of the child-woman's ability to tame the male savage through her romantic appeal, a taming that, in "pleasing uncertainty," may or may not have a sexual consummation. The same role might be assigned to an adult woman, but giving it to a child added an extra twist. Marah Gubar argues of nineteenth-century child performers generally, "Their prematurely developed skills and much-vaunted versatility enabled them to blur the line between child and adult, innocence and experience" in a way that fascinated Victorian audiences ("Drama" 64). Marketed off stage as well as on, the Phenomenon is said (at least by her father) to be the principal attraction of the Crummles troupe. We see her alienating a colleague whom she has upstaged; unsettling Nicholas, who refuses "some nice little part with the infant" with the suggestion that "perhaps it would be better if I had somebody of my own size at first, in case I should turn out awkward. I should feel more at home perhaps" (373); and impressing audience members from the Borum children to the theater critic Mr. Curdle, who considers her performances remarkable for "a unity of feeling, a breadth, a light and shade, a warmth of co-louring, a tone, a harmony, a glow, an artistical development of original concep-tions, which I look for, in vain, among older performers" (386).

Mr. Curdle's comments imply that Ninetta is to be judged by criteria nor-mally applied to paintings. And indeed, as Gubar observes, her role in *Nicholas Nickleby* is conducted almost entirely in dumb show. In contrast to the child actor upon whom Dickens evidently based her, and to the talkative Mr. Crum-mles, Miss Snevellicci, and Mr. Folair, she speaks only a single sentence that the narrator troubles to transcribe, although we are told that she gives an oration at the Lillyvick-Petowker wedding festivities and that she cries when Nicholas announces his impending departure from the company (Gubar, "Drama" 63, 75). The detailed descriptions given of her dancing and her treatment at the hands of the Borum children, who pinch her, purloin her parasol, and nearly tear her "limb from limb . . . dragging her in different directions as a trial of strength" (Dickens, *Nickleby* 388), all apparently without exciting her to speech, suggest that she exists to be looked at.

The body of this chapter begins, then, with a discussion of the emphasis on the visual, and particularly its association with stasis through paintings and tab-leaux, that is characteristic of Victorian authors' approach to the child-woman. Subsequently, the chapter considers what various arrested child-women—many of whom, including Dickens's Ninetta Crummles and Miss Mowcher, Dinah Mulock's Olive Rothesay, Rider Haggard's Gagool, and H. G. Wells's Weena, are represented as dwarfs or as unnaturally small—may reveal about Victorian unease and fantasy regarding the cessation of development. In an era preoc-cupied by change—technological, social, evolutionary, sexual—what was some-times seen as women's limited range for growth might look perverse, but it might also look desirable.

Looking at and by the Child-Woman: The Gaze in Dinah Mulock's *Olive*

A striking point of resemblance in many child-woman texts, whether early or late in the period, is that the child-woman repeatedly serves as a focal point for the gaze of narrator, characters, and readers. David Copperfield recalls the early days of his love for Dora by describing her as a performer, "sing[ing] enchanted ballads in the French language" while "accompanying herself on a glorified instrument resembling a guitar" (361). That he calls her a "spectacle" (443) seems exactly right. Elsewhere in the novel, Betsey Trotwood, commencing her acquaintance with another child-woman, commands David's mother to "take off your cap, child . . . and let me see you" (4), and the dwarf Miss Mowcher strikes David's friend Steerforth as a remarkable sight, "one of the seven wonders of the world" (301), because of the unexpected combination of her childish stature and her shrewdness. As the narrator, David gazes (and reports to us the results of his gaze) at a large number of the characters in the novel, but the child-women in this text are disproportionately objects for the gaze of characters other than David, on display in a way that Steerforth and Miss Murdstone, say, are not. And while Miss Mowcher instructs us, through David, "not to associate bodily defects with mental . . . except for a solid reason" (427), she also mourns that the physically able cannot "see" her, and her emotions, accurately; they perceive her as "a plaything . . . a toy horse or a wooden soldier" (424), just as David, who interprets her knock as a child's (423), perceives her as no more than her own "great umbrella that appeared to be walking about of itself" (423–24) "without the least appearance of having anybody underneath it" (428). Paradoxically, Miss Mowcher is so identified with her appearance as to be effectively invisible.

Other texts to be examined below similarly emphasize that the child-woman is a magnet for the gaze. Consider, for instance, Ayesha in Haggard's *She* (1886–87), who usually goes shrouded so as not to drive men to their death through passion, since "never may the man to whom my beauty hath been unveiled put it from his mind" (142–43); the bigamous title character of Mary Elizabeth Braddon's *Lady Audley's Secret* (1862), whose double life is exposed when her first husband sees the portrait that reveals her as "a beautiful fiend" (71); Wilkie Collins's Laura Fairlie in *The Woman in White* (1859–60), whose likeness Walter Hartright paints, individuating her even while he positions her as an object for contemplation indistinguishable not only from her double, Anne Catherick, but also from the first loves of all his readers, "the visionary nursling of your own fancy" (76); and Hetty Sorrel in George Eliot's *Adam Bede* (1859), who is ultimately an object for "all eyes" at her trial for the murder of her newborn baby (481). These examples—and one could list many more—suggest the range of uses of the visual that the Victorians associated with the arrested child-woman: public versus private, exterior versus interior, systemic versus individual.

In the interests of space, however, I consider here an especially well developed example of the child-woman as spectacle, Dinah Mulock's 1850 novel *Olive*. Like *David Copperfield*, *Olive* contains more than one child-woman, although whereas Dora Copperfield closely resembles her husband's dead mother, Olive and her mother are contrasting types. Olive is a child-woman in two senses—in infancy precocious and in her late twenties childlike (she is always "little Olive" to her future husband [see, e.g., 303, 309, 312]). In contrast, her mother, the "baby-bride" Sybilla (9), is an arrested child-woman from the outset. Born with a minor spinal curvature, Olive is imperfect physically and preternaturally developed morally, while Sybilla is known for her beauty but, until belatedly improved by maternity, is by nature superficial, cowardly, and immature.

Nevertheless, the narrative immediately establishes both women as simultaneously child and spectacle. In the first few pages, we are told that

> It would have done any one's heart good only to look at Sybilla Rothesay. She was a creature to watch from a distance, and then to go away and dream of, scarce thinking whether she were a woman or a spirit. As for describing her, it is almost impossible—but let us try.
>
> She was very small in stature and proportions—quite a little fairy. Her cheek had the soft peachy hue of girlhood; nay, of very childhood. You would never have thought her a mother. (8)

Meanwhile, when Olive's father first meets his daughter, then aged four, the sight excites in him "a gaze of frenzied unbelief":

> By her stature she might have been two years old, but her face was like that of a child of ten or twelve—so thoughtful, so grave. Her limbs were small and wasted, but exquisitely delicate. The same might be said of her features; which, though thin, and wearing a look of premature age, together with that quiet, earnest, melancholy cast peculiar to deformity, were yet regular, almost pretty. . . . She looked less like a child than a woman dwarfed into childhood. (23)

Even in establishing a vital contrast between mother and daughter, then, the narrator simultaneously establishes a similarity: both are objects for the gaze not only of the reader but also of the characters within the novel.

Indeed, both women are consistently positioned in an uneasy relationship to seeing and being seen. Olive's infancy involves a series of viewings leading to the recognition of her disability first by her nurse, then by the family doctor, and only subsequently by her parents. As a young adult hidden behind a curtain at a party, she overhears her best friend commenting that she should never expect to attract any suitors and for the first time realizes her own physical condition: "I see, as I never saw before" (67). Her "sense of personal deformity" inspires her to become a painter so that *she* can be the viewer and indeed the creator, "produc[ing] the grandest ideal loveliness" (113) instead of being on view herself, much as *David Copperfield*'s Miss Mowcher, equally self-conscious about her dwarfism, redefines herself from Steerforth's dupe to agent of justice. And the final lines of Mulock's novel create a tableau in which Olive's newly acquired husband directs his gaze away from his wife, while readers are asked to direct theirs toward her:

> Olive, with her clinging sweetness, her upward gaze, was a type of true woman. But Harold did not bend his look upon her. . . . He planted his foot firmly on the ground, lifted his proud head, and looked out fearlessly with his majestic eyes.
>
> "And I," said Olive, "thus."
>
> She stole her two little cold hands under his plaid, laid her head upon them, close to his heart, and, smiling, nestled there. (331)

In this narrative painting in prose, the figures are dressed in Scottish costume,[5] evoking the influential Scottish genre paintings of artists such as Sir David Wilkie and looking forward to John Everett Millais's *The Bride of Lammermoor* (1878), which depicts a couple clad in garb similar to Olive and Harold's and posed in much the same way, again with the woman's littleness and clinging, dependent pose accentuating her man's masculinity. But in *Olive*, at least, Olive's ostentatious smallness creates an impression of subordination to her husband that has not always characterized their relationship. If he saves her life by rescuing her from a fire, she saves his soul by restoring his faith in God, her status as child-woman belying his repeated claim that "no child can comprehend" religion (188). The visual enactment of their marriage as a tableau in costume, then, is a performance, self-conscious on the narrator's part, of the romantic convention in which the husband is to dominate over the wife. But it is also the reward for Olive's many years of competence and travail; she has earned, and must be seen to have earned, the luxury of stasis. Here she may be living out a fantasy of her creator, whose writings, in Elaine Showalter's reading, mingle an understanding of "the pleasures of success" with "a recurrent lament for the life that might have been: the dependent life, the life of the angel in the house, the 'safe negativeness,' the 'delicious retirement,' 'the exquisite absorption of home'" ("Craik" 10–11). That the novel ends here suggests that Olive's trials are over; the pose will be held forever.

Like her treatment of Olive, Mulock's treatment of Sybilla repeatedly emphasizes the visual. For one thing, Sybilla goes blind in early middle age, evidently a didactic device that recalls her initial coldness toward her imperfect child and her need to move beyond her daughter's appearance. And like Olive, Sybilla is the central figure in a number of narrative tableaux, often connected to sight. For instance, the second chapter ends when the young mother collapses in a faint immediately after learning of her baby's disability and "gaz[ing] incredulously on [the doctor], on the nurse, and lastly on the sleeping child" (Mulock, *Olive* 14). Similarly, her husband's return after an absence of several years is marred by the fact that he arrives as his wife is giving a party, so that although she is overjoyed to see him, "he was strangely bewildered by the scene which had flashed for a minute before his eyes," and must "[hold] her out at arm's length to look at her. . . . Trembling—blushing scarlet, over face and neck—she perceived her husband's eyes rest on her glittering dress. He regarded her fixedly, from head to foot. She felt his expression change from joy to uneasy wonder, from love to sternness, and then he wore a strange, cold look, such a one as she had never beheld in him before" (21).

As in the other tableaux in *Olive*, especially the one that concludes the novel, Captain Rothesay's stare here freezes the action. In emphasizing Sybilla's excessive display, it also functions as a rebuke, the follow-up to the elderly maid's earlier remonstrance, "Eh! Mrs Rothesay, ye're no goin' to show yoursel in sic a dress" (19), and the corrective to the lascivious stares that her revealing gown may have attracted. But although spectators may not grant its innocence, the sleeveless "short and airy robe," which reveals Sybilla's "tiny white-sandalled feet," recalls the dress of young children (20). Sybilla's clear desire, like Dora Copperfield's, is to remain youthful as long as the protectiveness of others will permit it. The stasis that her daughter achieves only after patiently endured hardship is Sybilla's from the outset.

Sybilla functions as spectacle at other moments in the novel as well. After being widowed in middle age, for example, she becomes an artist's model. Her blindness too turns her into a species of artwork, a "picture which lived on [in] Olive's memory evermore" and that may be studied the more intently because it cannot return the viewer's regard: "Her daughter looked at her with eyes of passionate yearning that threw into one minute's gaze the love of a whole lifetime" (202). But Sybilla's relationship to seeing entails more than merely being looked at, whether at first or second hand. Her name, of course, means "prophetess" or "seer," and its applicability is borne out by a dream that she experiences shortly after Olive's birth, in which she sees her child as an angel sent to guide her through a wild and dangerous landscape symbolic of life (12). The remainder of Sybilla's story, a tale of slow reclamation at Olive's hands, establishes the truth of this perception.

In *Annoying the Victorians*, James Kincaid remarks that "seeing is not just a single position but a process of movement in which the subject . . . possesses the object by relinquishing visual mastery, by momentarily *becoming* the object. In 'normal' seeing this activity . . . necessitates an ongoing repression of the position we were in a moment before and an elevation of the substituted position we are in now" (121). Similarly, in discussing the films of Josef von Sternberg, Gaylyn Studlar dwells on their "oscillation between stability and metamorphosis"; the focus on change plays to the audience's masochistic pleasure in being overpowered by the images on the screen and, by rejecting "society's demand for a single, recognizable, and permanent sociosexual identity," permits the subversion of "established gender-differentiated dominance/submission patterns" (51). Whereas Laura Mulvey argues in her classic essay "Visual Pleasure and Narrative Cinema" that the feminine object of the (masculine, heterosexual) audience's gaze is passive and that the male spectator occupies a position of power, Kincaid and Studlar, among others, suggest rather that power flows back and forth between the viewer and the viewed in a way that potentially disrupts societal expectations about gender, a point that Mulvey also makes in her 1981 revisiting of her earlier essay to consider female spectatorship, in which she sees the possibility of an "oscillation" between the feminine and the masculine, an "inability to achieve stable sexual identity" (12).

These ideas have resonance for *Olive*, and by extension potentially for other texts about the child-woman in which the gaze is emphasized. In witnessing Olive and Sybilla, opposed types of child-woman, alternate between the roles of spectator and spectacle for each other, the reader is invited to try out, and hence to judge, differing feminine strategies. Intimately linked in the narrative both to insight (prophetic vision) and to creativity (painting, narrative tableaux), sight operates as a metaphor for Mulock's vision of her own art, which held that fiction should be didactic. As Showalter and Sally Mitchell have separately noted, this didacticism in some degree takes the form, in Mitchell's words, of "explor[ing] women's hidden feelings and . . . educat[ing] their self-images" (*Craik* 110). The complementary child-women in *Olive*, then, are not turned into spectacles, raw material for art, or producers of art solely for dramatic effect. In looking at them, we are invited to discern, and potentially to critique, the relationship of Victorian femininity to art and performance. We are also to fathom the various difficulties and delights—for infantuation entails both of these—inherent in being at once the gazer and the one gazed upon.

The Flaw in the Glass:
The Child-Woman and Murderous Passivity

Olive, who thinks little of herself, prefers looking to being looked at and uses her vision to create paintings (including paintings of children) that possess a beauty that she believes herself to lack. She looks out, not in. In contrast, the erring child-women who may come most readily to mind for today's reader, Braddon's Lady Audley and Eliot's Hetty, are closely associated with mirrors. Lady Audley is introduced to us in the guise of a child. Her "very childishness had a charm which few could resist. The innocence and candour of an infant beamed in [her] fair face, and shone out of her large and liquid blue eyes"; in her adult clothes, "she looked like a child tricked out for a masquerade" (52). Yet as a bigamist, an arsonist, and a would-be murderess, Lady Audley is clearly a masquerader indeed, counterfeiting not adulthood but innocence, and the narrative confirms this identity by repeatedly placing her before mirrors, like an actress always making up for her next performance.[6]

In describing her mistress's rooms, the maid, Phoebe, thinks immediately of these mirrors, telling Luke of the "great looking-glasses that stretch from the ceiling to the floor" (27). We later learn that "the looking-glasses, cunningly placed at angles and opposite corners by an artistic upholsterer, multiplied my lady's image, and in that image reflected the most beautiful object in the enchanted chamber" (294). Moreover, when Lady Audley sets the local inn on fire in an attempt to keep her secret from getting out, her kindling is the lace adorning the "altar of starched muslin and pink glazed calico" that serves as the pedestal for Phoebe's mirror (323). The mirrors with which Lady Audley is ever surrounded—even her rooms in the madhouse, a parody of her boudoir at Audley Court, are furnished with "great expanses of glimmering something . . . which my lady mistook for costly mirrors, but which were in reality wretched mockeries of burnished tin" (389)—are so imbued with her image that her portrait, which reflects the demon within her, functions as one of them.

Lady Audley's narrator links the vanity that prompts mirror-gazing with the vanity that prompts murder, speculating about "that early time in which she had first looked in the glass and discovered that she was beautiful: that fatal early time in which she had first begun to look upon her loveliness as a right divine, a boundless possession which was to be a set-off against all girlish short-comings, a counter-balance of every youthful sin" (296). Looking glasses, it seems, not only reflect but also enlarge the self even while they simultaneously teach a lesson about woman's place in Victorian society. For Lynette Felber, "the mirrors reinforce the effect demonstrated by the portrait: woman's signifi-cance is constructed in the process of reflection or being looked upon" (482).

Adam Bede takes a somewhat similar tack, following Hetty into her room at a correspondingly "fatal early time" of admiration for her own beauty. If Dinah can readily persuade the suggestible Bessy Cranage to give up her ear-rings by telling of "a servant of God in the days of her vanity" who "thought nothing about how she might get a clean heart and a right spirit, she only wanted to have better lace than other girls. And one day when she put her new cap on and looked in the glass, she saw a bleeding Face crowned with thorns" (75), Hetty is harder to move from self-regard to looking outward. In Mrs. Poyser's acerbic estimation of her niece, "Adam Bede and all his kin might be drowned for what you'd care—you'd be perking at the glass the next minute" (140), and indeed, the astute reader will conclude from chapter 15, "The Two Bed-Chambers," that the difference between Hetty's bedroom and Dinah's is that while Hetty's contains mirrors (and adornments to put on before them), Dinah's contains a window.[7]

One point of comparison—and, generally, contrast—between the egotistical arrested child-woman and her male counterpart, then, is their relationship to mirrors. Dorian Gray, who receives from Lord Henry a silver mirror framed in cupids, uses it as a complement to his portrait, and eventually destroys it, is something of an exception to the prevailing pattern among nineteenth-century child-men. In Wilde's tale "the metaphor of the mirror" may be, as Donald R. Dickson argues, "a key to the structure of the novel" (13), very similar to the corresponding metaphor in *Adam Bede*, *Lady Audley's Secret*, and other child-woman narratives, but as a rule egotistical child-men such as Doyle's Tonga, Conrad's Kurtz, and Stoker's Dracula are not mirror-gazers. In *Bleak House*, for example, unlike Lady Dedlock and Esther Summerson, both of whom are associated with mirrors—Lady Dedlock in a way that suggests her expensive good looks, Esther in a way that repudiates vanity—Harold Skimpole is not mentioned in connection with these objects. And part of Dracula's horror, of course, is that he has no reflection.

In other words, Victorian age-inversion narratives sometimes draw a distinction between male and female egotism that comments upon the gender roles of the day. Egotistical as they are, for example, Kurtz and Dracula are capable of change, and Tonga is a figure of action rather than a frozen participant in a tableau. Wilde's tale associates Dorian Gray's narcissism with the homoeroticism of the circles in which he travels. The mirror and the portrait are designed to permit Dorian to take the same pleasure in gazing upon his beauty that other men (who are different from Dorian inasmuch as they are not cynosures) have without visual aids, so that he can be the complete androgyne, both erotic object and erotic actor. Thus Dorian occupies a gender position separate from all other characters in the work, much as contemporaneous sexology identified male homosexuals as a "third sex." Yet it is also noteworthy that Dorian's acquiescence in becoming an object for the gaze is represented as the error that destroys him. While Dorian's slayings of a man and woman who have looked upon him with desire meet with no (human) retribution, the object of the gaze is unique: by embodying the change that the living man has misguidedly traded for stasis, the portrait becomes the self, to such an extent that in seeking to stab the painted visage, Dorian inadvertently kills himself. Among the many social rules that he has broken is the expectation that the male gazer will differ from the object of his regard.

Meanwhile, in *The Strange Case of Dr. Jekyll and Mr. Hyde*, another text whose homoerotic overtones have attracted considerable critical attention, Jekyll's fatal attraction to a version of himself leads to his self-destruction. His admission that, apparently alone among those who have looked upon Hyde, he is initially "conscious of no repugnance, rather of a leap of welcome" when he gazes at his new form in the mirror (59) must be undone over the course of the rest of his confession. Jekyll's friends express surprise that his laboratory should contain a cheval glass, which, we learn, formerly had no place in Jekyll's quarters but was brought in as apparatus necessary to the experiment; that is, the appearance of the mirror is a symptom of Jekyll's moral decline. Yet elsewhere in the confession, Jekyll claims that he now looks in the mirror only briefly and usually in agony of mind, and as if in confirmation, the investigators find the glass tilted toward the ceiling rather than directed in a way that would show the dwarfish Hyde his own face. In this sense, Jekyll's masculinity is reclaimed.

But even though Dorian and Jekyll (or better, Hyde) seem more enamored of mirrors than is appropriate to the Victorian male, they and other egotistical arrested child-men are primarily motivated by a desire for experience without consequences. Standing at the mirror is not enough to content them; they expect their gratification to come from beyond the self. Their female counterparts, however, are much less drawn to experience; what they want is admiration, an affirmation that they neither need to change nor are doing so. Although Adam Bede believes that Hetty's "sweet baby-like roundness" of feature must betoken tenderness of heart and an affinity for children (197), in fact she is emotionally one of those "plants that have hardly any roots" (199), a child-woman too immature to feel what Victorian society assumed to be women's natural pull toward wifehood and motherhood. Her moments before the mirror seem at least as satisfying to her as her love affair, and for the same reason: it is not sexual fulfillment that she seeks, but the knowledge of her own desirability. Simply being a child-woman is enough for Hetty, who is pleased by stasis rather than by the potential for growth.

Similarly, Felber proposes that one "explanation for the curiously childlike and sexless nature of [Braddon's] protagonist" is "that her sexuality is projected onto Lady Audley," a projection accomplished by means of the male gaze (478). As Lucy Talboys, Lady Audley has married an attractive young husband and given birth to a child, yet these experiences, considered by her society to be what every woman should want, do not constitute a happy ending. Facing her husband's prolonged absence and an impoverished and unglamorous existence as a single mother, Lucy opts out, retracing her steps to girlhood and choosing a much older and wealthier second husband who will permit her to remain a girl indefinitely. As Lady Audley, her responsibilities consist principally in maintaining her beauty, and this emphasis on leisured nonaccomplishment is entirely satisfactory to her. Her efforts at murder are not designed to bring to her new experiences or possessions, but to preserve the existence that is already hers.

In depicting egotistical child-women such as Hetty and Lady Audley as oriented toward being rather than doing, Eliot and Braddon draw on a cultural belief in women's innate inertia that was to remain significant well past the mid-nineteenth century.[8] Writing in 1889, for instance, the biologists Patrick

Geddes and J. Arthur Thomson argue that sex difference begins on a cellular level observable in primitive forms such as algae:

> Some [cells] soon come to rest and settle down, and with these their more energetic neighbours by-and-by unite. We have here a very distinct beginning of the distinction between male and female elements. The comparatively sluggish, more nutritive, preponderatingly anabolic cells, which soon settle down, are female; the more mobile, finally more exhausted and emphatically katabolic cells—are male. As Vines says, "the one is passive, the other active." (128)

This distinction between passive, unmoving female and active, hungry male continues all the way up the chain of being, with profound social implications. In an oft-quoted line, Geddes and Thomson assert, "What was decided among the prehistoric Protozoa cannot be annulled by Act of Parliament" (267). Similarly, in *Civilization and Its Discontents*, a work written in 1930 but strongly influenced by nineteenth-century views, Freud writes that women are fundamentally "hostile" to civilization, a "retarding and restraining influence" over it (51), since "the work of civilization has become increasingly the business of men, it confronts them with ever more difficult tasks and compels them to carry out instinctual sublimations of which women are little capable" (50). The male, then, acts on culture; the female exists outside it, and this distinction is recorded in perverse form in the difference between villainous child-men and villainous child-women.

An extreme example of female stasis is the witch-woman Gagool in Haggard's *King Solomon's Mines* (1885). In a novel in which almost all the major characters express at one time or another their willingness to die in particular circumstances—for instance, if their children are appropriately provided for or if their death will serve a beloved or their king—Gagool is unique in her resistance both to change and to reaching her end. As she points out to one of her enemies, "Accursed fool, thinkest thou that life is sweet only to the young? . . . To the young, indeed, death is sometimes welcome, for the young can feel. They love and suffer. . . . But the old feel not, they love not, and, *ha! ha!* they laugh to see another go out into the dark" (204, emphasis in original). Although the source of Gagool's preternatural longevity is left to the reader's imagination, the narrative implicitly ties it to the only action that we learn to associate with her, the repeated sacrificing of the young. If the old-fashioned child often dies under the pressure of age indeterminacy and the internalized conflict between youth and age, Gagool has apparently succeeded in displacing her own death onto younger bodies in an eerie freezing of her personal mortality.

In identifying other targets for death, particularly the young women who are ritually sacrificed "on the day of the dance of maidens to the old ones who sit and watch on the mountains" (146), Gagool becomes a vampiric figure. In effect, she is a more dramatic version of the dialectic that Helen Small (drawing on the work of Theodor Adorno) sees at work between Little Nell and her grandfather, an aged child-man, in *The Old Curiosity Shop*, in which the child is "burdened with [the old man's] guilt and made its 'propitiatory sacrifice,'" essentially dying his death (188). Over many centuries, Gagool has moved not toward death but toward infancy and, indeed, toward humanity's animal ancestors. She is described as a "wizened monkey-like creature" who "crept on all fours" before "throwing the furry covering off its face" to reveal the visage of "a woman of great age, so shrunken that in size it was no larger than that of a year-old child," and a bald skull that "moved and contracted like the hood of a cobra" (121). As Teresa Mangum writes, Gagool is "monkey-like and savage in a terrifying reversal of Darwinian evolution in which a human paradoxically ages into the worst sort of racist stereotype—primitive, bestial infancy" ("Women" 79).

It is worth noting, though, that while Hetty and Lady Audley, as well as various other arrested child-women, such as Sybilla Rothesay, Laura Fairlie, and Wells's Weena, may be seen as "sluggish," be-ers rather than doers, such women are often paired with women substantially more active. Hetty is contrasted with Dinah, an itinerant preacher for whom the bounds of the self are inadequate; Sybilla with Olive, who takes her father's place by supporting herself and her mother while paying off his debt and watching over his illegitimate daughter; Laura Fairlie with Marian Halcombe, who plays a crucial part in uncovering the mystery of Collins's titular "woman in white." Lady Audley's "wax-doll" affect draws continual criticism from her energetic stepdaughter (56).[9] Even Gagool, whose problem is not passivity, is contrasted to the only other woman in the novel, Foulata, who not only has a healthier attitude toward mortality but also succeeds in killing the witch by crushing her beneath a door in a mountain labyrinth referred to as the "Place of Death." And although male characters in the works that contrast passive with active may find the sluggish, mirror-gazing child-women more sexually attractive than their more forceful foils, overall the narratives suggest that this preference is mistaken. Deterministic framings of femininity such as Geddes and

Thomson's or Freud's, then, are belied by the many Victorian novels that show the arrested child-woman as one point—and a problematic one at that—on a broad arc of feminine types. Female stasis was not universally accepted.

The Once and Future Child-Woman: Ayesha and Weena Meet the Anthropologists

The doubleness of Lady Audley, whose public child-face coexists with her secret criminality, evokes sensation through contrast. The title character of Haggard's *She* and its first sequel, *Ayesha: The Return of She* (1905), demonstrates that separate feminine archetypes may coexist harmoniously within a single body, although at a level of power disturbing to the male observer. A seemingly immortal goddess-queen, when we encounter her in *She* Ayesha has lived in unchanging beauty for millennia in an unknown African country, Kôr, awaiting the rebirth of her lover. Newly embodied as the young Englishman Leo Vincey, Ayesha's beloved does indeed reappear in her life, escorted by his foster father, Horace Holly. Their reunion is complicated by Leo's near-fatal illness and Ayesha's slaying of his African mistress, but eventually Ayesha and Leo seem poised for eternal life together if Leo can be made immortal by stepping into the same magic flame in which Ayesha bathed thousands of years earlier. In order to demonstrate the flame's safety and to purify herself before her marriage, Ayesha enters the flame once more, only to have its effects reversed: over a few moments she ages her full span and dies, promising to return. The return, of course, is accomplished in *Ayesha*, in which Leo and Holly search for Ayesha in the mountains of Tibet and find not only her but also the reincarnation of the wife of Leo's former self, Amenartas, murdered by Ayesha in ancient days. This time it is Leo who dies, "withered in Ayesha's kiss, slain by the fire of her love" (325), to be joined at last by a disembodied Ayesha.

The saga's central premise is that what the modern world may dismiss as myth is true and powerful. Hence in describing Ayesha, who inspires in him a religious awe, Holly's narration adopts a mystical tone that picks up something of Ayesha's archaic diction, essentially "the language of the King James Bible," as Norman Etherington observes in the introduction to his annotated edition of *She* (xxi). The volumes' framework, too, emphasizes the continuity of the ancient world—Egypt, Greece, Rome, Asia—with the modern world associated with Holly and Leo, partly through the awareness that Leo is the reincarnation of a remote ancestor but more particularly through the person of Ayesha, who, we are told, "never dies. She changes, that is all" (*Ayesha* 336). One way in which Haggard achieves this effect is to represent Ayesha as a manifestation of the Triple Goddess: mother, maiden, and crone in one.

While extensive commentary on the Triple Goddess is associated especially with Robert Graves's *The White Goddess* (1948), Graves's discussion draws upon Victorian predecessors such as James Frazer's *The Golden Bough* (1890) and the Hekate chapter of Lewis Richard Farnell's *The Cults of the Greek States* (1896) as well as upon Greek mythology; she was not a twentieth-century invention. The Triple Goddess also appears as a basis for potent female figures in Victorian fantasy contemporaneous with *She*. Katharine Bubel, for one, points out that George MacDonald invokes her in his *Curdie* books, particularly the second of the pair, *The Princess and Curdie* (1883), in which "the great old, young, beautiful princess" appears variously as "a grotesque crone," "a tall woman, 'large and strong as a Titaness,'" and "a young girl housemaid" (Bubel 5–6). Zee in Edward Bulwer-Lytton's *The Coming Race* (1871), whom Etherington mentions as a possible source for Ayesha, is at once an unmarried girl, a "healer" and "nurse" (193) who cherishes her patients "as a mother would tend and cherish her stricken child" (194) and who kisses the object of her romantic desire with "a mother's passion" (290), and "an erudite professor of the College of Sages" (58). And Etherington observes that Haggard's 1884 novel *Dawn* "contains three female characters who suggest aspects of Ayesha's character: a beautiful young lady of great learning, another who looks like 'an Egyptian sorceress' possessing the 'spirit of power,' and a wiser, older woman whose favorite retreat is her private museum of Egyptian antiquities" (xxx).

Ayesha unites all three modalities. The first volume locates her in the land of Kôr, a name that suggests not only the Latin word for "heart" (various Haggard critics have noted his predilection for landscapes recalling the female body) but also the Greek word *Kore* (*Κόρη*), "maiden." As an archaeological term, *Kore* refers to a genre of statue from the Archaic period. Kore statues were used as votive offerings or, less frequently, as funerary pieces, in both cases depicting mortal women whose beauty was sufficiently great to make them fit companions to the gods. Like the works of art associated with many fictional child-women and like Ayesha, who is frozen at a moment of biological youth and for whom marriage is a longed-for impossibility, the statue is static, a permanent tribute to the power of maidenhood—to which, Haggard reveals in the late installment *Wisdom's Daughter* (1923), Ayesha has long ago bound herself as a priestess and *child* of Isis, the latter term being repeated several dozen times. Thus while Holly emphasizes Ayesha's terrifying qualities, associating her with snakes and dwelling upon her deadliness, he also compares her to a child, writing that "she clapped her hands in childish glee" (*She* 137), "the dark eyes opened like the eyes of a wondering child" (*Ayesha* 224), and "she drew a footstool to his feet and sank upon it, looking up into his face with attentive eyes, like a child who listens for a story" (*Ayesha* 221).

Yet at the same time, Ayesha is a manifestation of divine maternity in both her healing and her punitive powers; she also moves into old age in *She* and back out again in *Ayesha* with horrific speed. The famous passage in *She* that describes Ayesha's abrupt aging moves her from maidenhood to old age to infancy in a few lines. As Holly puts it, "Smaller she grew, and smaller yet, till she was no larger than a baboon. Now the skin was puckered into a million wrinkles, and on the shapeless face was the stamp of unutterable age. I never saw anything like it; nobody ever saw anything like the frightful age that was graven on that fearful countenance, no bigger now than that of a two-months' child" (257). Conversely, in *Ayesha* She transforms from a Gagoolesque tiny "mummy-like shape. . . . unnaturally short for a full-grown woman," a "naked-headed Thing" simultaneously infantile and preternaturally old (215–17), into a woman of celestial beauty displayed before "the divine statue of Motherhood" (234). Neither the child-woman nor the crone is Ayesha's dominant mode; her most characteristic aspect is that of the queenly virgin goddess. Yet the emphasis on both transformation and—given Ayesha's longevity—permanence means that both child-woman and crone are constantly present, even if Holly does not always perceive them. Leo, who in *Ayesha* chooses fidelity to the crone over sexual fulfillment with Amenartas's beautiful reincarnation (and thereby brings about Ayesha's rejuvenation), in effect signals his awareness that whatever her form, Ayesha is always Ayesha. In a sense, then, if Oros is correct in asserting that She "never dies. She changes, that is all," this *aperçu* could equally well be reversed to state that She "never changes. She dies, that is all."

Holly's comparison of the aging Ayesha to a baboon (or, in some editions, a monkey) has prompted a number of critics to discuss the novel in terms of Darwinism.[10] But as some of these critics add, Darwinism is not all that is at stake here. For Bradley Deane, for instance, Haggard's romance depends upon "divergent constructions of the temporal. On the one hand Haggard gives us [in Leo] a transcendent and timeless ideal of manly beauty, and on the other [in Holly] a plucky struggler amid the forces of change who draws upon both the vitality of atavism and the wisdom that follows from experience" (396).

Similarly, Patricia Murphy sees in *She* a "frantic attempt to privilege male historicity over female ahistoricity," a battle between "the linear time of history associated with the masculine civilizing mission" and "the nonlinear time conventionally associated with female subjectivity through procreativity, natural rhythms, and infinitude" ("Gendering" 747–48; see also the chapter on *She* in Murphy, *Time*).

The discussion of atavism as a matter of primitivism in the case of the child-man thus becomes more complicated when we move to the child-woman. Some Victorian anthropologists considered women physiologically inherently child-like, much as the biologists Geddes and Thomson deemed the female half of creation innately passive, conservative, and inimical to development. In an 1868 article entitled "On a Characteristic Peculiarity in the Form of the Female Skull, and Its Significance for Comparative Anthropology," for example, Alexander Ecker writes that "the female character is in [cranial form], as in several other respects, approaching that of a child; woman, in fact, holds an intermediate position between man and child" (352). Yet whereas theorists such as Lombroso indicate that it is in part his resemblance to a child that identifies the male criminal as a lower order of being, Ecker puts the child, and thus the woman, above the man. The childlike forehead that, he says, is seen in many adult women "imparts something noble to the female head; and, according to Camper's facial angle, the cranium of a new-born child occupies a higher rank than that of an adult; and so does, by the same measurement, the female cranium occupy a higher rank than that of the male" (353).

Nor was this "higher rank" a sign of additional evolution. A generation later, Alexander F. Chamberlain, a British-born anthropologist working in the United States, argues that "woman and the child represent the most generalized forms of the human race, and Nature has kept woman nearer the child in order that, during the process of growing up, the latter might not altogether lose the fair promise with which he begins life, and that here and there a genius might be kept child-woman-like amid the mass of men who seem to approach the ape as they recede from childhood" (473). In this view, the evolutionary "progress" that might seem to be represented by the more specialized male is largely negative. Whereas the second law of thermodynamics (entropy), which became a topic for major scientific discussion in the mid-nineteenth century, suggests that stasis is associated with an alarming dissipation of energy and breakdown of complexity, these anthropological writings posit a more favorable stasis, in which women, and particularly child-women, may not need to evolve: they have already reached the ideal. Similarly, although (or because) she is a survival of the remote past, Ayesha is superior in power, beauty, and intellect to the modern Englishmen who encounter her, and the New Woman writer George Egerton (Mary Chavelita Dunne) identifies "the eternal wildness, the untamed primitive savage temperament that lurks in the mildest, best woman" as "the keynote of woman's witchcraft and woman's strength" (qtd. in Jusová 58).[11]

One of Chamberlain's authorities is Havelock Ellis, whom he quotes as writing in *Man and Woman* (1894),

> When we have realized the position of the child in relation to evolution we can take a clearer view as to the natural position of woman. She bears the special characteristics of humanity in a higher degree than man (as Burdach pointed out), and led evolution in the matter of hairiness (as Darwin, following Burdach[,] pointed out), simply because she is nearer to the child. Her conservatism is thus compensated and justified by the fact that she represents more nearly than man the human type to which man is approximating. (Chamberlain 484; Ellis 447)

Elsewhere in *Man and Woman*, Ellis cites "the precocity of women, [which] involve[es] greater rapidity of growth and its earlier arrest than in men. The result of this precocity is that women, taken altogether, present the characters of short men, and to some extent of children. The whole organism of the average woman, physical and psychic, is fundamentally unlike that of the average man, on account of this fact alone" (442).

Again, women and children are more "generalized," and better for it; "when women differ from men, it is the latter who have diverged, leaving women nearer to the child-type. The earlier arrest of development in women is thus connected with the variational tendency of men" (442). While he simultaneously suggests that woman may be more evolved than man, since "the pelvis of the modern woman is much more feminine in character than that of the primitive woman, and the modern man's pelvis is also slowly becoming more feminine" (447), and while (as we saw in chapter 2) his attitude toward childhood and evolution fluctuates depending on whether his focus is on women or on men, overall Ellis and his allies incline toward the position that man is associated with change, women and children with an admirable form of stasis that suggests where man should be headed. In other words, one might reasonably see atavism as something that Victorian life science tended to deem unnatural in men but appropriate in women. The more childlike the woman, the more closely some Victorian theorists believe her to approximate an evolutionary ideal.

This ideal is brought into question in *The Time Machine* (1895), which posits a remote future in which the feminized descendants of the privileged classes, known as the Eloi, live out their infantuated existence in a balmy England devoid of stinging insects but plagued by the Morlocks, the "ape-like" descendants of the poor, who inhabit subterranean tunnels from which they periodically emerge to devour the defenseless Eloi (46). Weena, whose attraction to Wells's Victorian narrator prompts him to single her out as the representative of her race, is described as "exactly like a child" (44), while, true to the anthropological speculations quoted above, both sexes approximate the feminine: "All had the same form of costume, the same soft hairless visage, and the same girlish rotundity of limb" (30). Yet the stasis of the childlike principle is, for Wells, sinister rather than ideal. Alfred Mac Adam observes in his introduction to one recent edition of the novella that Wells was unhappy with the prospect of a future society that saw no need for further evolutionary development: "Without a spur to force humanity into making new discoveries and expanding its physical or mental frontiers, Wells felt, we would be content with whatever satisfied our basic needs, but nothing more" (xix). Thus the Time Traveller hypothesizes that in having achieved a "balanced civilization," the aristocratic science of the future inadvertently destroyed humankind, since "the too-perfect security of the Upper-worlders had led them to a slow movement of degeneration, to a general dwindling in size, strength, and intelligence" (52).

Notably, however, degeneration takes different forms in the two groups. The Eloi are shallow but beautiful, making garlands of flowers and playing in the sunlight, their manner one "that inspired confidence—[typified by] a graceful gentleness, a certain childlike ease" (25), even though their intellectual development, which resembles that "of one of our five-year-old children," is as stunted as their height (26). As Mac Adam suggests, their problem is entropy rather than atavism (xxi). In contrast, the more energetic Morlocks exhibit a degeneration akin to the atavism of the Lombrosan child-man. They have hairy bodies and a foul smell, run either "on all-fours, or only with [their] forearms held very low" (48), and are "inhuman and malign" killers and cannibals (59). Although the Traveller once likens the Eloi's fingers to "tentacles" (25) and also perceives that they serve the function of "fatted cattle" for the Morlocks (65), he is considerably more prone to see the animal in the Morlocks, whom he variously compares to lemurs, spiders, deer, sea anemones, cavefish, worms, ants, rats, and "vermin" (53). Thus the Morlocks recall Carole Silver's observation that in Victorian discussions of the supernatural (as opposed to texts such as *David Copperfield* and *Olive*, in which the supernatural does not figure), "dwarfs were almost always thought of as male" (124); associated with "'primitive' sexuality," they are "perceived as disgusting phallic figures [who] suggest the grotesquerie of the erotic" (128).[12] In contrast, linked with debased romance rather than with debased sexuality, the Eloi, like the arrested child-woman more generally, suggest the epicene.

A distinction between the feminized Eloi and the masculine Morlocks, then, is that the former suggest a degenerate humanity that cannot progress beyond childhood, while the latter suggest a humanity that is going backwards, de-volving. As Marie Banfield has noted, entropy can appear in Victorian writing as the inverse of evolution, "things reverting to former, simpler states" instead of becoming more complex (183). In the Eloi and the Morlocks, Wells fore-casts a stage at which evolution will become its own opposite, resulting in two separate paths for humanity: one entropic and feminine, the other devolution-ary and masculine. Clearly, neither is desirable, but to invoke the terms that Murphy applies to Haggard's saga, Wells is even less happy with "male histo-ricity" than he is with "female ahistoricity." If feminine inertia leads to stagna-tion, masculine enterprise (in which the Time Traveller deems the Morlocks superior) has caused the Morlocks to slip still further back along the road to-ward the animal. In remarks such as "However great their intellectual degra-dation, the Eloi had kept too much of the human form not to claim my sympa-thy, and to make me perforce a sharer in their degradation and their Fear" (65), the Time Traveller allies himself with other Victorian narrators, including many representatives of anthropological science, who—anxiety about entropic stasis notwithstanding—prefer the arrested feminine to the degraded masculine.

Just Say No: The New (Child) Woman

Beginning in the 1880s but reaching its flowering in the final decade of the nineteenth century, the child-woman's asexuality took on a new coloration. As chapter 2 details, the arrested child-man in his more sinister manifestations has a perverse relationship to sexuality; he is associated with ideas disturbing to Victorian sensibilities, such as homosexuality, miscegenation, promiscuity, and even bestiality. Asexual child-men seem less destructive than their sexual-ized brothers, perhaps in part because they do not threaten to reproduce themselves, whether such reproduction happens in the usual fashion, by recruitment, or by scientific experiment. In contrast, the asexuality of the arrested child-woman increasingly came to lack the comforting qualities associated with such virtuous male counterparts as *David Copperfield*'s Mr. Dick. While we have seen that the good Victorian man may perceive the asexual child-woman, rightly or wrongly, as appealingly innocent and thus desirable, the childlike aspects of the New Woman, in particular, have a political dimension that, for many of her contemporaries and especially after 1895,[13] calls her innocence decidedly into question. Whereas the arrested child-woman of the Dora Copperfield type remains childlike in part because the men who surround her seem to demand this, the New Woman often offends by using maidenhood as a refuge from men: she consults her own desires, not theirs. The celibacy advocated by numerous turn-of-the-century feminists was intended not as a means of attracting or cleansing men but as a means of evading some of the physical and societal dangers, from pregnancy to subservience to a husband, associated with female heterosexuality.

In other words, the childlike New Woman, presented by her advocates as an alternative to such social evils as syphilis, prostitution, and the gynecological difficulties and sapped female energies imposed by excessive childbearing, impressed her detractors as rebellious and unnatural, associated with a chastity as perverse as any male unchastity could be. The stasis of a Sybilla Rothesay or a Hetty Sorrel betokens a moral weakness that, in the Victorian context, was venial because it was understandable. It bolstered existing perceptions that some women were naturally passive, self-regarding, and trivial even while others might be natural moral leaders. The stasis of an Ayesha or a Gagool is the stuff of fantasy, clearly intended to be symbolic and archetypal rather than as a representation of real femininity. The stasis of a dead Chloe or a dead Violet in the 1870s magazine stories by Graham and Vernon renders these women all the more appealing as wives who will now be forever fixated on their men. John cries out to the dying Chloe immediately before her love dawns, "Oh, child! if you could only have learnt to love me before you went, you would never have forgotten the lesson even in God's own heaven" (Graham 63). But the self-chosen stasis of the New Woman, who seeks to retain the perquisites of girlhood while simultaneously demanding masculine privileges such as the vote and access to the professions, had dismayingly real social implications. According to her detractors, writes Murphy, her "agenda countered the natural progress of civilization and hampered the female's primary reproductive function" (*Time* 6).

Thus, for instance, Kathleen Blake argues of Thomas Hardy's *Jude the Obscure* (1895) that Sue Bridehead, "sophisticated but infantile, passionate but sexless" (706), has adopted a "model of freedom [that] comes from childhood" (707); growing up, for her, would mean accepting the limitations imposed upon adult women, and her stated desire to "'get back to the life of my infancy and its freedom,' 'to remain as I began,'" requires a repression of adult female sexuality (709). As Jeffrey Berman observes, "Sue's need to be loved by men has little to do with the wish for sexual gratification" (164). Hence, Blake notes, *Jude*'s association of Sue with windows, which—like the mirrors that permit other arrested Victorian child-women an erotic relationship that is safely asexual because it involves only the self—afford her a degree of protection and separation from the risk of consummated male desire: she "mak[es] spiritual love with a window in between" (717). Indeed, in the serial version of the novel published in *Harper's New Monthly Magazine* in 1894–95, Jude and Sue do not consummate their relationship; the child killed by Little Father Time is theirs by adoption. Throughout, Sue's anxiety about marriage is intimately connected to what Shanta Dutta calls "her rebellion against a society which conditions women into accepting the passive role of being the 'chosen'" (119).

Hardy's treatment of Sue, like the vituperative reception of the novel that contains her, has been explored in detail by too many critics to need extensive discussion here. Rather, I invoke her as a particularly familiar example of a type of arrested child-woman that had wide currency at the end of the nineteenth century and that was influenced by Nora in Henrik Ibsen's *A Doll's House* (1879, translated into English 1889), a text that many nineteenth-century Britons found profoundly shocking. Nora's initial willingness to play the child within marriage did not offend dominant Victorian sensibilities; in contrast, her decision to leave husband, children, and sexual role-playing, in effect to retrace her path to girlhood in an effort to find a different way of growing up, provoked criticism as vitriolic as that meted out to Hardy's Sue.

Egerton, who had read Ibsen in the original during her two-year residence in Norway in the late 1880s, was one of many New Woman writers to explore the sexuality of the child-woman. Egerton's first two books of stories, *Keynotes* (1893) and *Discords* (1894), were admired in "advanced" circles but shocked more conventional reviewers.[14] While these volumes have received the bulk of the scholarly attention devoted to Egerton, their successor, *Symphonies* (1897), is also worth examining for its comments on the child-woman, a figure that appears in several of the seven tales and that seems to have struck some readers as the most positive aspect of the collection. Correspondence between Egerton and her publisher, John Lane, suggests that in the wake of the Oscar Wilde trials and under stress financially because her husband had recently left her, Egerton was feeling pressure to distinguish herself from the Decadent movement: "I have had to change a great deal [in writing *Symphonies*]," Egerton complains (qtd. in Ledger xi). But even (or, for more daring readers, because) "water[ed] down," Sally Ledger observes, "*Symphonies* fail[ed] to strike a chord with the literary market" (xi–xii). While the *Literary World*, like many other reviewing organs, considered that "a blight appears to have fallen upon [Egerton's] imagination; a disaster has overtaken her literary promise," its reviewer nevertheless singles out two of the stories about child-women to save from the wreck:

> "A Chilian Episode" is very nearly completely successful (we expect so much from George Egerton that we feel it necessary to judge her by a high standard), [although] it is not of a value to take an honoured position beside the best work in the two books which appeared before *Symphonies*. . . . But there is one triumph, as it seems to us, in *Symphonies*, though even this is an echo as far as the subject is concerned. Our reference is to "Heart of the Apple." ("Group" 67)

"A Chilian Episode" initially appears to center on the "child-girl" Betty, a coquette who encourages all of her many beaux (although feeling a preference for the naval cadet Samuel), on the theory that "one is only young once!" (18). Like Eliot's Hetty or Graham's Chloe, however, Betty is primarily interested in being admired rather than in reciprocating desire: "she shrank involuntarily" at seeing the passion in Samuel's eyes (24) and "turned her mouth aside" from his kiss (27). When Samuel's involvement in a failed plot puts him in front of a firing squad, we learn that Samuel's mother's love is far superior to Betty's. As Graham's John discovers of Chloe, the "child-girl" is not yet capable of serious love. In contrast, "the mother love of an unwarped woman for the son of her soul is stronger than the love of man, more tender than the love of woman; for it asketh nothing in return,—just gives, gives, gives, as the ocean gives salt and savour and healing!" (Egerton 40–41). The ocean image here suggests a "nothing" that is womblike rather than sexual, all-embracing rather than focused on the genitals.

Eventually Samuel realizes, "Oh, it is hardest on you, noble, good, dear mother; I care most, now that it has come, at leaving you" (35). And indeed, after Samuel's death,

> when the moon peered in, it found Betty smiling in her sleep, her cheek all dimpling, dreaming of love and green woods, for the woman in her was yet untouched. This episode [the love affair with Samuel] was but the caress of a sun ray, the sear of the great fire had not yet come. For when the nameless charm of youth is yet upon a maid, and the breasts are still like half-blown white buds, and the senses only stir uneasily, as yet half awake, and the mystic witchery of the unknown only whispers in the blood, the heart takes trial trips on many streams before it embarks on the one great fatal torrent that engulphs it forever. (38–39)

But Egerton also suggests that the issue is not simply that Betty is not yet ready for romantic love but that the appropriate object of the child-woman's love may always be child rather than spouse. Significantly, Samuel's mother, thirty-five at the time of the story, married at sixteen and was promptly widowed: "Young, beautiful, barely eighteen, she turned each would-be lover away, until no more came; wore the sombre colours of a widow, and devoted herself solely to her son, her *hijito*" (32). Maternal love may necessitate an act of intercourse before its inception, but it does not itself involve sexuality. Having apparently accomplished her aim by producing a son, Samuel's mother is free to retire from romance and focus upon a type of love that she may find more satisfactory. Because she has once been sufficiently sexual to fulfill her biological purpose, asexuality becomes a legitimate option for her. Egerton's commitment to her protagonists' sexuality diminishes once they have become mothers.

A somewhat similar situation exists in "At the Heart of the Apple," the other story that the *Literary World* reviewer approves. Set in Norway, the story focuses on the orphan girl Evir, who, having been brought up on a small island only rarely visited by representatives of the outside world, retains an "absolutely fresh, unspoiled nature, all her basic instincts intact" (206). As "a thing of perfect health, sound in mind and body, all her apperceptions unconfused by the scrapment system of modern education" (207), Evir feels no shame at having borne an illegitimate child at fifteen to a passing artist. A former suitor of Evir's mother seeks "to develop her keen intelligence, but the way was beset with difficulties. The child was a bar to every plan he formed for her future" (207), since she rejects as "unnatural" the suggestion that the child be quietly farmed out so that she can receive an education (210). Motherhood, that is, offers her a stasis with which she is content; she will stay on her island, a child of nature who resists all pressure to change.

But as Evir's response to the return of the artist when their son is seven years old implies, her imperviousness to the demands of conventional society, as represented specifically by dominant sexual and matrimonial practice, also has a political dimension:

> Simply, you have no claim on him, that is all; he is mine absolutely. That is the compensation the world offers the woman if she'd only recognise it. . . . I don't want to be claimed. I like it best so. I am one of the race of women, and they are many, to whom the child is first—the man always second. He fills life for me, and I should be jealous of your claim on him. Marriage does not attract me; indeed, except as a means of making me a mother when I chose, I would loathe it. (215–16)

Angelique Richardson writes that "At the Heart of the Apple" may be seen as a voice against the project, engaged in by a number of New Woman writers, of censorship of fiction that engaged in the "frank representation of sexual desire" (11); as "a perfect eugenic specimen; a Darwinian success story," Evir is "made for mothering" (12). Similarly, Jusová contrasts Egerton to other New Woman novelists, chief among them Sarah Grand, on the ground of Egerton's "resistance to the bourgeois ascetic ideal of feminine behavior" that repudiated female eroticism (58). Yet while Evir is certainly described in terms that convey her erotic appeal—for example, we read of her "supple strength, skilled grace, her white arms cleaving the water for her beautiful body to follow" (213)—she asserts her own freedom from sexual desire. When her erstwhile lover insists that "you had some affection for me that summer, I know you had. I never met any one like you since; I have never had the same feeling for any of them as I had for you," Evir's rejoinder is, "No? As a matter-of-fact I didn't know what you call affection meant, and I don't know now" (216). Egerton's fallen child-woman is in fact unfallen, maternity completing her as a woman without compromising her fundamental virginity.

Whether flirtatiously asexual like Sue Bridehead or postsexual like Egerton's virginal mothers, the arrested child-women found in the ranks of the New Woman are presented as complex, and particularly as sexually complex, in ways that the men around them find difficult to fathom and to live with. (Many readers of *Jude* assume that Sue bears some responsibility for the death of the undergraduate who was her first suitor.) The childlike New Woman, then, is not the female counterpart of the child-man skewered by Grand in "The New Aspect of the Woman Question," the 1894 article (discussed in chapter 2) in which she remarks that "man morally is in his infancy. . . . now woman holds out a strong hand to the child-man, and insists, but with infinite tenderness and pity, upon helping him up" (273). Ruled by desire and impulse, Grand's child-man is a simple creature who may readily be controlled by the more sophisticated woman. In contrast, as Evir's comments to her son's father in Egerton's "At the Heart of the Apple" indicate, the type of child-woman who is also a New Woman can emerge as the victor in the sex war because her desires harmonize with what her advocates see as natural morality. Much as Mulock's Olive asserts the right to direct others' gaze rather than serving as its object, Evir and her fellows assert their right to live outside the dictates of convention. Their chance of achieving this freedom rests upon their transformation of sexuality into maternity, a state revered by dominant Victorian ideology in a way that paternity was not.

In *Time Is of the Essence*, Murphy contends that the Victorians were obsessed by both time and gender, as female threats to invade male strongholds such as professions, higher education, and the polling place coincided with new understandings of geological time, the human evolutionary past, and the truncation of time associated with processes (manufacturing, communication, transportation) in an industrializing world. She sees in *fin-de-siècle* fiction, including Haggard's *She*, both a body of work in which anxiety about time and anxiety about gender converge in the New Woman and a pattern of using time as a means of exploring, and ultimately recuperating, cultural anxiety about femininity. Time, which could seem both menacing and reassuring, could be constructed in a way that reified gender boundaries that the New Woman might appear to undermine.

Although Murphy considers that commentary on time and gender "tended to converge in early texts [i.e., those written before the advent of the New Woman] only obliquely or infrequently if at all" (*Time* 3), I would suggest that her insight about the difference between men's and women's relationships to time in the nineteenth century helps to illuminate more than New Woman fiction. The arrested child-woman, clearly a gendered figure, embodies an antagonistic attitude toward the forward movement of time. That she appears throughout the Victorian era and in such a wide variety of genres, from the feminist short story to the domestic novel, from the sensation novel to speculative fiction, is suggestive; clearly, this figure is not simply a convention of a particular form but rather the embodiment of matters much on the public mind. The arrested child-man may be found in the same genres within fiction and in the discourses of the same disciplines—primarily anthropology, sociology, and psychology—yet the arrested child-woman carries different emotional and moral valences, different implications for society.

Perennially, the stasis with which she is associated dramatizes issues that were crucial to the woman's role in Victorian Britain, particularly the question of the relationship of the self to others. Dora Copperfield, for instance, cannot move beyond the pleasures of play to take up the responsibilities of housekeeping and wifehood, an incapacity that directs attention to the costs of homemaking for the woman. Similarly, Weena is literally devoured by the Morlocks, a denouement that suggests the extent to which masculine energies require the consumption of pretty feminine innocence. Child-women who attempt to live upon the reflected energy of the male, however, are doomed as well; neither Lady Audley nor Hetty Sorrel is permitted to bask for long in the luxuries provided by masculine admiration. Yet as Robson observes in her discussion of Sarah Ellis's best-selling conduct manual *The Daughters of England* (1843), the domesticated middle-class daughter is associated "not only with the lost years of individual males, but [also] with a communal, preindustrial past, the golden age of England" (52); her purpose is "to transport her father back to . . . a sensuously realized past that stands in sharp distinction to the longueur of the working day" (53). The example of Mulock's Olive, one of the relatively few unambiguously positive Victorian depictions of child-women, hints that stasis is least frightening when it comes as the reward for movement already accomplished— or when it exists within a framework that benefits the male.

four

Girls as Women

Rhetoric associated with the Victorian cult of domesticity held that society was organized around separate spheres, with men having primary responsibility for the public and economic, and women for the domestic realm. So "natural" was this system that it supposedly operated even at the cellular level, as in the distinction (discussed in chapter 3) that the biologists Patrick Geddes and J. Arthur Thomson drew between the stay-at-home female cell and the roving male cell. But in fact, of course, the separateness of the spheres was perennially, and disturbingly, troubled. Just as many men rejected their assigned role by being threats instead of protectors or by failing to support their families, working women were a feature of all classes, from the very poor up to the monarchy, while the stuff of the private and domestic was regularly commercialized via phenomena such as prostitutes, cooks, nannies, and wet nurses. In this context of uncertainty about whether private and public could maintain an appropriate distance from each other, the figure of the arrested child-woman may seem to insist upon the viability of separate spheres, the figure of the precocious child-woman to insist upon their impossibility.

In other words, if arrested child-women such as *David Copperfield*'s Dora function in part to advertise their male protectors' ability to bestow upon them a leisured existence in the private realm, precocious child-women often testify to the opposite situation. In a society in which eighty-five percent of the population belonged to the working classes and from thirty to forty percent were aged fifteen or younger, relatively few women, and relatively few children, could afford to remain free of responsibility. Approximately one-third of the paid workforce was female (Mitchell, *Life* 47), and many more women put in arduous but unsalaried days keeping house, working on the family farm, making clothing for their husbands and children, and so on. Beyond the privileged classes, daughters were an important part of the female labor economy inasmuch as their ability to perform household tasks—caring for younger siblings, for instance—often made it possible for their mothers to take on paid labor or for their families to function when the mother's absence was permanent. And beyond the home, Sally Mitchell points out, even in 1900, after decades of legislation designed to curb child labor, "most young people were in full-time employment by the age of thirteen or fourteen," and those under age twelve could legally work part time "in agriculture, retail trades, and domestic service" (*Life* 45). Childhood leisure was a luxury, not a birthright.

The same might be said of sexual innocence. The birth rate peaked at thirty-six births per thousand members of the population in 1870 (approximately three times the 2011 figure), and nineteenth-century commentators estimated the number of prostitutes in London alone at somewhere between ten thousand and eighty thousand (Acton 15). As W. T. Stead's 1885 exposé "The Maiden Tribute of Modern Babylon" pointed out, a number of these "lost women" were in fact lost girls, tricked into error by the cupidity and appetite of the adult world. Notoriously, it was not until 1875 that the age of consent for girls was *raised* to thirteen.[1] Catherine Robson observes of exposés published in the 1840s that not only did "the horrifying visions of exploited girl-labor threate[n] to demote innocent girlhood from the status of an universal phenomenon to an economically contingent construction," but in addition these revelations' "focus upon the active body of the working-class girl revealed it to be disturbingly sexual" (51). In terms of social expectations, the working-class girl was always a precocious child-woman.

This precocity troubled many observers. Arguably, one of the aims of nineteenth-century reformism was to make available what we call childhood (or would like to call childhood) as far down the social ladder as possible; thus, for instance, Robert Polhemus describes Stead's successful "Maiden Tribute" campaign to change the age of consent from thirteen to sixteen as "meant to extend girlhood, setting aside three more years as a protected age of innocence" (199). As Hugh Cunningham notes in *The Children of the Poor*, the "story of the history of childhood" in Britain is a Cinderella tale in which the misprized working child endures centuries of abuse and, in Carolyn Steedman's paraphrase, is "finally rescued and given a 'proper' childhood" (Steedman 6). Because Victorians had substantially established this aim but had not achieved it by the end of the era, Victorian commentators were conscious that the privileged state that many hoped to tie to youth was in fact more closely tied to class. Accordingly, many nineteenth-century visions of the precocious child-woman of the working classes present her as an outgrowth of serious social problems, from dissolute fatherhood to upper-class callousness.

But the precocious child-woman is not only a working-class figure, and although she may be symptomatic of societal problems, she is usually not presented as the problem herself. Sometimes, indeed, she is the solution to the impossibility of widely extending the luxury of ideal childhood. This chapter examines two principal modalities within the type: the economically precocious girl, who typically belongs to the proletariat, and her sexually precocious counterpart, who may well come from the privileged classes. Although negative examples of both exist, the economically precocious child-woman is frequently represented as a heroine, an exemplar of family values that the adults around her may be failing to uphold, while the sexually precocious child-woman is often praised for the very prematurity of her passion, which demonstrates for the Victorian observer a womanliness—and an appreciation of adult masculinity—that is ipso facto virtuous.

That, if anything, Victorian writers tended to represent the precocious child-woman more sympathetically than the arrested child-woman does not inevitably demonstrate that precocity was the ideal, though for some writers it clearly was. Rather, while both conditions deviate from Victorian understandings of developmental norms, economic precocity could readily be used, as Malcolm Andrews observes of Dickens's use of such child-women, "to elicit from the reader . . . pity and indignation" (85). But Andrews continues by noting the existence of a sharp gender divide in Dickens's writings, since "nearly all the *delinquent* grown-up children are boys: nearly all the pure, idealised grown-up children are girls" (86, emphasis in original). For Andrews, this dichotomy is traceable to the similarity that Victorians perceived between women and children; the precocious child-woman seemed less unnatural than her precocious brother.

But class as well as gender inflects the condition, so that precocity among the poor looked different during this period than precocity among the well to do. If we wish to generalize about age inversion overall, then, I suggest that we see it as a kind of generational colonization, in which adults and children covet each other's qualities and perquisites but generally do not cross class boundaries to do so. If the stasis associated with the arrested child-woman is to some degree attributable to what Robson sees as a masculine longing for innocent girlishness, as I propose in chapter 3, the precocious child-woman offers us the converse situation. "Idealised" she may (or may not) be, but she is also a figure who either claims or is assigned adult power. Instead of clinging to childhood, she has moved on to identify and appropriate something desirable about adulthood, which, depending on circumstances, may be economic independence, male romantic companionship, the ability to keep the family going, or the power of the femme fatale. In her pragmatic coveting of aspects of the adult condition, she functions to assure adults that maturity is enviable and, moreover, that what their role demands of them (labor, homemaking, romantic commitment) cannot be excessive, since a child can accomplish it. While the adult may variously exploit, sentimentalize, or lament her, all three responses entail a recognition of her success in achieving agency, which in turn may prompt efforts to reclaim that agency for the adult world. Often, then, the precocious girl associated with an underperforming adult male functions to nudge him into assuming his responsibilities vis-à-vis the family. That she is still simultaneously often associated with the unnatural reminds us of the ambivalence with which many Victorians regarded adulthood even in themselves, let alone in children.

"The Woman That Works for Their Bread": Girls and Economic Precocity

A type of child-woman particularly visible in quotidian Victorian society, since her livelihood depended upon being noticed, was the child street trader. The journalist Henry Mayhew estimated the number of London's street children (of both sexes) at ten thousand in 1851;[2] this population included entertainers, beggars, thieves, and crossing sweepers, among others, but the largest subgroup by number was composed of itinerant vendors, whose wares ranged from flowers and fruit to toys, cheap jewelry, and household goods such as rubber bands, clothespins, tinware, matches, and flypaper (Steedman 115). In contrast to infantilized figures such as Dickens's Dora, whose environment is limited to the home and whose "labor" consists primarily of efforts to train her dog to do simple (and unremunerated) tricks, the street trader was an important part of the public panorama and of her family economy. And if the anxiety surrounding Dora is that her childhood has been extended so that it is coterminous with her married life, the anxiety surrounding the street child is that she has never had a childhood.

David Copperfield was published in volume form in 1850. In December of that year, Mayhew visited the Farringdon watercress market as part of the research behind his *Morning Chronicle* series "Labour and the Poor," which would later appear as *London Labour and the London Poor*. At the market, he encounters a young watercress seller who, he observes, had "entirely lost all childish ways, and was, indeed, in thoughts and manner, a woman" (157). This blurring of boundaries dismays him; he notes with concern, "I did not know how to talk with her." She looks amazed when he tries to "[treat] her as a child, speaking on childish subjects," and he finds her "cruelly pathetic" (157). Nevertheless, he bows to her self-description, asserted most vigorously in her comment that "I aint a child, and I shan't be a woman till I'm twenty, but I'm past eight, I am" (158). Watercress sellers had been a feature of British art since the eighteenth century,[3] but as Steedman details, Mayhew's Watercress Girl in particular fascinated the Victorian public, becoming a source for a number of similar figures in fiction, ballads, and stage melodramas. These fictionalized versions of Mayhew's subject typically pick up on the idea of the aged child. For instance, Sarah Maria Fry's watercress seller has a "thin, old look, which ill suited her childish age and figure," while Mary Sewell's, who calls herself "the woman that works for [her family's] bread," is a child in "nought but the size . . . /And quaint were her speeches and womanly wise" (qtd. in Steedman 122–23). Perhaps especially because the venue is a public one, earning her living has stripped her of the childishness that would presumably be hers if she belonged to the bourgeoisie.

While the arrested child-woman is commonly depicted as a magnet for the gaze, this is less true of the precocious child-woman. To be sure, Mayhew incorporates into his Watercress Girl's testimony a physical description, designed to permit readers to picture her "little face, pale and thin with privation [and] wrinkled where the dimples ought to have been" and her "long rusty hair [that] stood out in all directions" (157). And, indeed, this description is more visually oriented than many that Mayhew provides. By way of contrast, consider his portrait of a coster girl, a fine-grown young woman of eighteen. She had a habit of curtsying to every question that was put to her. Her plaid shawl was tied over the breast, and her cotton-velvet bonnet was crushed in with carrying her basket. She seemed dreadfully puzzled where to put her hands, at one time tucking them under her shawl, warming them at the fire, or measuring the length of her apron, and when she answered a question she invariably addressed the fireplace. Her voice was husky from shouting apples. (47)

In this vision, the coster girl has a physical presence without having an appearance,[4] while the eighteen-year-old featured in "Of the Life of a Flower Girl" is vouchsafed no corporeality at all, as most of Mayhew's attention goes to detailing her prison record.

Yet although the Watercress Girl is certainly turned into an object for the reader's prolonged scrutiny, her statement focuses on her life and thoughts rather than on the visual. Steedman notes that "the transcript of her narrative is much longer than that of any other child [Mayhew] interviewed" (117), reflecting a fascination that has less to do with her appearance than with her experience and outlook. Her inability to resemble the eight-year-olds who populate the comfortable world inhabited by Mayhew and his readers renders her pathetic in a way that is at once fascinating, horrifying, and age-related: she would not have this quality if she were genuinely an old woman or even if she were the age of the coster girl or the flower girl mentioned above. Because she is eight rather than eighteen, Mayhew suggests that she is not to be defined as a working-class woman, but rather as something that should concern his readers far more, a child displaced from childhood.

In general, discussions of the economically precocious child-woman are more concerned with her actions than with her body. She does not share the arrested child-woman's static quality but seems, like Becky Sharp in William Makepeace Thackeray's *Vanity Fair* (1847–48), who also starts life as a child-woman, to slip readily from environment to environment. In addition to working as a peddler, Mayhew's Watercress Girl has looked after a baby cousin, assisted her mother in the fur trade by sewing up slits in pelts, and tended the fire in a Jewish house on the Sabbath. To complete this picture of virtuous industry, we learn that she has voluntarily taken over the cleaning of her family's two rooms and is careful to bank her money, mindful that she is "one who's got a living and vittals to earn" (158). The interviewer's questions, which are not provided in the transcript but are occasionally deducible from her responses, bring the girl continually around to money and her own earning capacity. But in contrast to Becky Sharp's case, there seems no taint of the mercenary here, since we are invited to assume that the child is working for her family rather than for herself alone. Selflessness, of course, is a key attribute for the iconic Victorian woman but not necessarily for the iconic child. By associating this trait with the Watercress Girl, Mayhew establishes her right to be considered a woman morally as well as practically. And because she is old in virtue rather than old in sin, the reader's difficulty in placing her mentally is compounded. We can assign her neither to the workhouse nor to the middle-class home, and if we wish her off the streets, we are condemning her and her family to privation.

Yet this preternatural and selfless competence coexists with the narrative's underscoring of the Watercress Girl's "child" side. Even as (or perhaps because) she asserts her adulthood, she is led to expose the limits of her mathematical knowledge: "I knows how many pennies goes to a shilling . . . but I don't know how many ha'pence there is, though there's two to a penny" (158). Nor is this the only occasion on which this issue is raised. Either this watercress seller or one very like her arouses the pity of members of her own class; earlier in the volume, the eighteen-year-old apple seller has reported to Mayhew, "There's a little gal, I'm sure she an't more than half-past seven, that stands selling water-cresses next my stall, and mother was saying, 'Only look there, how that little one has to get her living afore she a'most knows what a penn'orth means'" (47). Here childishness is used both to heighten and to ameliorate tension. While the Watercress Girl's inability to multiply two by twelve renders her more vulnerable—will she be shortchanged? will she ever gain the knowledge needed to better her condition?—it simultaneously hints that she has not been rendered excessively commercial or excessively sophisticated. Her precocity, like her power, has its limits.

Somewhat similarly, as late as the penultimate page of Dinah Mulock's *Olive*, a novel whose contrasting child-women I discuss more extensively in chapter 3, the title character's husband, who has recently been seen in a somewhat infantile position himself, "look[ing] up to her, helplessly, yet peacefully as a child" (314), refers to her as "little Olive" (330). Such moments help to temper social fears that the child-woman too accustomed to responsibility may forget her place. "Little Olive," in her adulthood sometimes presented as arrested but in her childhood precocious, will submit to her husband even though she has demonstrated her superior maturity, spirituality, and commitment to family from earliest childhood, while the Watercress Girl, for all her competence and industry, may not have the information necessary to function independent of parental authority. They are adultlike without threatening the adult system. Thus, within the substantial body of fiction describing economically precocious child-women, it is common for the narrative to describe such figures as attempting to shore up the authority of their lawful guardians rather than to challenge it.

Alton Clyde's "Effie's Trial" (1867) typifies this pattern. This brief story begins by establishing the maturity of its title character, who is "only a child in years, but a woman in feeling and thought," and detailing how, "at an age when most children are still wrapped in the shelter of the home-nest," "the thoughtful premature child-woman of thirteen" has been "forced out into the world to take her place among its struggling bread-winners; to work, and strive, and care for herself and others, until her little feet often trembled by the way" (578).[5] Yet we quickly learn as well that Effie's role has been bequeathed to her by her mother, whose dying wish it was that Effie should not only be a mother to her younger siblings but also "be the means of leading [her] father back to a better life," as his addiction to gambling has kept him from shouldering his family responsibilities (578). Moreover, when her father steals and pawns a valuable piece of fabric that Effie is embroidering, she shields him even when she is threatened with prison. The spectacle of her dutifulness and filial feeling—her emotional maturity, in other words—finally coaxes forth her father's long-buried virtue. He confesses, returns to work, and renounces gambling, and "in due time the mother's dying prophecy was fulfilled; for Effie was the means of leading her erring father to a better life. They had a home once more, and the little ones, for whom she had prayed so often, did not want for their daily bread" (580). Unlike the children in Mayhew's volume on street life, Effie, a seamstress, has always worked at home, within the private sphere; the story's ending takes Effie's separation from the public and the adult still further by cancelling her achievement in providing a home and food for her siblings, inasmuch as this task is reassigned to her father. The reader is permitted to conclude that once the father assumes his responsibilities, Effie may be a child again.

Like many of the texts on this theme, "Effie's Trial" thus demonstrates that if extended immaturity, such as that manifested by many of the arrested child-women discussed in chapter 3, is often cause for narrators' anxiety, there is anxiety also concerning the power inhering in its opposite. Whether or not the economically precocious girl is admirable, she is also unnatural. Effie is so effective in her precocity that the happy ending must entail her precocity's dissolution. Something similar happens in more sinister cases. Consider a phrenologist's reading of the head of the title character in George Knight's *Sapphira of the Stage* (1896), who is three or four years old at the time. When he finds that her "basilar-phrenometrical angle" is thirty-five,

> his face wore an expression of unfeigned awe.
>
> "[Sapphira's father's] was thirty-seven," he added; "it ought only to be twenty-five at the most. Over thirty it is the stamp of the Destroyer—the index of the human tiger. . . . What that child becomes will depend on you, more or less, but she will always be a modified fiend. She is her father's daughter, and she is a woman. Therefore she will probably go one better—or worse." (32)

In other words, Sapphira may be two degrees less cranially abnormal than her father, but since she is already identifiable as a "woman" even in her early childhood, she is likely to outstrip him in fiendish power.

And, indeed, Sapphira proceeds to confirm for the reader her tigerishness, if not her womanhood, by smashing the doll that she has earlier been seen nursing "with a curious gravity totally unchildlike" (21). Yet like Mulock's Olive, Sapphira moves from the precocious to the arrested; whatever her physical age, her manner will invert it. When we next encounter her, aged twenty but "a girl still" (87), she is earning her living on the stage and has a lengthy track record of leading men to their death. In this avocation she is assisted by her girlish appearance, since, as the narrator puts it, "the palpably mature woman is always more or less unpleasant to a refined taste" (42). The comment hints that the unnatural—the juxtaposition of youth and independence, girlishness and sophistication—does not merely coexist with the working-class girl's erotic appeal but is to some extent its basis. Meanwhile, the chronicle of Sapphira's ill-starred conquests, which is provided in a form suggesting its equivalence to a criminal dossier, testifies that her power is as substantial as it is misused. Thus the ending of this story necessarily involves a return to the "natural" via Sapphira's acknowledgment of the superior strength of her final suitor and subsequently her death at his hands.

A less destructive but nonetheless disturbing example of the unnatural in the precocious child-woman occurs in journalist George Augustus Sala's 1859 glimpse of a member of a troupe of strolling players. Sala describes this individual as "a diminutive child-woman or woman-child, I scarcely know which, who, with her dark eyes and hair and slight figure, would be pretty but for a preternaturally large and concave [*sic*][6] forehead—a forehead that seems to argue wrong and mismanagement somewhere beyond the inevitable malformation of nature" (323). This mismanagement appears to be associated with the girl's very presence in the group. Like the "pitiably half-human" bears and the wolves—"not performing wolves, nor dancing wolves, nor learned wolves," but wolves hungering for a meal specifically of children (317–18)—who also accompany the entertainers, she is out of place and tormented, tied to another girl in the troupe by a "bond of love and suffering" (326). And like the peculiar cranial angles of Knight's Sapphira, the crooked body of Dickens's dwarflike Jenny Wren, and the "wrinkled" face of Mayhew's eight-year-old Watercress Girl, the misshapen physiognomy of Sala's strolling actress testifies to a wrongness that, as with Effie's experience, is most immediately a family problem.

For one might observe that not only the economically precocious child-woman but the great majority of literary child-women, arrested as well as precocious, exist in conjunction with missing or inadequate parents. Dora is the daughter of an emotionally distant widower; the first Mrs. Copperfield was an orphan; in other Dickens novels, Jenny Wren's father (a child-man) is a drunkard, Amy Dorrit's is in debtor's prison, Judy Smallweed's and Esther Summerson's are dead, and so on. Mulock's Olive Rothesay is the child of unhappily married parents, a mother who is initially cold and rejecting and a father who is absent during her infancy and a source of trouble during her young adulthood. Braddon's Lucy Audley has a dead mother and a worthless father. Wilkie Collins's Laura Fairlie is the ward of an unsatisfactory uncle, whose neglect and unconcern embroil her in a conspiracy that reduces her to "[speaking] as a child might have spoken . . . [showing others] her thoughts as a child might have shown them" (458), and only the emergence of a quasi-parental set of protectors, Walter Hartright and Marian Halcombe, can restore her to a state approximating normal adulthood. H. G. Wells's Weena inhabits a society that seems to be organized communally rather than around the nuclear family, while Rider Haggard's Ayesha, as a goddess, has no need of parents. And Stead's "Maiden Tribute," in detailing the premature metamorphosis from child to woman of working-class girls tricked into selling their virginity, blames the situation largely upon "the culpable refusal of mothers to explain to their daughters the realities and the dangers of their existence" (6).

Mayhew's Watercress Girl is no exception to this pattern of absence within the family, to which the precocious child-women respond by taking on an adult role, and the arrested child-women by clinging to childhood. Although she has a mother, who defends her from an abusive schoolmaster, has taught her to sew and to knit, and is "so very good to me. She don't often beat me," she notes that she "ain't got no father, he's a father-in-law. No; mother ain't married again—he's a father-in-law. He grinds scissors, and he's very good to me. No; I dont mean by that that he says kind things to me, for he never hardly speaks" (158). "Very good," in this latter context, seems merely to mark the absence of abuse in a man already defined by the absence of a blood tie, a marriage license, and even language itself. It appears that the economically precocious child-woman is a child functioning as an adult because the real adults cannot fulfill their responsibilities owing to absence or incapacity, while the arrested child-woman is often an adult who fails to grow beyond childhood because she lacks suitable parental models. Together, these two figures represent contrasting responses to a single phenomenon.

That the working-class child-woman is perennially described as the product of an inadequate home, and particularly of a financially inadequate father, should not surprise us. Nineteenth-century British sociological commentary on the poor, most of it written by members of the middle classes, is rife with discussions of the ways in which "grinding poverty . . . checks [parents'] natural impulses, and turns them from good to evil," as one 1850 *Fraser's* article put it in urging the establishment of day-care centers (qtd. in Nelson, *Men* 177). Working-class fathers were a favorite target of reformers, who often associated them with drunkenness, brutality, and incest. Against this backdrop, readers must view as a blessing the emergence of competent child-women who can both stand in for their fathers as economic providers and do their mothers' job by keeping the household running smoothly. Clyde's Effie; Mayhew's Watercress Girl, who scrubs the family floors after her long day's work; and the Little Mother of the 1884 *All the Year Round* series *Travels in the East*, who looks after the children and does the family wash after her own stint selling watercress or matches (99–105), all belong to families that might well collapse without them. Thus although the narratives that contain this type of child-woman speak of her with conscious pity as sacrificial victim, they simultaneously present her as powerful benefactor.

What might seem more striking is that the inadequacy of the impoverished parent appears to affect other reaches of society as well. It is not only the working-class girl who may be asked to mature early in response to the failings of her seniors. Although the class status of figures such as Amy Dorrit and Esther Summerson has been jeopardized by their parents' misbehavior, their own deportment is that of the gently bred, and the clash between their circumstances and their inclinations makes them women before their time. A less noble figure, Thackeray's Becky Sharp, evidently owes her amorality to an early and intimate acquaintance with the difficulties of maintaining a genteel façade when her dissolute father can provide no economic support and her opera-girl mother no breeding; hers is "the dismal precocity of poverty" (21). In contrast, in the family of Mulock's Olive poverty cannot be invoked to excuse parental misconduct; nevertheless, the sins of Olive's aristocratic father, which eventually include sexual infidelity, illegitimate fatherhood, drunkenness, and business failure, are the stereotypical failings of the working-class male as described in countless middle-class periodicals.

Mulock (later Craik) was herself an erstwhile child-woman in that her unstable father abandoned his motherless children both physically and financially to her care when she was still in her teens. In commenting on her tendency to provide her heroines with dysfunctional families, Mitchell argues that "by killing and dishonoring the fathers, Craik also rejects the world they represent— the world of rigorous systems, irresponsibility, selfishness, and repressed emotion. Thus she destroys the need for daughters to become fixed in childish dependency because they worship adult male strength, intelligence, and power." Mitchell adds that the many dead or enfeebled mothers in this author's fiction demonstrate the extent to which "the value of [feminine] tradition . . . in the form imposed by society, is dubious" because it offers only "womanly dependence" (*Craik* 111). One way to read the pattern of the economically precocious child-woman, in other words, is as feminist protest, a rejection not only of unfortunate personal experience but also of the patriarchal structures upon which nineteenth-century society was based.

More generally, such child-women may also be seen as metaphors for other kinds of social dysfunction. Writing of Dickens, Arthur Adrian argues that "just as family after family is portrayed with the natural guardian assuming no control, so Victorian England is to be viewed as one vast family with incompetent and indifferent leadership. In short, the defaulting parent and the neglected child are to be recognised as the domestic equivalents of the bungling statesmen and their abandoned constituents" ("Parenthood" 11). Back in the home, child-women of the Effie or Little Mother type offer sites for the expression of cultural anxiety about parenthood in a world in which domesticity was both undergoing significant changes and being required to serve as a kind of secular religion. I have argued elsewhere that Victorians often used the working-class father as an outlet and scapegoat for the expression of concern inspired more immediately by middle-class family life (*Men*, ch. 6). The economically precocious child-woman, token of a social disharmony that may or may not be resolved at the end of her story by a diminishing of her agency, functions as another way of articulating such concerns.

Wives and Daughters: Sexually Precocious Child-Women and Their Fathers

Implicit in many narratives about the economically precocious child-woman, but by no means limited to this form, is the eroticization of the father-daughter bond, wherein a daughter becomes a substitute wife to her widowed father rather than merely a housekeeper. While nineteenth- and early twentieth-century fictions do not typically suggest that this type of union has an overtly sexual side, it is often characterized by caresses, possessiveness, and expressions of passionate devotion. Seven-year-old Sara Crewe's relationship to her father in Frances Hodgson Burnett's *A Little Princess* sets the tone: the narrator terms them "the dearest friends and lovers in the world" (222).[7] Sara begins the novel as her father's "comrade" (16) and "companion" (10), his "Little Missus" (65), and it is expected that after she completes her schooling in England (where she is sent more to safeguard her health against the presumed dangers of the Indian climate than to improve her mind, since she is already an indefatigable reader), she will live with him, keep his house, and preside over his table. When he leaves her at Miss Minchin's Select Seminary, having first purchased for her a trousseau of clothing adorned with ostrich feathers, ermine, and Valenciennes lace, Sara assures her father, " 'I know you by heart. You are inside my heart.' And they put their arms round each other and kissed as if they would never let each other go" (17). Although Sara's relationship with her father appears to end with his death, it finds alternative expression when his best friend adopts her, showers luxuries upon her, and makes her the center of his emotional life.

Significantly, while Burnett's narrator stresses that the "old-fashioned" Sara strikes various other characters as "queer" or unattractive, her relationship with her father is not presented in this light, and its validity is asserted by its reincarnation at the end of the story when Sara settles down with Tom Carrisford. There is no anxiety on the narrator's part about excessive agency for Sara, but only about agency's curtailment. And Sara's filial passion, an important source of her agency, is contrasted favorably with the more distant bond experienced by other girls, such as Ermengarde St. John, whose father decries her stupidity; Lottie Legh, whose father considers her too spoiled to remain in his household; and the working-class Becky and Anne, who have no fathers. Closeness to a father is evidently the luxury that Sara most misses when she loses her surviving parent and her fortune, to judge from the longing glances she casts at the neighboring Carmichael family and its jolly paterfamilias, and the narrative's delight in establishing Sara as the exclusive love of her new adoptive father indicates that this position should be considered enviable rather than "queer."

While Sara's happy ending involves finding a second father, Victorian child-women novels frequently suggest that especially when interrupted, an innocent but quasi-erotic passion for the father helps to prepare a girl to form a deep and permanent attachment to her future husband. That these novels concern themselves with the girl's viewpoint much more than with the male's is an implicit guarantee that no abuse is taking place, while the emphasis on romance establishes that the girl is using her agency responsibly by embracing, however prematurely, her appropriate social role. Polly Home (later known as Paulina de Bassompierre), whose experiences form a subplot in *Villette*, is only one of a number of small girls who upon separation from their adored fathers transfer their affections to a substitute some years their senior. Consider *Daisy Burns*, a three-volume novel published in the same year as *Villette*, which recounts an emotional history of this type in more detail than Charlotte Brontë affords.

Although the author of *Daisy Burns*, the Irish novelist Julia Kavanagh, allied herself with her mother rather than with her feckless father when her parents separated, Kavanagh's title character is the motherless only child of a man whom she loves "passionately and exclusively . . . years have not effaced either his memory or his aspect from my heart" (6). When, at ten, she loses her father, Daisy goes to live with his erstwhile protégé, Cornelius O'Reilly, who is then about twenty. During her father's lifetime little Daisy is jealous of his fondness for Cornelius and rejects the latter's suggestion that she kiss him. "I never kissed any one but my father," she tells the reader (11). But when Cornelius expresses sympathy over the older man's sudden death, "the thrill of a strange and rapid emotion ran through me. I disengaged my hands from those of Cornelius, and, with a sudden impulse, threw my arms around his neck. My cheek lay near his; his lips touched mine; I mutely returned the caress. I was conquered" (19).

Girls of this sort may be said to partake of an emotional stasis akin to that of the arrested child-woman, but, significantly, it freezes them at a more developed stage, so that their interactions with men do not take place in a presexual Eden that might permit the men to leave sexuality's burdens behind. Daisy's feelings for Cornelius undergo little further alteration, but then they need no retailoring for adult life. After she becomes passionate about him as a ten-year-old, she remains so. Her dilemma is caused, not by discomfort with the intensity and implications of her emotions or by any uncertainty on her part as to how to interpret them, but rather by others' inability to see that a child's love may be deep and steadfast. When Cornelius does not take her seriously, her frustration is patent. She complains that

> in vain I showed him how devotedly fond I was of him; he treated me with the most tantalizing mixture of kindness, carelessness, and indifference.... I worked hard to give him satisfaction, but he only took this as a matter of course; called me a good child, and, as I was quiet and silent, generally allowed me to sit somewhere near him for the rest of the evening, and this was all: he seldom caressed, he never kissed me. (62)

Although Cornelius becomes more affectionate toward Daisy in response to her evident love for him and her eagerness to sit as his model while he tries to establish himself as an artist, when she is twelve he becomes engaged to the twenty-six-year-old Miriam, which is to Daisy "a thought so bitter, so tormenting, that it worked me into a fever, which fed eagerly on the jealousy that had given it birth" (107). Much of the remainder of the novel is concerned with extricating Cornelius from his ties to Miriam and bringing him to see Daisy in the light—the appropriate light, asserts the first-person narration—of desired romantic object. Although both Daisy and, to a lesser extent, Cornelius are described or addressed as "child" throughout the novel, and although this identification may be the reason that their marriage does not produce offspring, in Daisy's case child status is clearly to be seen as compatible with lasting, mature, and erotically charged love, a love originally grounded in love for the father.

The emotional undercurrents of this triangle are on display during Daisy's apotheosis as Cornelius's model, her sitting for his best work, *The Stolen Child*. The painting ostensibly depicts an aristocratic child who has been abducted by Gypsies, but it also serves as an unconscious expression of Cornelius's guilt in falling heir to love originally destined for Daisy's father. Dr. Burns was himself a thief of children in that he eloped with Daisy's mother without her father's consent, and, Cornelius notes, he

> bitterly . . . repented this act of his youth. He often spoke of it to me. "Cornelius, never rob a man of his child," he said, "it is a great sin." He was right, Daisy; it is a great sin; I felt it then; I feel it far more now; for though you are not my child, I have reared you, and I know that affection is jealous; that to resign a daughter to a stranger must always be bitter; but that to have her actually stolen from you, to be robbed of the pleasant thing which has for years been your delight and pride, to feel that it is gone beyond recall, the property of another, I know that this is too sharp a pang for speech, almost for thought. (358)

That Cornelius casts himself in this passage as Daisy's second father, subject both to stealing and to being stolen from, paradoxically establishes his right to be considered her lover and underscores the novel's point that because the two roles are essentially identical, Daisy's pursuit of Cornelius is not unmaidenly.

The theft motif also surfaces in *Villette*, in which Polly/Paulina's father, on realizing that she is not twelve or fourteen, as he has thought, but eighteen and the declared lover of Graham Bretton, laments that while he has always liked Graham, "Now he betrays me by this robbery! My little treasure used to love her old father dearly and truly. It is all over now, doubtless" (391). Agonized, Paulina promises her father, "I won't leave you, papa: I'll never leave you. I won't pain you! I'll never pain you!" (394). She solves the dilemma by determining, in effect, to marry both of them, "the father, the daughter, the future husband, now united" and agreeing to live together (397). This resolution at once exemplifies what various scholars have identified as Paulina's privileged status within the novel—she has much better luck than Lucy Snowe throughout—and helps to justify it, since Paulina is able to provide both the daughterly and the wifely devotion that her society demands of her. While Paulina in *Villette* and Daisy in *Daisy Burns* must each defeat a female rival for her lover's affections, the more important conflict is Oedipal, and both narratives consider that this conflict is most satisfactorily resolved through another version of the conflation of father and lover that has existed from the outset.

To be sure, other authors suggest that there may be cause for anxiety about father-daughter relationships of the intensity of Sara's, Paulina's, and Daisy's. Adrian details Dickens's dismay at cases in which the daughter has assumed the role of her father's wife, or even her father's mother. One example is "the relationship between Agnes Wickfield and her father [in *David Copperfield*], where the parent does not deliberately exploit the child, but becomes so dependent on her that she voluntarily makes his happiness the 'utmost height' of her hope." So much is she the focus of " 'the concentration of his whole mind' . . . [that] she considers herself the 'innocent cause of his errors,' " while Wickfield himself comes to realize that his emotions were inappropriate: "My love for my dear child was a diseased love, but my mind was all unhealthy then" (*Relationship* 122–23).

Adrian contends that Dickens uses these inverted family structures to illustrate society's "withdraw[al] from personal responsibility. Why should a girl of thirteen years [Charley in *Bleak House*] take on a woman's work by supporting two younger children?" (*Relationship* 124). Yet Dickens's dismay at working-class instances of this phenomenon appears significantly greater than his dismay when the participants are middle-class and not being asked to earn their bread. Emotional precocity is to be preferred to economic precocity, since agency achieved within the former state may be repurposed as successful matrimony. If we are given cause to worry about Reginald Wilfer's infantilization in *Our Mutual Friend*, it is not on his daughter's account, since Bella's feeling for him is presented as her best quality. If Amy Dorrit's tender regard for her father has found an unworthy object, the praiseworthiness of her emotion is undimmed. And if Wickfield's excessive reliance upon Agnes has problematic consequences for the father, Dickens (who seems to have been substantially closer to his own adult daughters than he was to his sons) does not appear to suggest that the daughter is the worse for it. Agnes, for instance, emerges from daughterhood perfectly suited to wifehood and eventual motherhood, able to construct for David the kind of companionate marriage that he now seeks, because she has in effect already provided it for Wickfield. All three of these Dickens child-women move from a quasi-marital relationship with a childlike parent to a more "natural" union with a husband who is represented as mature.

A number of these novels demonstrate that it is not only male authors who hint that child-women may find gratification and empowerment in an intense father-daughter relationship. As a final example, let us turn to Mary Elizabeth Braddon's *John Marchmont's Legacy* (1862–64). Mary's position in the title as her father's "legacy" establishes from the outset that she is an object to be willed by one man to another. Part of her assigned role, then, is to be passive, and she is treated in ways that recall the situations of Laura Fairlie and Anne Catherick in *The Woman in White*, a strong influence upon Braddon's work. That is, Mary is falsely stigmatized as "weak-minded" (221), her marriage is questioned, and for some years she is shut out from the action by being hidden away with her baby son by the villain who covets her estate. In her adulthood, in other words, her status as "child" is emphasized, as she is excluded from adult purviews such as marriage and the intellect and is confined to a nursery so private that only a very few are even aware that it exists.

But Mary's childhood has worked in just the opposite way. Here again we meet a child-woman whose mother is dead and whose father is a failure physically, financially (until he inherits his estate, he has great difficulty making a living), and religiously; the narrator criticizes him as "too weak to trust blindly in his God" (Braddon, *Legacy* 99). Since her mother's death, which occurred shortly after Mary's third birthday, Mary has been responsible for shopping, meal preparation, and keeping her father virtuous. To be sure, the narrator introduces her via a discussion of why we should feel "sorry for this little girl," who "had never been a child" (18). Yet while the loss of childhood is lamentable, the eight-year-old Mary has gained something that her society considers valuable: she is

> a woman invested with all that is most beautiful amongst womanly attributes—
> love, tenderness, compassion, carefulness for others, unselfish devotion, uncom-
> plaining patience, heroic endurance. . . . At three years old she had bidden fare-
> well for ever to the ignorant selfishness, the animal enjoyment of childhood, and
> had learned what it was to be sorry for poor papa and mamma. (18)

Practically and emotionally if not sexually, she has stepped into the role of her father's wife. While this perception sometimes gives the narrator pause—we are told that "[their] affection . . . was almost morbid in its intensity. . . . The little girl loved her father *too much*" (19, emphasis in original)—Mary's noble "womanly attributes," the heightened capacity for sympathy and altruism that is evidently attributable to the role she fills for her father, garner her more agency and narrative respect than will typically be the case once she has attained woman's estate.

Agency, then, is a vexed question here. If Mulock's Olive is finally rewarded with childlike dependence for having been precocious and dependable in youth, Braddon's narrative suggests that for Mary there are at least two possible readings: either her excessive agency in childhood must be punished (not merely balanced, as in "Effie's Trial" or various Dickens novels) by diminished agency in adulthood or the movement between competence and incompetence, power and helplessness, has always been determined not by Mary but by the adults around her. John, after all, both needs his daughter to be an adult and, because of his feelings of guilt over this need, insists upon her status as child; the narrator remarks at one point that at John's invitation, Mary "sat on his knee still, though she was thirteen years of age" (50). It is perhaps this unresolved anxiety over whether his offspring is child or wife that prompts him, newly heir to a large estate, to make the serious error of marrying again, a decision ostensibly due to his belief that he has not long to live and will need to lay in a substitute caregiver for his "little" daughter. Predictably, Mary, unaccustomed to receiving care in any case, is unhappy at being supplanted by a stepmother. John's remarriage forms part of an extended narrative pattern of triangles in which two women vie for the regard of one man. Indeed, Mary and her stepmother, Olivia, are also rivals for the love of the novel's hero, Edward Arundel, toward whom Mary has nurtured romantic feelings since age nine, continuing the pattern of filial love developing into romantic love that is elsewhere evident in figures such as Daisy Burns and Polly Home.

John Marchmont's Legacy thus moves its title character back and forth between the status of child and that of adult in a way that seems to have little to do with chronological age. Tellingly, however, it is principally Mary's ability to feel passionate love, first for her father and subsequently for Edward, that makes her an adult in the narrator's eyes, even while (as is also the case with Daisy Burns) the people surrounding her continually overlook or misinterpret this passion, which they consider incompatible with her childish exterior. Edward, for instance, is drawn to the newly grown-up Mary because he is uncomfortable with strong emotion in women and believes that one "as childlike now, in her early womanhood, as she had been womanly while she was a child" must feel no more than "naïve tenderness" toward the opposite sex. Whereas he has successfully avoided noticing the fatal passion for himself contracted by Olivia, who is tall, dramatic-looking, and commanding in her demeanor, what he takes to be Mary's mild fondness "bewitche[s] and enrapture[s] him" (142). Meanwhile, Olivia, who "ha[s] never yet learned to think of Mary as a woman," holds her in contempt as a rival for Edward (140) and because of that contempt connives at Mary's incarceration,[8] while the principal mover behind that incarceration, the mercenary Paul Marchmont, affects to believe Mary a victim of seduction, too inexperienced to be able to tell a real marriage ceremony from a sham.

Thus to Karen Odden's argument that "the childlike Mary represents the danger of reading naïvely and confusing life with literature" (29) we might add that Mary's childlike quality also heightens her risk of *being* read wrongly, much as Miss Mowcher's customers insist upon using her dwarfism to deny her interiority. Daisy Burns too seems to function more successfully as a model for Cornelius's painting *The Stolen Child* than she does interacting with others in the flesh, since in the painting she is a legible symbol rather than a three-dimensional being with an agenda of her own. James Kincaid suggests that "the child is the perceptual frame we have available to us for fitting in just about anything we choose—or nothing" (*Child-Loving* 62). In *John Marchmont's Legacy*, Braddon explores repercussions of this cultural tendency to project certain qualities (or certain absences) onto the figure of the child-woman.

The ambivalence with which some Victorian novels represent the precocious and passionately devoted daughter is akin to the Victorian lack of unanimity on whether stasis is a good or a bad thing where girls are concerned. On the one hand, like Mayhew's Watercress Girl and her counterparts, the precocious daughter has been shut out from childhood, a circumstance evoking fears of exploitation, inadequate protection, and destruction of innocence. Becky Sharp, for instance, "sate [*sic*] commonly with her father . . . and heard the talk of many of his wild companions—often but ill-suited for a girl to hear" (21). When he dies, Becky mourns not only the loss of his companionship but also the loss of her freedom (22), which throughout the novel she seeks to restore via bad behavior. Becky's example hints that concerns about the loss of female childhood may be as much on society's behalf as on that of the girl: without a protracted period of sheltered naïveté, what might she not do with her sexual allure?

On the other hand, the devoted daughter may be seen as displaying precisely those qualities that her society wants her to develop, such as altruism, tenderness, commitment to family and to the home, and, in particular, a recognition of something almost magically desirable about adult masculinity—a recognition that adult men may themselves lack and that perhaps will help them to develop it. How regrettable can it be that the precocious child-woman has lost what Braddon identifies as "the ignorant selfishness, the animal enjoyment of childhood," when selfishness and kinship to the animal are what we are to regret about her inverse, the arrested child-man? Moreover, when the father, who is the object of her special devotion, is so often flawed in his masculinity, lacking competence or strength or the ability to protect, his daughter's readiness to adore him may hold out the promise that to her, at least, his masculinity does not suffer these humiliating lacunae—or, more sinisterly, the threat that her involvement with him has somehow caused them. It is noteworthy that Thackeray, wishing to establish Becky's distance from the ideal woman, identifies her as not really a devoted daughter; although she is prey to fits of sobbing after her arrival at Chiswick, we are told that her "fanc[y that] she was consumed with grief for her father" is only fancy (22). That she feels no genuine devotion, no real commitment to furthering a man's welfare above her own, makes it easier for a Victorian audience to grant that Becky may be precocious and selfish at the same time.

Victorian Responses to the Child-Wife

To some writers, at least, the precocious daughter's passion for her father looked admirable. While it might be taken too far, might be a response to unacknowledged but undesirable impulses on his part, or might cause her pain when another woman entered the picture, nonetheless it was usually considered to demonstrate impulses both beautiful and appropriate. As we have seen, that same passion transformed into an erotic fixation upon another man might also be represented sympathetically, yet the objects of the child's devotion, from *Villette*'s Graham Bretton and *Daisy Burns*'s Cornelius O'Reilly to *John Marchmont's Legacy*'s Edward Arundel, do not initially take it seriously, a sign that they do not view these girls in a romantic light. If, as Alison Hoddinott puts it, Paulina "has a deeper understanding of the dangers and vulnerability associated with love than [Graham] has" (8), this affinity for romance remains opaque to their prospective partners until the girls may readily be defined as marriageable. To the observer, in other words, any abnormality in these child-women's erotic attachments is traceable to the girls and/or to their fathers, not to the future husbands, whose comparative lack of interest identifies them as safe partners, gentlemen rather than the out-of-control drunkards and brutes who populate Victorian child-abuse court cases. By contrast, the type of child-woman often designated the "child-wife" tends to be the object rather than the subject of passion. Tellingly, she is more likely than the devoted daughter to be associated with the term *unnatural*. Even so, the Victorian debate over the extent of her agency continues, and is reflected in the fact that some child-wives (for instance, those in the stories by Jeffrey Graham and John Richard Vernon discussed in chapter 3, whose signal accomplishment is their death) are arrested child-women, while others are precocious.

Thus, writing in the *Contemporary Review* in 1891, a few years after Stead's exposé of child prostitution and the successful campaigns (which had their counterpart in India) to raise the age of consent for girls, F. Max Müller comments, "When we hear of child-wives or of child-widows in India, we almost shrink from realising all that is implied in these words. Our thoughts turn away in pity or disgust. We think of our own children, and to imagine them as wives when ten years old, or as mothers of children when twelve, sends a shiver through our hearts" (183). Yet Müller's purpose is, if not to defend the practice of child marriage, at least to argue that it is not invariably abusive: "Nature is wonderfully kind even towards those who seem to us to disregard her clearest intimations. There is such a thing as loving devotion even among children, and the absence of all passion surrounds those early attachments with a charm unknown in later life" (184). The article focuses on a couple aged twelve and nine at the time of their marriage, a union whose success seems in Müller's account to have depended in large measure on the blend of precocity and youthfulness represented in it, since "they were happy as children all day long, and yet their thoughts were engaged on subjects which form but a small portion of the conversation even of more mature married couples in England. Young as they were, they were old enough to think of serious subjects" (185). Being a child-wife is here associated with hypermaturity: Srimati Ray adopts Christian-influenced beliefs (for Müller evidence of her superiority to her Hindu kinfolk) and becomes an exemplary money manager, student, housewife, and eventually mother.

The *Review of Reviews*, a periodical edited by Stead, expressed dismay at the article:

> Professor Max Müller, of all people in the world, writes a paper which, however it may have been intended, undoubtedly will be read as constituting more or less of an apology for Hindu child-marriage. The Professor guards against this as best he can, but the peep which he gives us into the sanctuary of the wedded life of Srimati-Soudamini Ray, the wife of one of the leading members of the Brahmo Somaj, will probably leave an impression that will tell in the wrong direction. ("Reviews Reviewed" 173)

The anxiety apparent in this comment reflects an awareness of the extent to which the idea of girls entering as emotionally powerful partners into lifelong romantic commitments (as opposed to falling prey to seducers or rapists, a situation upon whose evils public opinion was agreed) appealed to some members of middle-class society in the late nineteenth century. While Müller, a philologist and Orientalist, might draw a distinction between the "we" whose "thoughts turn away in pity or disgust" from the concept and the "natives" born "under the warmer sky of India," who "dwell with rapture on the days of their boyhood and boyish love as the most blissful of their whole lives," writers focusing on British relationships might perceive the same bliss in precocious romance that Müller, who acknowledges that "these childish or boyish attachments are not unknown among ourselves," seeks to locate primarily in the supposedly more passionate tropics (184).

Consider, for instance, Captain Mayne Reid's autographical novel *The Child Wife* (1868), based on his relationship with Elizabeth Hyde Reid, whom he married in 1853, when she was fifteen years old. Told from the point of view of the hero, Captain Maynard, the narrative describes the pair's first encounter as follows:

> Turning to go below, [Maynard] saw a face so wonderfully fair, so strange withal, that almost mechanically he stayed his intention, and remained lingering on the deck.
>
> In less than ten minutes after, *he was in love with a child!* There are those who will deem this an improbability; perhaps pronounce it unnatural.
>
> Nevertheless it was true; for we are recording an actual experience.
>
> As Maynard faced towards the few passengers that remained upon the upper deck, most of them with eyes fixed upon the land they were leaving, he noticed one pair that were turned upon himself. At first he read in them only an expression of simple curiosity; and his own thought was the same as he returned the glance.
>
> He saw a child with grand golden hair—challenging a second look. And this he gave, as one who regards something pretty and superior of its kind.
>
> But passing from the hair to the eyes, he beheld in them a strange, wondering gaze, like that given by the gazelle or the fawn of the fallow-deer, to the saunterer in a zoological garden, who has tempted it to the edge of its enclosure.
>
> Had the glance been only transitory, Maynard might have passed on, though not without remembering it.
>
> But it was not. The child continued to gaze upon him, regardless of all else around. (108, emphasis in original)

Although the passage casts Blanche as vulnerable animal and Maynard as part of the species that has imprisoned that animal, the implication is nevertheless that it is the thirteen-year-old, not the adult, who is somehow controlling his response. Elizabeth's memoir of their courtship, in contrast, indicates that the fictionalized version may be influenced by wishful thinking on Reid's part; in her rendition, whereas "the gallant Captain . . . as he himself expressed it, had 'fallen in love with me at first sight,'"

> on my part, the gallant hero had made no impression whatever; for when I was asked that night by someone who had not yet had a look at the lion, "What is Captain Mayne Reid like?" "Oh! he is a middle-aged gentleman," was my reply, giving no other description of him at all. This was afterwards repeated to Mayne Reid, and he allowed that his vanity was much wounded thereat. (123)

To add injury to insult,

> On the following morning, my aunt said to me: "Captain Mayne Reid has fallen desperately in love with you, my child! He did nothing but talk of you the whole of the evening."
>   To which I replied, "You can tell Captain Mayne Reid that I have not fallen in love with him." (123)

While Elizabeth reiterates her lack of interest by informing the reader that she is sewing clothes for her doll when he first declares his love, Reid nonetheless engages in an aggressive courtship of his future wife, interrupted by a two-year absence. Upon their reunion, she begins to reciprocate his feelings, and they marry shortly thereafter.

Both the discrepancies and the resemblances between the accounts are suggestive. Reid's novel puts Blanche in the care, not of an aunt, but of a West Indian servant, Sabina. When on her fifteenth birthday Blanche tells Sabina that she is in love, Sabina, evidently more conservative than Elizabeth's aunt, tells her that she is too young. Responding to Blanche's question about the age considered appropriate for this emotion, however, Sabina, presaging Müller's remark a generation later about the precocity-inducing effect of the "warm Indian sky," concedes that the matter is affected by environment: "Dey do say it 'pend berry much on the nater ob de climate. In dem Wess Indy Island wha it ar hot, dey fall into de affecshun sooner dan hya in Englan'. I know lots ob young Badian girl get married 'fore dey am fo'teen, an' dey falls in lub sooner dan dat." Blanche points out, "You must remember I lived three years in the West Indies," at which Sabina shifts her ground from physical to cultural environment: "No matter 'bout dat. It no diff'rence make in 'spect ob de rule. In Englan' you only chile yet." Blanche, however, has the last word, rejecting stasis by protesting, "Only a child! Nonsense, Sabby! See how tall I am!" (227).

Reid's account, in other words, locates gratification at the man's interest not in the girl's caretaker but in the girl herself, since Blanche is eager to experience romance and considers it a privilege that should not be withheld from her if it is granted to Barbadian girls. Elizabeth's account emphasizes her childishness, suggesting that she views adult men as alien beings whose sexual appeal she is ill equipped to judge. Blanche, that is, instantly recognizes through her fixed gaze the fascination of Maynard's masculinity, while Elizabeth wishes the reader to understand that she remains oblivious to it until well into his courtship. Elizabeth presents her thirteen-year-old self as anything but precocious; if she has a "would-be boy-love[r]" close to her own age and finds him handsome (125–26), she is simultaneously still sufficiently emotionally invested in her dolls to sew them elaborate wardrobes. Robson notes of Sarah Stickney Ellis's popular conduct manual *The Daughters of England* (1843) that it urges girls "to fend off maturation, to 'endeavour to prolong rather than curtail the season of their simplicity and buoyancy of heart'" (55), and Elizabeth's passion, similarly, is for her rapidly receding childhood, not for adult romantic adventures. In contrast, Reid depicts Blanche as a child in years but invested with "the sageness of a woman" (177). Her lack of inhibition manifests both innocence and passion, but it is additionally the sign of an early-onset wisdom and good taste, the "sage" ability to recognize the adult man's desirability. Unlike the arrested child-wife in Vernon's "Dog-Violet and Mignonette" (discussed in chapter 3), Blanche is sometimes to be seen outside her future husband's company and thinks of herself as an adult rather than as a child or a pet.

Despite Reid's narrator's acknowledgment that some readers may consider it "unnatural" for a man in his thirties to fall in love with a thirteen-year-old, and while Blanche is a child-woman in a way that Elizabeth, who wants to be seen simply as a child, is not, both texts ultimately consider the pairing of a mature man with a girl of fifteen romantic and appropriate. It is clear that for both narrators, Elizabeth/Blanche's blend of childlike qualities and evident sexual attractiveness is the source of her appeal, although Elizabeth stresses the former element and Reid the latter. Conversely, however, both novel and biography also indicate that adult masculinity, as manifest in the dashing adventurer and successful novelist, is something that the girl is expected to covet.

Whatever our response today to either account,[9] and despite the mentions of the unnatural raised by Reid's narrator (and later, in another context, by Müller), Victorian culture seems to have accepted the romance with equanimity, and until at least 1930 the novel, for whose serial rights Frank Leslie paid

Reid eight thousand dollars, enjoyed multiple reprintings and translations. To be sure, the *Overland Monthly*, an American periodical edited by Bret Harte, condemns the novel on the grounds that "the tone . . . is low" and the characters are marked by "vulgarity" ("Current Literature" 295), but the reviewer's distaste is not associated with the title character or her age. For this reader, "The 'Child Wife' is an inconspicuous young person, appearing late in the book, and chiefly useful to give a title to the story" (296). Similarly, the *American Quarterly Church Review* expresses horror that the story describes "an evanescent physical passion arising from an accidental glance at the person of a bathing woman. . . . introduces a disgraced and degraded soldier—drunkard, coward, bully, gambler—who first sells his wife's honor, and then attempts her murder. . . . depicts a licentious English nobleman, who grants a fraudulent title to conceal his own criminal amour" ("Child Wife"), but in cataloguing the inappropriateness of these various subplots for child readers, it does not mention the titular romance. In contrast, the *Ladies' Repository* of the Methodist Episcopal Church considers the novel "a charming story" ("Contemporary Literature" 157), and the *Congregational Review* praises it specifically on account of the romance: "The original part is that of a military man and author falling deeply in love with a little girl, and following love's tight noose through all desperate opposition and fortune until the exciting and well sustained plot ends in success, which of course makes his head swim" ("Literary Notices" 109). In other words, the warmth of the novel's American reviewers seems to track directly—not inversely—the extent to which the romance with Blanche strikes each reader as central.

Reviews in Britain also seem to have been generally accepting of the central concept, if less enthusiastic than reviews of those Reid novels set on the American or Mexican frontiers with which the author had made his name. Like the American notices, even those British responses that express dislike for the novel tend not to base this view on Maynard's relationship with Blanche, but on issues such as his politics: "He reveals himself as the stern, fanatical revolutionist, the ardent and aggressively militant Republican," complains the *Westminster Review* of the 1888 reprint ("Belles Lettres" 115). By 1891 Reid could be the subject of an admiring profile in the family magazine *The Strand* that comments on his novels' autobiographical element, mentions *The Child Wife* several times, singles out his marriage as happy and successful, and notes, "It is the merit of Captain Reid's works that they are all as thoroughly manly, healthy in tone, and good in purpose, as they are entrancing. Not an ignoble thought or word is to be found in them" (Holyoake 95). While reviews of this title are certainly mixed, I have found no reviews that suggest that the love story is inappropriate or unnatural. Rather, it appears that for Victorian readers, not only the respectability of the hero's intentions (marriage, not statutory rape) but also the sexual maturity of the heroine is evident.

Louise Jackson notes that in Victorian Britain, "sexual deviancy in men was clearly linked to notions of class, work and social status" (131), so that men of the professional classes were considerably less likely than working-class men to be convicted of indecent assaults upon children (125). This circumstance may help to explain the discrepancy between the dismay expressed about child marriage in India, including the critique of Müller's apparent willingness to see positive aspects in such marriages, and the apparent equanimity with which *The Child Wife* was received. As a non-Western, primarily non-Christian nation, India was by definition deviant in the eyes of many Britons, who perceived it as a land much in need of the moral teachings and resocializing efforts of Western missionaries. In contrast, Reid was a successful author particularly noted for his "manly, healthy" books for boys. Anxieties about his own manliness and healthiness would have had alarming implications for his potential effect upon his young readership.

Moreover, as late twentieth-century scholars, most controversially Kincaid, have discussed, Victorian examples of adult men romantically drawn to girls are plentiful. The affection, in our own era sometimes viewed as abusive and sometimes excused, of Charles Dodgson/Lewis Carroll for Alice Liddell and his other "child-friends" is merely the most notorious instance of a larger phenomenon. But while today the inclination is often to condemn all manifestations of this phenomenon as perverse occurrences to be mapped along a single continuum, the Victorian tendency was rather to separate erotically motivated attachments that found illicit sexual expression from those that did not. That is, Victorian public opinion was outraged by child rape, incest, and seduction, though not, as we may see from the tolerant response to *The Child Wife* and an earlier Reid novel, *The Scalp Hunters* (1851), whose protagonist successfully woos a twelve-year-old, by sex with a girl in her mid-teens if it occurred within the bounds of a marriage sanctioned by religious authority and by the girl's father. In other contexts, public opinion was again relatively complacent about encounters that, however gratifying to the adult man, did not seem to pose an immediate threat to girlish innocence; whereas marriage to a willing child might seem to obviate the need for stasis, romantic friendship might seem not to endanger it. While there is some doubt about why Alice Liddell's mother may have begun to find Dodgson an unwelcome participant in her daughters' lives, the mothers of his other child friends appear to have welcomed his interest and readily acceded to his requests, punctiliously made through them, for permission to photograph them, even in the nude.

If Reid, like a number of other authors, suggests that the girl capable of appreciating the romantic appeal of an adult man is admirable because she is "sage," we have also seen Knight remarking in *Sapphira of the Stage* that for the "refined taste," "the palpably mature woman is always more or less unpleasant" (42). In *Sister-Songs: An Offering to Two Sisters* (1895), written for the young Monica and Madeline Meynell, poet Francis Thompson explores the nature of the girl's superior appeal:

> *O thou most dear!*
> *Who art thy sex's complex harmony*
> > *God-set more facilely;*
> > *To thee may love draw near*
> > *Without one blame or fear,*
> *Unchidden save by his humility:*
> *Thou Perseus' Shield! wherein I view secure*
> *The mirrored Woman's fateful-fair allure!*
> *Whom Heaven still leaves a twofold dignity*
> > *As girlhood gentle, and as boyhood free;*
> > *With whom no most diaphanous webs enwind*
> > *The barèd limbs of the rebukeless mind.*
>
> (sec. 2, lines 282–93)

For Thompson, then, to love a girl enables the same appreciation of erotic "allure" as to love a woman, but without the potential for guilt; the innocent girl will not suppose herself a romantic object and thus will neither lose her girlhood nor ask anything of the man.

This formulation implies that courtship involving consciously flirtatious behavior and the awareness that the process might end in sexual intimacy— precisely the aspects of the relationship between child-woman and adult man that Mayne Reid celebrates and Elizabeth Reid downplays—is disturbing to Thompson, who prefers what he sees as the delicacy and freedom of a relationship in which sexual consummation will never take place. Even when, early in

Thompson's poem, the speaker refers to a fleeting encounter with a child-woman who may be a prostitute—"like thee, a spring-flower; but a flower / Fallen from the budded coronal of Spring, / And through the city-streets blown withering"—and notes that her path takes her through "unchildish days," he asserts that in kissing Madeline ("Sylvia") he kisses "Her, [the street] child! and innocency" (sec. 1, poem 8, lines 19–21, 29, 32). This insistence upon girls' innocence apparently remained persuasive for many readers. In 1921 L. S. Wood included portions of *Sister-Songs* (titled as separate poems) in his collection *A Book of English Verse on Infancy and Childhood*. Although a number of his selections from Thompson, such as "Daisy," "To Olivia," and "To Monica Thought Dying," might strike readers in the early twenty-first century as love poems, Wood assures us that they are expressions of the poet's "deep reverence for childhood" (351).[10]

As with Elizabeth Reid's memoir of her husband, today's readers have at their disposal the love object's response to her adult suitor, since as a young married woman in 1909 or 1910 Monica Meynell Saleeby produced a poem of her own, entitled "Retrospect." In its entirety, the poem reads as follows:

You loved the child of fifteen years:[11]
I knew not this vast thing;
Your great heart shrank beneath your fears;
You left me wondering.

Now fourteen years have passed us by;
Our souls meet once again;
And, meeting, I have asked you why
Our ways apart have lain?

And now your answer comes at last:—
"I loved you in that day."
Oh, strange reply! Oh, tender past!
Oh, long love locked away!

And now, yes, I have climbed Love's hill:
My heart is bound, yet free;
And is there not some young child still
For you to love in me?

You have the right to love her yet,
For he who loves me grown
Knew not the child you'll ne'er forget;
I give her for your own.

Oh, keep her young within your breast,
Allow her to survive;
For love of you I'll do my best
To keep your child alive.

Like Thompson, Saleeby (by that time the wife of the prominent eugenist Caleb Saleeby) makes a distinction between the untouchable child-woman and her more experienced older self. The child-woman is not the wife and is therefore free to be the romantic object of a man who is content to adore from a distance. Identifying for herself a position midway between Elizabeth Reid's and the fictional Blanche's, Saleeby indicates her young self's half-awareness of Thompson's feelings, which left her unawakened but "wondering," and suggests further an interest on the part of her adult self in encouraging and participating in them retrospectively.

Thompson's address to the child-woman associates her appeal with pent-up power but present lack of agency. While he predicts that as a poet Monica is destined to rival her mother, Alice Meynell, and chronicles her profound effect on him, he also celebrates her confinement; she is "Born of full stature, lineal to control;/And yet a pigmy's yoke must undergo" and "ripe for kingship, yet must be/Captive in statuted minority!" (sec. 2, lines 321–22, 329–30). The adult Saleeby concurs, presenting her child-self as vulnerable, uncomprehending, and evanescent—yet as desirable for precisely those characteristics. Lack of agency, then, is for both poets essential to agency in another form, since innocence is presented as crucial to the girl's powerful allure. This formulation helps explain why Elizabeth Reid, whose memoir expresses no regret over having been courted and married so early in life, should insist upon her initial childlikeness and obliviousness to Mayne Reid's sexual interest: she exists within a framework in which these traits are often the tokens of virtue and of female authority. If the sexualizing of the girl has its unnatural aspects, the girl's cultural power may depend upon situating conscious eroticism elsewhere. It is the man, not the child-woman, to whom the stigma of unnaturalness should pertain. Thus the identity of the instigator in all the texts discussed in the present section seems to some degree uncertain; neither male nor female is entirely prepared to claim it.

We may wish to locate Thompson's and Saleeby's poems, at least, within the further context of Roman Catholicism, as a somewhat similar example is provided by *The Mirror of True Womanhood* (1876), an oft-reprinted didactic work by the Irish-born Canadian priest Bernard O'Reilly. Under the heading "Glorious examples of fidelity—the child-wife," O'Reilly details the story of a girl married at thirteen to a much older and more sinful man. "Transformed" by the knowledge of his infidelity, "in a day, she passed from the guilelessness of the child to the majesty of a woman sensible to her wrongs." The husband, aware that "the peerless flower of beauty and spotless purity which had been laid upon his bosom was drooping before his eyes; the atmosphere of evil which surrounded him had blighted its freshness," becomes "conscience-stricken, and filled with reverence, if not yet with love, for the angelic creature of whom he deemed himself unworthy" (119). Reformed, he develops at her instigation into the "Father of his Country," while she, his equal partner, is its "patron-saint and protectress" (121). Although the marriage begins unhappily, it is the wife's status as *child*-wife, a latter-day Mary who can combine the roles of wife and virgin, that enables her to surmount both domestic and national evils. Rhetoric of this sort helps to identify in Victorian Christianity, with its tendency to laud Mary as virginal girl-mother and to emphasize scriptural texts such as Christ's "Suffer the little children to come unto me, and forbid them not: for of such is the kingdom of God. Verily I say unto you, Whosoever shall not receive the kingdom of God as a little child, he shall not enter therein" (Mark 10:14–15), one potentially potent influence on some strands of age inversion.

While, as examples such as Becky Sharp and Knight's Sapphira illustrate, precocious child-women are not uniformly innocent or virtuous, as a group they seem morally superior to their arrested counterparts. This superiority may be traceable to their connection to the male within Victorian and Edwardian culture. If the arrested child-woman often seems primarily interested in what the man can give her, such as jewels, status, or protection, precocious child-women are typically represented as interested either in emotional connection with the man or in the taking on of some part of his role, be it providing for the family or asserting erotic engagement. Yet because their social power is necessarily limited—in Thompson's phrase, they are "Captive in statuted minority"—they seem less of a threat than, say, Haggard's Ayesha, known as She-Who-Must-Be-Obeyed, who usurps male prerogative in every dimension, from sexual aggression to physical aggression to absolutist rule. Thus they function less as rivals than as adjuncts, facilitating the accomplishment of goals, such as earning a living or forming a lasting romantic connection, that men may find taxing or frightening. Even the conniving "little woman" Becky Sharp originally impresses men from George Osborne to Rawdon Crawley as the ideal wife, not despite but because of her agency; that her competence facilitates Rawdon's continued boyishness is one reason that he marries her and that other men envy him.

Yet it is also one reason that Becky must be punished, expelled from her marriage and from her social successes and confined to the limited space of Jos Sedley's quarters. If the appeal of the arrested child-woman is sometimes that she provides a model authorizing her man to be a child as well, the appeal of the precocious child-woman is sometimes that she provides a shelter in which his childlikeness can flourish. In both cases, this appeal may have a threatening obverse. That the denouements of tales about precocious child-women often involve the wished-for or actual diminution of their agency, whether through their restoration to child status, their death, or their marriage to a bona fide adult, is one measure of the discomfort we may feel not only on their behalf but also on society's.

five

Boys as Men

As we have seen, Victorian authors use two main typologies to describe precocious child-women: impoverished, in which case the child-woman's primary raison d'être is financial, and affluent, in which case it is romantic, whether the chief romantic partner is father or future husband. To be sure, we may find instances of liminality. The erstwhile child-woman Becky Sharp, for one, devotes herself to improving her economic and social standing, but she does so by parlaying her sexual attractiveness into advantageous unions, whether temporary or long-term. Nevertheless, it is hard to think of Becky as motivated by either heart or libido, since she is so clearly a climber, not a lover.

Just as the arrested child-man differs from his female counterpart, the precocious child-man does not parallel precisely the dual typologies described above. While some closely resemble their working-class female counterparts, having been required to take on adult responsibilities in the workplace at an early age, others mirror adult inadequacies instead of attempting to compensate for them. Sexually precocious child-men are rare. Although Victorian novelists sometimes trace romances between children that continue into adult life, à la Cathy and Heathcliff in *Wuthering Heights*, the boys in such pairings are typically described as boys, not men. In *Villette*, for example, it is not the teenaged Graham Bretton but the "infant" Polly Home who, shortly before she develops her lasting passion for him, is described as "old and unearthly" (7).[1] Male precocity is more commonly expressed through behavioral modes other than the erotic, such as "old-fashioned" mind-sets; habits such as smoking or profanity; and participation in adult ventures, often specifically financial in nature.

For precocious child-men of all classes are typically united by a close engagement with money, whether the texts that contain them are comic or tragic. Indeed, when faced with a choice between pursuing sexual gratification and pursuing monetary gain, they unhesitatingly choose the latter. Whereas the narrative centering on the arrested child-man often explores the dangers that unbridled sexual desire poses to domesticity, the narrative centering on the precocious child-man is more likely to concern itself with the threat to domesticity posed by too great an interest in money. This trope reflects a number of related Victorian preoccupations—the tension between the male role as breadwinner and the spiritual or emotional world, the anxiety about the potential incompatibility of family and work, the jeopardizing or destruction of the purity of idealized childhood by the corruption associated with the marketplace, the conflict between lasting value and what Naomi Wood, in an essay about the role of money in *Treasure Island*, calls "the grammar of circumstance" (74). Like child-women, too, the precocious child-man is associated with fractures and vacant spaces in the family, but instead of endeavoring to heal these flaws, which is often the task of the virtuous child-woman, even the well-meaning child-man often has the effect of exacerbating them.

"All the Airs and Manners of a Man": Dickensian Precocity as Critique of Adulthood

Charles Dickens again affords a useful starting point, partly because he offers some early examples of a type that was to become more common in narratives written after his death and partly because of the marked moral difference that is often apparent between his precocious boys and their female counterparts. Underdogs by virtue of poverty, disability, social marginalization, motherlessness, and other handicaps, most of Dickens's precocious child-women nevertheless strive, often successfully, to look after their younger siblings or feckless fathers, providing islands of morality in a society that may seem to place little value on their efforts. The boys, however, rarely share this high ground. Consider the precocity of Jack Dawkins, the "Artful Dodger" in *Oliver Twist* (1837–39). The Dodger and his sidekick, Charley Bates, observes Karín Lesnik-

Oberstein, are "not so much 'bad' children as not 'children' at all by the definitions of the novel" (94), which, she argues, associates the child as an ideal or sentimentalized abstraction with silence, sleep, and death. And, to be sure, the demeanor of all Fagin's boys but Oliver is adult, whether we see them en masse, "smoking long clay pipes, and drinking spirits with the air of middle-aged men" (105), or individually in the case of the Dodger, who wears a man's coat despite his short stature and has "all the airs and manners of a man" (100). Yet Dickens's 1841 preface remarks on the shock that some early readers experienced at being forced to recognize the existence, not of criminality in general, but of child criminality in particular; having the airs and manners of a man does not make one an adult. Neither safely unconscious nor safely grown up, "the boys are pickpockets, and the girl is a prostitute" (33).

Larry Wolff examines the "emphatic gendering of prostitution and juvenile crime" contained in this binary, which extends beyond Victorian fiction into Victorian sociological writings such as those of Henry Mayhew and William Acton (229). By implication, Dickens's categories are mutually exclusive, so that girls do not pick pockets (are not illicitly associated with money) and boys do not prostitute themselves (are not illicitly associated with sex). At least in the action to which the reader is witness, the gendering of children's criminal activity is maintained, sex crimes kept distinct from property crimes. Yet as Wolff points out, Victorian realities, which included boy prostitutes, were otherwise, and Nancy's upbraiding of Fagin makes clear that in fact his pupils may move between the two businesses. As a child "not half as old as [Oliver]," Nancy too "thieved for [Fagin]" (qtd. in Wolff 228). Dickens's own narrative, in other words, undermines the very gender distinctions that his preface draws.

Similarly, of course, the Dodger, like Fagin's other male apprentices, undermines the age distinctions that Oliver—so innocent, so not-adult—simultaneously enables Dickens to insist upon. Monica Flegel finds that this quality appears to render the Dodger ineligible for "child" status:

> Through his adult attire, [he] calls into question the stability of the distinction between childhood and adulthood, and thus his own right to the claims that childish helplessness makes upon the reading audience. As such, he cannot be salvaged as Oliver can, and is sentenced to the very adult punishment of transportation. His "queerness" cannot be left as an undecidable, and he is determined by his clothing and his behavior to be more adult than child. (" 'Work' " 69–70)

But within *Oliver Twist*, in which most of the action takes place on a social level where childhood is an unaffordable luxury, the Dodger is the norm, Oliver the freak. Of all the novel's children and teenagers, it is only Oliver and his workhouse friend Dick (known narratively, Lesnik-Oberstein points out, as "the child" [94]) who encourage readers to think of "the child" as something qualitatively different from "the adult."

That Oliver, the embodiment of middle-class ideals of childhood, is so unusual in the realm of the undeserving poor is the result of planning, not misfortune. The novel hints that precocity is something that unscrupulous adults impose upon children precisely in order that the children may be seen not as victims (which would imply an adult victimizer and the possibility of punishment for that person) but rather as agents—a status that Dickens, the erstwhile child laborer, rejects in his anguished recollections of his own case. When the Dodger is jailed for theft, Fagin imagines for Charley's benefit a trial in which the Dodger will be assertive, impudent, and unchildlike, "addressing of 'em [the assembled court] as intimate and comfortable as if he was the judge's own son making a speech arter dinner," as Charley expresses it. This maneuver succeeds in its psychological object: "Master Bates, who had at first been disposed to consider the imprisoned Dodger rather in the light of a victim, now looked upon him as the chief actor in a scene of most uncommon and exquisite humour, and felt quite impatient for the arrival of the time when his old companion should have so favourable an opportunity of displaying his abilities" (391). If the Dodger does not seem helpless when in the grasp of the Law, his conviction and transportation presumably will not move Charley to blame Fagin and perhaps rethink his own associations. Yet Dickens has earlier made visible for the reader Fagin's attempts to corrupt Oliver by embroiling him in criminality—in effect, his plot to steal his youth, an indication that he has already stolen the Dodger's, Charley's, and Nancy's.

In other words, to render children, and perhaps particularly boys, precocious is for Dickens a prime mechanism of their victimization, not (as might be assumed by those who have not had the benefit of the glimpses into Fagin's secrets that Dickens's privileged narrator shares with us) the signal that victimization is impossible. Theft, Wolff concludes, is a useful crime to ascribe to children in Fagin's world because children in the 1830s could still be transported for it—assigned agency, identified as the guilty parties, and removed from England without risk to their adult corrupters (246). As Wolff also observes, however, the theft that the child may be forced to commit seems to be the least of it:

> The tremendous displacement of emphasis on theft achieves its high point when Oliver goes down on his knees to beg Bill Sikes, "Oh! pray have mercy on me, and do not make me steal. For the love of all the bright Angels that rest in Heaven, have mercy upon me!" . . . The focused nature of Oliver's spiritual agony permits him, and the reader, to make juvenile crime into a matter of theft, but the extraordinary, even religious, intensity of the boy's outburst also suggests that there is more at stake here than stealing. Dickens underlines the metonymic implications of theft, even as he dramatically evades their criminological denomination. (234)

While the particular metonymy for which Wolff is arguing is one in which theft stands in for prostitution, I propose that we take a broader view still by seeing not the commission of property theft but the incitement to it as a theft of morality more generally. Even while readers are led to prefer Oliver (who appears throughout to possess less agency than any other child in the novel but the moribund Dick) to the Dodger, we are also led to feel that Fagin is significantly more guilty than the Dodger, notwithstanding that at his own trial Fagin is broken and passive, engaging in none of the saucy if profitless repartee that, as Fagin predicted, we have indeed seen from the Dodger in a similar situation. That is, despite Fagin's best efforts and the Dodger's uninterrupted cockiness, we may after all be inclined to see the Dodger as Fagin's puppet and victim—fallen, certainly, but retaining the smallness of the child even though dressed in adult garb. Children have their disturbing side for Dickens as for many other Victorian writers, but adults who prey upon children are more disturbing still. Laura Berry contends that during the nineteenth century, "representing the victimized child becomes an important means of articulating an autonomous and socially indebted self, bound but self-determined" (19). The ambiguity of this vision, with its mixture of the subject and the object, seems particularly well embodied in the Dodger as precocious child-man. Perhaps, then, on some level it is the Dodger, not the beautiful and virtuous Oliver, who most closely represents the resentments and anxieties of those Victorian readers who perceived adulthood, à la Wordsworth's "shades of the prison-house," as an inexorable movement away from the divine.

Oliver Twist, one of Dickens's earliest novels, encourages the assignment of guilt to individuals; we may, if we choose, lay Nancy's or the Dodger's failings at Fagin's door rather than at the system's. Later Dickens works move away from this scenario of victims and tempters, preferring a vision in which corruption comes from a sort of antimoral miasma in which, to differing extents, almost all members of society are implicated. Thus in *Bleak House* (1852–53), the precocious child-man Bart Smallweed is described to us in the context of heredity and environment. Son, grandson, and great-grandson of men described as "going out early in life, and marrying late," Bart, at fourteen, is one of a string of "complete little men and women" that the family has produced in lieu of children (342). Instead of reading fairy tales and playing cricket, the pastimes that the narrator associates with a normal childhood, he is already "an old limb of the law" who spends most of his time at the office (327). Indeed, his true family is as much the court system as the Smallweed dynasty, since "in his bringing up he has been so nursed by Law and Equity that he has become a kind of fossil imp," "a weird changeling, to whom years are nothing. He stands precociously possessed of centuries of owlish wisdom. If he ever lay in a cradle, it seems as if he must have lain there in a tail-coat. He has an old, old eye, has Smallweed: and he drinks and smokes, in a monkeyish way; and his neck is stiff in his collar; and he is never to be taken in; and he knows all about it, whatever it is" (329).[2]

While the narrative makes clear that the Smallweed family is given over to parsimony and sharp practice—Grandfather Smallweed is a usurer, and we may wonder about the truth of his claim to have been Krook's brother-in-law, which enables the Smallweed family to hunt through the dead man's papers for information about Captain Hawdon—it appears that unlike the Dodger, Bart and his family stay on the right side of the law. Drinking and smoking aside, Bart might indeed seem to be a model boy by the prevailing standards of his society: he is gainfully employed in a respectable business, saves his money, and demonstrates filial obedience by adhering to his grandfather's precepts. But, of course, one of Dickens's points here is that these qualities are inadequate without heart. Moreover, heart is largely formed by the experiences of childhood, experiences that Bart has been denied because of his family background and too-early association with what *Bleak House* presents as the morally dubious world of the law.

Bart, then, forms a dramatic contrast to precocious child-women such as Henry Mayhew's young watercress seller. On the one hand, he seems better equipped than she to function in a complex society. Whereas she cannot use her knowledge that there are twelve pennies in a shilling and two halfpennies in a penny to calculate how many halfpennies make up a shilling, Bart, brought up by a miser, is well grounded in the mathematics of money. Witness his bravura performance totting up a luncheon bill:

> Mr. Smallweed, compelling the attendance of the waitress with one hitch of his eyelash, instantly replies as follows: "Four veals and hams is three, and four potatoes is three and four, and one summer cabbage is three and six, and three marrows is four and six, and six breads is five, and three Cheshires is five and three, and four half-pints [of] half-and-half is six and three, and four small rums is eight and three, and three Pollys is eight and six. Eight and six in half a sovereign, Polly, and eighteenpence out!" (337)

The Watercress Girl's employment history (as childminder, pieceworker, and household help, in addition to her cress selling) has been a matter of circulating among unskilled jobs in multiple fields. In contrast, Bart's financial acumen and work as a lawyer's clerk may mark him as one of all too many figures in *Bleak House* who will spend their lives in the arid atmosphere of the courtroom, but it also places him somewhere in the lower middle class.

On the other hand, while both children are fatherless, the watercress seller seems to have a considerably more successful family life. By some Victorian conventions, this should not be the case, since not only is she much more impoverished than Bart, bringing to mind nineteenth-century stereotypes about the attenuated domestic ties of the very poor, but she is also the child of a mother who is cohabiting with a man not her daughter's father. (The absence of marriage lines among the poor was common but deplored by middle-class observers.) Meanwhile, Bart and his twin sister, Judy, are the posthumous legitimate children of a legitimate father. Their mother having died shortly after their birth, they have had a stable home with their next of kin, their grandparents. Yet while the Watercress Girl speaks with gratitude and affection of her mother and her "father-in-law," the Smallweed home is a place of unmitigated spite, particularly evident in Grandfather Smallweed's animus against his senile wife but extending to the rest of the family as well. Judy, for instance, is a rare exception to the usual Dickens paradigm in which precocious child-women occupy the moral high ground, and Bart evidently feels no compunction about falling out with his friend Mr. Guppy, once something of a center to his emotional life.

Far from being the locus for morality that the home often is in Victorian fiction, the Smallweed ménage, Barbara Gottfried points out, "figures symbolically the reproduction in the domestic sphere of the corruptions and abuses of the (patriarchal) world outside the house" (4). In the Smallweed family, as Karen Chase writes of *The Picture of Dorian Gray*, "age is a punishment: the accumulation of experience weathers and soils" (208). This soiling is figured in Bart and Judy by precocity and in their grandparents by a parodic infantilism, a state of tantrums, pillow fights, babbling, and physical helplessness that recalls the comment of the narrator of *The Old Curiosity Shop* that "we call this a state of childishness, but it is the same poor hollow mockery of it, that death is of sleep" (99). A parallel point might be made of Bart and Judy's premature and equally repellent old age. Thus Grandfather Smallweed compares himself to a "Brimstone Baby" (437), while Mr. George looks at Judy "as if, she being so old and so like her grandfather, it is indifferent which of the two he addresses" (354). "This confusion of youth and old age is a recurring and unstable feature" in Dickens, Chase observes (13), and in the Smallweed family its primary function is to signal the complete breakdown of morality.[3]

In short, while Bart's precocity enables him to function effectively in the world of law, monetary transactions, and investigation, this is all that it enables him to do, since the home that has nurtured this precocity by feeding him on calculations instead of fairy tales is indistinguishable from the corruption of the moneylender's office and the courts. If in other homes money is valued because it enables the continuation of family life, the Smallweeds tolerate family life only insofar as it enables the retention or accumulation of money. Thus although the clerks joke about Bart's supposed romantic entanglements, which might in other circumstances be a sign that a normal domestic life may be possible for him, we have no reason to suppose either that these relationships actually exist or that if they do, the outcome will be a happy family. Bart has learned his grandfather's lessons too well; in his case money will always trump heart.

Poor and precocious child-women such as Mayhew's watercress seller or Dickens's Jenny Wren are described in ways meant to elicit readers' sympathy. Mayhew's showcasing the Watercress Girl's financial ineptitude works to draw us closer to her, just as showcasing Bart's calculating savvy or the Dodger's willingness to extract coins or personal property from passers-by is one of the ways in which Dickens distances us from the latter figures. We feel for these child-women, in part because we perceive that they too feel. But while we are also expected to feel sympathy for the unworldliness of many of Dickens's arrested child-men—such as Mr. Dick, Joe Gargery, and Smike in *Nicholas Nickleby*—we are not given emotional access to such precocious child-men as Bart, the Dodger, or young Tom Gradgrind in *Hard Times* (1853), who, as his sister Louisa says of herself, "never had a child's heart. . . . never dreamed a child's dream. . . . never had a child's belief or a child's fear" (79).[4] Even the death of little Paul Dombey may elicit our tears primarily because of the grief that it engenders in Florence. As I discussed in chapter 1, Paul is often represented as a "goblin," a figure of otherness, rather than as a being whose feelings persuade us that he is like us. And while we might be tempted to diagnose an autobiographical element in this particular author's tendency to see precocious child-men as emotional cripples victimized morally as well as economically by those who thrust them into the world of work too early, it will become clear over the remainder of this chapter that Dickens is by no means unique in suggesting that precocious child-men are characterized by emotional opacity.

Since we may also find it difficult to enter into the rather stunted emotional lives of arrested child-women such as Hetty Sorrel, Sybilla Rothesay, or Weena, we may posit a tendency in Victorian texts of age inversion to group together most precocious child-women and some (generally virtuous) arrested child-men as figures with whom readers, however different their own circumstances, are encouraged to identify. Conversely, arrested child-women and precocious child-men are likely to be constructed in ways that repel our identification. One reason for this pattern may be the Victorian tendency to associate successful negotiation of the private sphere with altruism. The virtuous precocity of child-women such as the young Olive Rothesay, Sara Crewe, Esther Summerson, and their ilk is a precocity that stresses engagement with others, while virtuous arrested child-men from Joe Gargery to Little Billee care much more about personal relationships than about financial success or class rise. In contrast, the self-absorption of the typical arrested child-woman and the commercial preoccupations of the typical precocious child-man offer neither models for the Victorian reader's emulation nor a sense that these characters are much inclined to reach out to us.

Paired Child-Men:
Contrasts and Similarities in *Vice Versâ* and *Kidnapped*

As the example of young Tom Gradgrind suggests (and as we have seen in a feminine context in various novels discussed in chapters 3 and 4), sometimes a precocious child goes on to become an arrested adult. Tom changes little between our first sight of him as a boy in his early teens and our last, when he is a nominally adult fugitive preparing to flee the country; throughout, he is discontented, shifty, and above all selfish. Force-fed a utilitarian and adult point of view in childhood, he appears immature in young manhood. Other texts, however, compare precocious youth to arrested adulthood by employing two separate but paired figures. The perception that there may be commonalities between the situation of the boy-man and that of the man-boy, so that indeed the two may best be considered side by side, animates several works of the 1880s, among them the 1882 comic fantasy *Vice Versâ: A Lesson to Fathers*, by Thomas Anstey Guthrie (usually published under the pen name F. Anstey). Here a magical object known as the Garudâ Stone is discovered to have the power to grant wishes when Dick Bultitude inadvertently transforms his father, a pompous businessman, into a schoolboy identical to himself. Ordered to put matters right immediately, Dick, who is not eager to return to his prep school, takes over his father's appearance and occupation. Under these admittedly unusual circumstances, we may find it hard to decide which Bultitude is the precocious and which the arrested child-man.

Yet it is clearly Paul, the erstwhile father, who evinces to a greater extent the traits of the precocious type. Shrunk to boy's size, Paul performs disastrously in the arena of interpersonal relationships afforded by the school, offending his son's sweetheart, Dulcie (daughter of the headmaster, Dr. Grimstone), by telling her that she is too young for romance and "ought to think about—about your dolls, and—ah, your needlework" (89) and running afoul of countless unwritten laws of schoolboy interaction. Dick has evidently been one of the more popular boys in the school; Paul, taking his place, is an instant pariah. Nor is this result unexpected, since the narrative emphasizes that even in his own body Paul is more or less estranged from his entire circle: his wife is dead,[5] he is on the coldest possible terms with his ne'er-do-well brother-in-law, he has acquaintances but apparently no friends, and his interest in his children's company is minimal. Introduced to us by business (not home) address and profession as "of Mincing Lane, Colonial Produce Merchant" (1), he clearly has no talent for family life, being

> one of those nervous and fidgetty persons who cannot understand their own children, looking on them as objectionable monsters whose next movements are uncertain—much as Frankenstein must have felt towards *his* monster.
>
> He hated to have a boy about the house, and positively writhed under the irrelevant and irrepressible questions, the unnecessary noises and boisterous high spirits, which nothing would subdue; his son's society was to him simply an

abominable nuisance, and he pined and yearned for a release from it from the
day the holidays began. (4, emphasis in original)

Over much of the novel, this impatience with childhood persists despite his
bodily transformation.

Dick, meanwhile, performs as ineptly in his father's place, giving rise to a
belief in the City that Paul has lost his mind—or, rather, become "reprehen-
sibly eccentric and extravagant" (296). The latter adjective suggests where the
problem lies; like precocious child-men in other narratives, the counterfeit
adult has an inappropriate relationship to money and work. As one shocked
witness reports, "Business was, I understood him to say, 'all rot!'" (297). Rather
than concentrating on the chief responsibility associated with his gender,
position, and apparent age, that of increasing his fortune, Dick seems to
think that he can perform the duties of an adult man by focusing his energies
on the home. Much to the delight of the two children left at home, their supposed father now vigorously plays with them, invites clowns to dinner, gives
elaborate children's parties, and generally acts, as the young daughter of the
house puts it, "quite jolly and boyish—only fancy! [so that] we are always
telling him that he is the biggest baby of us all" (172). In a twist that particularly horrifies Paul, his wayward impersonator has even been romancing the
cook.

Yet although both are out of place (a shared experience that finally recon-
ciles them after they are restored to their proper bodies), there is clearly a difference between father and son in this narrative, which suggests that the boy-
man may be distinguished from the man-boy along the crucial axes of intimacy,
money, and work. Nicholas Tucker points out that in one of the novel's central
lessons, "Mr Bultitude is forced to realise how much his previous power and
security had always rested on the possession of a full pocket-book. This is exactly the economic powerlessness most children have always had to acknowledge and often suffer from, a point Anstey hammers home unsparingly."
Moreover, with "no money and few rights," even a precocious boy has "virtually no way [to] assert himself in the world around him" (141). After unwill-
ingly substituting for his son, Paul becomes sufficiently understanding of this
problem that upon his restoration he gives Dick a munificent back-to-school
tip, to be split between Dick and a school friend who was kind to Paul. In contrast, while Dick is occupying his father's body, we do not see his money itself,
but rather the uses—most of them family-oriented—to which he puts it.

By the standards of the adult male world of business, then, the transformed Dick is excessively interested in domestic and romantic intimacy and insufficiently interested in work. By juvenile standards, the transformed Paul (who, ironically, has diminished what turns out to be his own power by earlier having furnished his son only five shillings instead of the desired sovereign) has no understanding of his responsibilities toward his fellow children and, humiliatingly, is still more of a dunce at lessons than his son. If anything, Dick functions somewhat better in the throes of the magic than Paul does, since Dick (like his arrested namesake in *David Copperfield*) is at least good at establishing domestic ties, while Paul, both financially and socially inadequate at Dr. Grimstone's academy, can navigate neither personal relationships nor the exigencies of school, from which he ultimately runs away.

In this regard, the novel's subtitle, *A Lesson to Fathers*, is telling. Dick will effectively be rewarded for having usurped his father's body, since Paul decides to grant his heart's desire by sending him to Harrow. True, some penalty is also involved, thanks to Paul's mishandling of Dick's personal relationships. Paul's behavior at Dick's prep school has been such as to cause the other boys to hold him in contempt and, worse still, to lose him Dulcie's affections, "a very real and heavy [punishment]" (363). Yet by judicious use of his fists, Dick otherwise "gradually succeed[s] in recovering all the ground his father had lost him" (362), and the narrator hints that even Dulcie may restore him to favor in time. Paul, however, must deal not only with the need to dismiss his treasure of a cook (who has assumed from Dick's manner toward her that a proposal of marriage is imminent) but also with a loss of reputation in the City, which, unlike Dick's troubles with his classmates, is in some measure permanent: "Probably Paul will never quite clear himself of the cloud that hangs over a man of business who, in the course of however well regulated a career, is known to have been at least once 'a little odd'" (361). Brian Stableford ascribes the "dramatically unequal" punishments to the fact that "the social positions of the two identity-exchangers are far from equal" (68). In addition, Paul's comparatively more severe treatment reflects his crime in having allowed himself to become so estranged from his family that only literally stepping into his son's shoes could bring him into sympathy with his children.

The "lesson to fathers" that the novel promises, in other words, is effectively a lesson in age inversion. If from Dick's perspective the principal lesson to be learned may be merely that he is better at being a schoolboy than his father is and that it is more fun to be, in Tucker's phrase, "a spoilt, prosperous grown-up" than a powerless boy (140), Paul must discover that the kind of manhood that he has been practicing is inadequate, that even arrested development is morally preferable to precocity and its attendant disdain for boyhood, and that he must learn from his son how to be a good father. Seeing that "his experiences, unpleasant as they had been, had had their advantages: they had drawn him and his family closer together," Paul understands the value of the "warmer and more natural feeling" that now exists between him and his children (360), controls his impulse toward resentment as more information about Dick's behavior during the imposture trickles in (since "he valued the new understanding between himself and his son too highly to risk losing it again by any open reproach" [362]), and becomes a reformed man: "Mr. Bultitude would never after this consider his family as a set of troublesome and thankless incumbrances; thanks to Dick's offices during the interregnum, they would henceforth throw off their reserve and constraint in their father's presence, and in so doing, open his eyes to qualities of which he had hitherto been in contented ignorance" (360). Like other moral tales, then, *Vice Versâ* requires its protagonist to recognize the benefits of having been chastised and to come at last, like his namesake and apparent inspiration, Mr. Dombey, to a condign sense of the faults of being too businesslike, too practical, and too "adult."

In effect, the adult reader is expected to participate in this lesson as well—and indeed necessarily participates in the sort of juvenility that the novel validates, inasmuch as enjoying the tale requires accepting the idea of a magic wishing stone, cheering on the punishment of pompous and unboylike behavior, and generally rooting for the side of frivolity and immaturity. The precocity of the "old head on young shoulders" that Paul embodies while he bears Dick's appearance is condemned not only throughout the narrative but in the fantasy's very format. And while *Vice Versâ* has been enjoyed by many children over the years, has been adapted into children's films and other children's texts (such as Mary Rodgers's 1972 *Freaky Friday*), and occasionally shows up, as in the Puffin edition of the early 1980s, in imprints marketed to children, the intended audience was at least primarily adult.[6] This work is thus an example of a Victorian form examined in more detail in the conclusion to the present study, the "children's book for adults," which, I argue, seeks to bring about a kind of temporary age inversion in its audience, often for moral purposes.

Pairings of precocious boy and arrested adult also figure in works by another author of children's (in this case specifically boys') books for adults, Robert Louis Stevenson. As I have noted in a different context elsewhere,[7]

Treasure Island (1881–82), for example, repeatedly returns to whether Jim Hawkins can be said to occupy a man's role and, still more urgently, whether any of the novel's nominal adults are not better described as children. Ben Gunn, the Squire, the mutineers—all are represented as children at various points in the narrative, while Jim and his fellow boy, the young sailor Dick, are easily manipulated by those who, like Long John Silver and Israel Hands, are willing to flatter them by calling them men. Clearly, what is at stake in the term *man* in this tale is not maleness alone but rather a complex combination of sex, gender role, adulthood, and particular personality traits such as daring, trustworthiness, and toughness. In fact, *Treasure Island* contains few or no "men" beyond Captain Smollett and perhaps Dr. Livesay, but it contains any number of males of various ages who will do much to be thought men, and one, Silver, whose success derives from his willingness to defy categories of age and gender both. The juxtaposition of precocity and arrested development, apparent in almost all the characters in the novel, is thus strategically useful for Stevenson inasmuch as it helps to illustrate the range of possibilities through which one may fall short of manhood or, conversely, may retain the outlook of childhood.

I sketch this reading of *Treasure Island* by way of providing a context for a more detailed discussion of *Kidnapped* (1886), which employs a somewhat similar pattern but focuses more extensively on the interaction of a single pair, David Balfour and Alan Breck Stewart. Shanghaied at the behest of his uncle, who fears that the boy has come to displace him from the family estate of Shaws—note that the practice of giving the eldest son of the eldest son legal precedence over a mere second son of the older generation suggests an institutional willingness to foster precocity—David finds himself at the mercy of an unscrupulous ship's crew and makes common cause with Alan when the latter is brought on board after his own ship is wrecked. Together they triumph over the crew and over hunger, pursuit, and other dangers on land, but their relationship is always uneasy, not only because David is a Lowlander and a Whig while Alan is a Highlander and a royalist, but also because they represent contrasting types of male. Alan, boyish in his short stature, "childish vanity" (79), and "childish propensity to take offence and to pick quarrels" (107), strikes David as immature and undependable, while Alan considers the seventeen-year-old David, who is young enough to be Alan's son, excessively practical and elderly in his outlook.

Stevenson, of course, is well known for his use of doubling, which undergirds the mutual hatred and mutual dependency of figures such as Dr. Jekyll and Mr. Hyde and the brothers Durie in *The Master of Ballantrae* (1888). Yet his handling of the alter ego in *Kidnapped* is somewhat unusual, since, as John Kucich indicates, the relationship between David and Alan is for all its volatility considerably less destructive than is usual for a Stevenson text (42). Some commentators see this bond as a (positive) kind of father-son pairing. For Susan Gannon, for instance, "the essence of Stevenson's story [is] David's awkward, moment-to-moment struggle to appreciate and assimilate the virtues of his alter ego, Alan Breck, in order to become a more complete human being" (98), while John Steiner compares Alan to a psychoanalyst and David to his analysand, noting that as their most serious quarrel seems about to erupt into violence, "the older and stronger man [is enabled] to recognise that he [is] dealing with a child and hence to desist and to climb down" (442). The maturity with which Alan is invested in such readings accentuates his heroic qualities in a way that David's narration, which stresses his juvenility, does not.

Ann C. Colley cogently points out that Stevenson himself was keenly aware of the deceptive aspects of "chronological age. Referring to himself in a letter to his cousin Robert Alan Stevenson, he explained, 'You are twenty, and forty, and five, and the next moment you are freezing at an imaginary eighty; you are never the plain forty-four that you should be by dates'" (176). The fluidity of Stevenson's perception of his own age status, Colley continues, resulted in an equally fluid approach to the ages of his fictional creations. She notes that "Stevenson had difficulty in portraying an adult without making some reference to a childish feature or characteristic in the person. . . . Consequently, in Stevenson's fiction protagonists move effortlessly back and forth between childhood and adulthood" (176). David and Alan are no exceptions; they "alternate between 'the rude, silly speech of a boy of ten' and the measured phrases of maturity. Their vacillating responses to each other and to themselves reflect the giddiness of their shifting identities" (177). Thus, for example, after the pair triumphs in a fight against the ship's company, Alan addresses David as an equal and an adult—" 'David,' said he, 'I love you like a brother. And O, man,' he cried in a kind of ecstasy, 'am I no a bonny fighter?'" (88)—while projecting a contradictory sense of his own age; David compares him in successive sentences to "a man trying to recall an air" and to "a five-year-old chil[d] with a new toy" (88). Meanwhile, David himself is so horrified at the adult part that he has played in having done his "fair share both of the killing and the wounding" that he "beg[ins] to sob and cry like any child" (89). Alan's habit of addressing him alternately as "lad" and "man" suggests not imprecision of language but the difficulty of fixing age where David, like Alan himself, is concerned.

Even while David and Alan share the quality of being simultaneously boy and adult, however, chronological age remains relevant because of its role in how readers and other characters in the novel perceive them—a point that, in a comic vein, is crucial to *Vice Versâ*. David's naïve acts (such as boarding the *Covenant* at the behest of an uncle whom he already knows to be murderously disposed toward him) seem natural rather than self-destructive, given his inexperience. It is rather his moments of adult presence, his movement from behaving "like a sick, silly, and bad-hearted schoolboy" to asserting himself as a "gentlem[a]n" (226–27), that may appear unexpected. Conversely, Alan may be most striking when he speaks or behaves in ways that undercut his adult status. As David remarks, "Wheedling my money from me while I lay half-conscious was scarce better than theft," but this behavior is memorable less for its dishonesty than because "Alan had behaved like a child, and (what is worse) a treacherous child" (220).

Alan himself is clearly aware of the importance of others' perceptions of age, since at one point he secures shelter for himself and David by "do[ing] a bit of play-acting" that involves hand-feeding David "like a nursery lass" while intimating that the boy is a Jacobite on the run from the authorities (247). Their audience, a sympathetic waitress in a pub, exclaims, "And him so young!" To which Alan responds, " 'He's old enough to—' and Alan struck his forefinger on the back part of his neck, meaning that I was old enough to lose my head" (250). While David resents being "treated like a child" (250) when minutes earlier Alan has been referring to him as a "gentleman" (247), we are glad to see that he is nonetheless ready to profit from her help, which involves not only free food but also transportation to the next stop on their journey. The tension between his evident youth and the dangers that he is ill equipped to face without help elicits sympathy both from the waitress and from the reader; we are more concerned for David than for Alan not only because he is the narrator but also because he is a boy navigating a man's world without the support of family.

Just as *Treasure Island*, another novel about a boy engaging in the life-and-death adventures and range of movement more usually reserved for adulthood, is centrally concerned with the acquisition and (re)distribution of money, *Kidnapped* is structured at key moments around David's fascination with financial questions—again, a hallmark of the novel of precocious masculinity. Thus David's claim to Shaws motivates his uncle Ebenezer's attacks on him; David's quarrel with Alan is caused by Alan's having gambled away David's small hoard of money; and David introduces Alan to us under the chapter title "The Man with the Belt of Gold" (70), an identifying characteristic that explains why the newcomer is in danger on the *Covenant*. Furthermore, Oliver Buckton observes, the novel concludes by leaving David "in limbo outside 'the doors of the British Linen Company's Bank' . . . on the threshold (literally) of recovering his birthright, the inheritance of the House of Shaws. His physical position reveals a state of indeterminacy: being at the very doors of the bank, David is neither inside nor outside the space of wealth" (231). This "indeterminacy"—the same term that Chase uses to describe old age in the Victorian era (6)—is clearly related to the "vacillating" quality that Colley notes, and it reflects the bind in which the precocious child-man is caught; neither fully adult nor fully boy, he aspires to money without being in a position to advance his claim with entire success.

Moreover, again like *Treasure Island*, *Kidnapped* stresses the ease with which money, however hard won, may disappear. David is repeatedly the victim of monetary loss. His uncle provides him with only thirty-seven guineas of his rightful inheritance to add to the small stake with which he begins the novel. Of this sum, the ship's crew steals about one-third, David loses all but a few pounds and is then made to pay excessively for help on the Isle of Mull, and Alan usurps the remnant, although his opponent at cards, Cluny, makes good the latter loss. An obsessive chronicler of financial outflow, David is grieved to the point of feeling unmanned by every subtraction from his exchequer.

These thefts are especially disconcerting in the context of precocity because of the novel's suggestion that cash and other valuables are connected to adult male sexuality. David describes the debonair Alan, who proves to be expert at manipulating women, as having "a belt full of golden guineas round his loins" (75), while on their trek across Scotland the pair encounters a man who carries Alan's silver button—token of Alan's friendship and inherited by Alan from his father—"in a hairy purse that hung in front of him in the Highland manner (though he wore otherwise the Lowland habit, with sea-trousers)" (196), a description that seems evocative of male genitalia. Furthermore, Ebenezer, who shares his first name with Dickens's miserly Scrooge, was David's father's rival in love, and the brothers agreed that if the elder were to have the wife, the younger should have the estate. David, then, is the product of a marriage that depended upon the divorce of love from coin, while Ebenezer has redirected the one toward the other: "Money was all he got by his bargain;

well, he came to think the more of money," explains the lawyer Rankeillor before advising David to "be a good husband of [his] money" (269, 287). Penniless and bereft of Alan on the novel's final page, David feels stripped as well of any claims to mature manhood, confessing that "I felt so lost and lonesome, that I could have found it in my heart to sit down by the dyke, and cry and weep like any baby" (289).

All is not lost, of course, since both Alan and money will return in *Catriona* (1893). But the repeated pattern of David's diminishment, even infantilizing, in *Kidnapped* seems morally necessary, parallel in some ways to Paul Bultitude's in *Vice Versâ*. Throughout, Stevenson associates David with the unromantic—the Lowlands rather than the Highlands, the Hanoverian cause rather than the Stuart, the bourgeoisie rather than the clan system. The contrasts between David's relationship to money and Alan's are an important part of these associations. No risktaker or maker of grand gestures, David seeks to hold on to his money or to spend it sensibly. He sees it as individual property and not a family or communal asset; moreover, he seems inclined to value it above less tangible systems of exchange. Thus, for instance, he commits a grave social error in offering a shilling to a Highlander in exchange for help rather than showing him Alan's button, which in that neighborhood has much more power to command loyalty than any amount of cash. In other words, David's instincts as a precocious boy keenly aware of the point that Tucker makes about *Vice Versâ*, namely, that a boy has "no money and few rights. . . . virtually no way [to] assert himself in the world around him," coincide to a dangerous extent with those of his penurious uncle, for whom the world appears to contain only money and the self.

Alan, in contrast, is a gambler for whom adventure, personal and group loyalties, and romance will always come first. The narrative stresses that the belt of gold in Alan's possession is not his own money and not regarded as such; rather, it is voluntary tribute that he has collected from his clan on behalf of the exiled Stuart monarch, signal of the Highlanders' willingness to set aside practicalities (such as the financial hardships entailed in paying taxes to two separate kings) for an ideal. Alan's major form of currency is not coin but his set of silver buttons, which, unlike David's shillings and guineas, appear to buy an inexhaustible supply of assistance without ever being spent. As an arrested child-man, that is, Alan is diametrically opposed to David when it comes to personal economy. And despite the financial and ethical irresponsibility implicit in Alan's gambling away David's funds, the reader may well conclude that Gannon is correct in arguing that David has more to learn from Alan than Alan does from David.

Buckton suggests that David "depend[s] on Alan for his identity. . . . David can only function, it appears, in Alan's presence" (235), which is why *Kidnapped* must end immediately after the two are separated. Another way to put this might be to postulate that Alan functions as the antidote to the tendency, fully formed in Ebenezer and incipient in David, to rate money too highly, so that Alan in effect switches David onto a new track, redefining him as fighter, fugitive, and Jacobite. David's efforts to repudiate these romantic identities lead to his infantilization and loss of individuality (he is "like any baby") at the end of the first novel. From that nadir, however, he can climb back in *Catriona*, where we see him pursuing Highland loyalties, reaching sexual maturity, falling in love for the first time, and forming a new family by moving to Paris with his wife and Alan. With these signs that his switchover has been successfully accomplished and that he is now a domestically oriented man rather than a precocious money-oriented boy, the narrative permits him to come into his inheritance.

We saw in chapter 3 how Dinah Mulock uses pairing in *Olive* first to distinguish the good child-woman from the bad and then to reclaim the bad. Similarly, both Stevenson and Guthrie use paired child-men to indicate that the evils associated with precocity are remediable. If only approaching death brings Dickens's Tom Gradgrind to repent having persuaded his sister into a disastrous marriage for his own benefit and rejected his well-meaning though erring father, Paul Bultitude and David Balfour survive their trials, learning to think less of money and to build a functional family life. Even for them, however, the process of recovering from precocity requires drastic measures: magic in Paul's case and repeated imprisonment, penury, and helplessness in David's. That these child-men experience significant losses of agency, which for David is figured explicitly as a return to infancy, points to the emotional value that Victorians influenced by Romantic views associated with ideal childhood.[8] Even malevolent arrested child-men are associated with power, if only the power to harm, just as even the most socially marginalized of their benign brothers (the mentally handicapped Mr. Dick, for example) prove unexpectedly effective or artistically talented. Similarly, precocious child-women, especially of the working classes, as I argue in chapter 4, typically have more agency than society is comfortable seeing them exercise. In contrast, precocious child-men often seem peculiarly incapable of making their mark, a point that hints at the futility sometimes ascribed in the nineteenth century to the commercial enterprise.

Tragic Precocity at the Turn of the Century

The examples of precocious masculinity discussed thus far have focused on the comic, the mock heroic, and the satiric; although the Artful Dodger, say, may be the victim of adult crimes against childhood, his demeanor is unfailingly jaunty. Yet particularly in the late nineteenth and early twentieth centuries, precocity may be found within the tragic mode as well, a major distinction here being the implication that redemption is impossible for either the precocious individual or the family that has generated him.

The greater the family tragedy, it appears, the more exaggerated the unnatural discrepancy between calendar and metaphorical age. Consider Sarah Grand's novel *The Heavenly Twins* (1893), one of a number of New Woman fictions to address the collateral damage brought about by male sexual license.[9] One of the three main female characters in this work, Edith Beale, is a bishop's daughter reared in ignorance of the ways of the world. Because she does not understand the risks involved in marrying a man of impure life, she accepts the proposal of Sir Mosley Menteith, a roué who has selected her "for her health and beauty" (281). Since he promptly infects her and her unborn child with syphilis, she retains neither quality for more than the first few months of their marriage. Suffering from the pangs of insanity and approaching death, she shrieks, "I want to kill—I want to kill *him*." But the object of her murderous rage at that moment turns out to be not her erring husband but her baby son, "that monstrous child" (304, emphasis in original).

At birth "apparently healthy," the infant "had rapidly degenerated" (277). His mother can feel no love for him, and his existence—like Edith's discovery that he is half-brother to another, illegitimate syphilitic infant—seems to accelerate her own madness and fatal illness. The son's appearance in the novel is brief; only a few months old, he is never individuated, and his function is primarily symbolic. For the purposes of the present study, then, the most noteworthy aspect of this child is that the narrative describes the stigmata of inherited syphilis only in terms of old age. While today's medical lore lists a wide variety of symptoms for congenital syphilis, including rashes and skin lesions, fever, irritability, an abnormally small head, deformities, nose running with clear or bloody mucus, jaundice, anemia, swelling of the liver, seizures, and mental retardation, Grand's description of Edith's child suggests none of these problems, with the possible exception of the failure to thrive that was associated not only with venereal infection but also with many other conditions.[10]

The baby is, rather, "a little old man baby" (288), "old, old already, and exhausted with suffering" (289). He is said to resemble his maternal grandfather, the bishop, to whom Edith assigns a large share of the blame for her disastrous marriage. In addition, of course, his condition is clearly his father's fault, so that in his person he simultaneously recapitulates and indicts two varieties of male irresponsibility, sexual license on the one hand and withholding vital knowledge from women in the name of "innocence" on the other. That both forms of irresponsibility are associated with male maturity helps to explain why the baby, the physical manifestation of these crimes, is represented as already an old man. In addition, just as old people may be described as children in order to separate them from "the hegemony of adulthood" by linking them to "a group set apart as different, as 'other'" (Hockey and James 138), the phrase "little old man baby" distances this infant from normalcy, thus identifying Monteith's sin as a crime against nature.

Edith's baby is too young to be an active participant in financial matters, so that he is one of the rare exceptions to the pattern of connection between precocious child-men and money. In compensation, his connection to family dysfunction seems, if anything, stronger than that of the typical precocious child-man. His condition signals at once the failure of maternal love (Edith is unable to bond with her damaged child), the irretrievable breakdown of Edith's marriage, and the end of her hitherto tranquil relationship to her parents, especially her father, whom she rejects not only as private father but also in his public capacity. As William Driscoll notes, when Edith assembles her father, her husband, and Dr. Galbraith at her bedside, the narrator "refers to Edith's father as 'the bishop' not as her father. As a result, 'the gentlemen' shift from characters to allegorical representations of the 'arrangement of society,' the church, the medical establishment, and sexual double standard (embodied by a military man)" (para. 19). As Edith's father, Beale has erred on an individual level in considering that a sexually experienced older man might be an appropriate husband for his unworldly young daughter. But as a representative of the church, and thus still more damagingly because of the potentially widespread nature of the harm done, he has erred by condoning sexual sin, whose consequences are embodied in the infant. Tellingly, the punishment meted out to Menteith as he leaves his wife's deathbed (which he does without guilt or regret, eying attractive women on his way out) is that a Bible is thrown at him, break-ing his nose. Still more tellingly, the wielder of this missile is not a member of the male clergy but a female contemporary of Edith's.

Both precocity and gender help to inscribe the baby as "monst[er]" as well as victim; he is a figure simultaneously of innocence and of disease. As a somewhat similar case, consider Little Father Time in Thomas Hardy's *Jude the Obscure* (1895), who is not only preternaturally old for his years but also frail, enervated, and distanced from life. Indeed, Elaine Showalter argues that like Edith's baby, little Time—whom Hardy's narrator describes as "Age mas-querading as Juvenility, and doing it so badly that his real self showed through crevices" (290)—is framed by *fin-de-siècle* feminist "conventions relating to the prematurely aged and psychologically disturbed syphilitic child" ("Syphilis" 108). The child's nickname was conferred on him "because I look so aged they say," to which Sue responds "tenderly" by terming him "preternaturally old" (294). Nor, having introduced Time in these terms, does the narrative retreat from its insistence on his age inversion. Adjectives applied to him include *octo-genarian* (327), *quaint* (321), and the reiterated *aged* (312, 352), and throughout he is also linked to misery, although the narrator claims that his advent "rather helped than injured [Jude and Sue's] happiness" (303). Jude and Sue "try every means of making him kindle and laugh like other boys" (306), but unsuccess-fully; even in good times, he is the "one immediate shadow" in their lives (312), the source of "a great deal of pain and sadness" as the reporter of what people are saying about the family (312), and the possessor of an "incurably sad na-ture" (358).

Time's sojourn in the household concludes, of course, with the murder-suicide that eliminates all three of the children and its famous note of explanation, "*Done because we are too meny*" (355, emphasis in original). The clear implication of this note is that the adults in the family, particularly Jude, cannot provide a proper home for their offspring—in other words, that the child perceives the inade-quacy of the father and understands his duty to step into the breach, in the tradition of the many precocious child-women who shoulder their families' financial burdens. In this case, however, the solution arrived at is different. Instead of working to increase the family income so that they can find better lodgings (the immediate problem), Time kills himself and his half-siblings in order to decrease the family expenditures and alleviate the overcrowding that has pushed Jude out of the house. This reasoning is fully in line with the mor-bid practicality of what the boy describes as his early training at the hands of his biological mother, Arabella, who never had him christened, "because, if I died in damnation, 'twould save the expense of a Christian funeral" (294). Moreover, as Jeffrey Berman contends, Time's fate is also partly attributable to Sue's misguided decision "to be 'honest and candid' with him, as if he were a mature adult rather than a terrified child"; she treats him as "an extension of herself" instead of recognizing his youth (160). In a sense, this is the practice followed by most of the adults who surround precocious children, boys and girls alike, in the literature of age inversion during this period. Typically, precocity is a response to adult needs and behaviors rather than an expression of the intrinsic nature of the child in question.

Since Sue herself, as discussed above in chapter 3, is a variety of arrested child-woman, we may read *Jude the Obscure* as another late-century text that pairs an age-inverted child with an age-inverted adult. Yet because of the gender difference involved, *Jude* does not offer the reader an implicit choice between two models of masculinity, after the fashion of Alan and David in *Kidnapped* or Paul and Dick in *Vice Versâ*. Indeed, *choice* seems too optimistic a term for a text in which individual disasters appear to have been fated over generations. Instead, we may hypothesize that Sue's refusal to mature fully helps to maintain Time's tendency to take on adult worries and responsibilities. But since in this novel obsessed with both nurture and nature Time is the product of three parents and not of Sue alone, we must acknowledge also the contributions to his personality made by Arabella during his loveless existence in Australia (before she rejects him as an inconvenience, prefiguring his treatment of himself and Sue's children) and by genetic inheritance from his father. For as a boy, Jude, himself a failed suicide, seems poised on the balance between precocity and arrested development. Having "felt the pricks of life somewhat before his time" (5), he longs to "prevent himself growing up! He did not want to be a man" (13) and is described at age eleven as "an ancient man in some phases of thought, much younger than his years in others" (22). Little Time, it would appear, is doomed both by environment and by heredity.

Sally Shuttleworth explains why, given Hardy's interest in contemporaneous theories of inherited personality traits, it is inevitable that Time, who is seen by most critics as an allegorical figure, should embody precocity rather than some other state. In Shuttleworth's cogent reading, "logically, a child who is burdened by the thoughts and feelings of his forebears . . . must cease to be a child. The very category of childhood, as a state characterized by innocence and inexperience, must cease to [exist]. Age will be forced to masquerade as Juvenility" (150–51). Shuttleworth fits Jude's son into the twin contexts of views on heredity held by eminent Victorians such as the psychologist Henry Maudsley and well-publicized late nineteenth-century instances of child suicide, suggesting that Hardy was responding both to ideas about ineradicable features of the human condition and to accounts of events attributed to grim peculiarities of modern life. As should be clear by now, however, Time may also be seen as part of an extensive network of disturbingly precocious children in Victorian literature, many of whom substantially predate him in what U. C. Knoepflmacher calls "their steady subversion of a prevalent Romantic/Victorian typology" ("Child" 78). Knoepflmacher's contention that "Hardy's constructions of childhood are not only antisentimental but also programmatically antiliterary" (78–79) thus seems, at least where Jude's son is concerned, to overlook an alternative but nevertheless literary tradition connecting precocity with the uncanny, with adult domestic failure, and/or with financial or sexual crisis.

Accordingly, it should come as no surprise that my final example of tragic precocity is drawn from a work by a twentieth-century novelist whom modernist critics tended to dismiss as traditionalist: Arnold Bennett's *Clayhanger* (1910), which traces the ineffectual attempts of young Edwin Clayhanger to rebel against his controlling father, Darius. After the fashion of other patresfamilias in turn-of-the-century British novels, Darius represents the stifling of his son's creative impulses (Edwin wants to be an architect but is instead forced into the family printing business), the authority of money and age, and the potency of a kind of bourgeois death-in-life, from which Edwin is unable to emerge fully until his father's demise. What Edwin does not fully understand, however, is that the roots of Darius's drive to dominate are to be found in his origins as a precocious child-man. The reader becomes privy to this information in a chapter entitled "The Child-Man," in which "the man Darius" (33), then aged seven, labors in a pottery factory as a "self-supporting man of the world" (38) who, like a male version of Mayhew's watercress seller, plays an important part in the family economy.

Clayhanger provides a grim history of young Darius's work experience as a boy in the mid-1830s, when he takes a series of physically demanding and poorly remunerated jobs carried out in stifling and airless spaces. Through the repeated use of ironic phrases such as "the brawny arms of a man of seven" (34) and "seasoned men of the world aged eight" (37), the narrator emphasizes the disjunction between society's expectations for an impoverished child and that child's capacities; here again, precocity has been forced upon Darius rather than representing the early upwelling of some innate quickness. And in stressing the harshness of an environment in which the child quickly learns, for instance, that in the morning "nobody would provide him with kindling for his fire, that on the contrary everybody who happened to be on the place at that hour would unite to prevent him from getting kindling, and that he must steal it or expect to be thrashed before six o'clock" (35), the narrator establishes the beginnings of the trauma that will later result in the adult Darius's "intense and egoistic sense of possessing in absolute ownership the business which the little boy out of the Bastile had practically created" (384) and consequently in his unwillingness to share either freedom or the hard-won fruits of his labor with his son.

Still more traumatic than this early employment is the revelation that it is not enough to accomplish its aims. Whereas other precocious workers, from Jenny Wren to the Watercress Girl to Effie of "Effie's Trial," are described as earning funds adequate to their families' needs (even the Artful Dodger is successful in his assigned labor of picking pockets), in *Clayhanger* the working boy must leave his factory job because his father has been blacklisted by the local employers for taking part in a strike, "and Darius, though nine, could not keep the family" (39). The family enters the workhouse, a lasting shame and a signal of the father's failure to provide that reverberates throughout Darius's life. It is not their appropriate protector, the paterfamilias, who redeems them, but a more adequate replacement, Mr. Shushions, the local Sunday school teacher, who wants to help the family because he is drawn to Darius's intelligence. Thus Darius functions, not as his father's assistant and second-in-command, but rather as the instrument of his supplanting, which may help to explain why he is subsequently so adamant about forcing Edwin into the former role. So potent is the bond formed by Mr. Shushions's rescue of the family that the aged teacher's death many years later (in the workhouse from which his protégé has been unable to extract him in time) is the signal for Darius's decline. As Robert Squillace puts it, "The onset of Darius Clayhanger's fatal softening of the brain coincides precisely with the death of the last objective remnant of his childhood" (165).

Yet in another sense Darius never entirely moves beyond childhood. After they hear of Mr. Shushions's death, Edwin feels "secret superiority" at his father's emotional response to the news, being

unaware, with all his omniscience, that the being in front of him was not a successful steam printer and tyrannical father, but a tiny ragged boy who could still
taste the Bastile skilly and still see his mother weeping round the knees of a
powerful god named Shushions.

"I—I don't know," said Darius with another sigh.

The next instant he sat down heavily on the stairs and began openly to blub-
ber. His hat fell off and rolled about undecidedly.

"By Jove!" said Edwin to himself, "I shall have to treat this man like a bloom-
ing child!" (404–5)

In the context of the discourse of the child-man, Squillace's insight might
prompt the reader to see precocity as a protracted illness that has the effect of
both cutting off the maturing process of Darius's inner child and advancing
the destruction of his domestic relationships. Gradually distanced emotionally
from his parents first by his early employment and subsequently by the family's brief incarceration in the workhouse, Darius becomes accustomed to con-
ceiving of family bonds wholly in financial terms.

In the days of Darius's success, for instance, the narrator characterizes his
pleasure in his home life by suggesting that he classifies his children with other
consumer goods that testify to his solvency, noting, "It was wonderful that
he had three different suits of clothes, none of them with a single hole. It was
wonderful that he had three children, all with complete outfits of good clothes.
It was wonderful that he never had to think twice about buying coal, and that
he could have more food than he needed" (170). Similarly, the comment that
"with all its inevitable disillusions [his marriage] had been wonderful, incred-
ible. He looked back on it as a miracle" is immediately followed by comments
that make clear that its pleasures were essentially those of having pulled off a
complicated business transaction: "For he had married far above him, and had
proved equal to the enormously difficult situation. Never had he made a fool of
himself. He often took keen pleasure in speculating upon the demeanour of
his father, his mother, his little sister, could they have seen him in his purple
and in his grandeur" (170). The use of the term *speculating* here, following the
remarks on his children's clothes and immediately preceding a peroration to
his business, clearly has financial overtones, while the hint that all his adult
achievements have been a drama enacted for the imagined audience of the
family of his childhood suggests his failure to grow beyond his youth.

The autobiographical elements of *Clayhanger* have not been lost upon the various critics who note Darius's similarities to Bennett's own father, Enoch Bennett, who died in 1902 and by whom the author had been unhappily employed in early adulthood before he moved to London and began his writing career. But the novel may also be read in a more general light than as a *roman à clef* about the Bennett family. The increase in the number of fictions about precocious child-men in and after the 1880s reminds us of the contemporaneous changes in the way British society understood childhood, as the anticruelty movement, the diminishing of fathers' legal rights over their offspring, and the erosion of paternal authority as the twin onslaughts of Darwinism and a "God is love" religious sensibility ate away at the divine right of fathers and a protective sensibility was increasingly extended even to the children of the poor. The historian John Tosh sees a "public undermining of private patriarchy during the 1880s and 1890s" (*Place* 146) and finds that "the standing of children and childhood was rising, as that of fathers and fatherhood was falling" (150). In this context it is hardly surprising that *Vice Versâ*, for instance, should deem the child superior to the paterfamilias or that an Edwardian novel such as *Clayhanger* should represent the erstwhile child laborer as a traumatized victim of early Victorian barbarism, unable to come to satisfactory terms with his stolen childhood. While selfish arrested child-men of the *fin de siècle* such as Dracula, Hyde, and Kurtz pose significant threats to society, they at least exhibit energy and a certain grandeur. Precocious child-men of the same era tend to be smaller than life.

Moreover, the number of precocious literary child-men is smaller than either the number of precocious child-women or that of arrested child-men. It seems no irony, but rather cause and effect, that this comparative dearth corresponds to a glut of such figures in real life. Tosh notes that even among the middle classes, most

> boys ended their formal education in their mid-teens. . . . At an age when many of them had scarcely entered puberty, boys began to keep long hours at work, surrounded by people much older than themselves. . . . Parents, employers and teachers were often intent on forcing their charges through the remaining stages to manhood as quickly as possible—a distinctive feature of English upbringing much noted by foreign observers. (*Place* 105)

Dickens's youthful employment in the blacking factory, in other words, which seemed to him so patently abusive, was not at all unusual; rather, it is the standard to which he sought to hold his parents, and by which they fall on a continuum somewhere between callous and criminal, that was peculiar for his day. This recognition helps to explain why, with the exception of works by Dickens, we see so few precocious child-men in works written before the final decades of Victoria's reign, when childhood began to lengthen for middle-class boys and not merely for their sisters: the acceptance of connecting boys early to their work was so widespread as to be taken for granted. Jude, growing up a generation earlier than little Time, seems less precocious in his employment as bird-scarer than Time does as the apparently leisured child of poor parents, not only because Time concentrates qualities derived from Arabella and Sue as well as from Jude but also because the conditions of life and the expectations for childhood have changed.

Hence, perhaps, some of the differences between the handling of precocious working girls in Victorian and Edwardian literature and that of precocious child-men. Although many girls and women were employed outside the nineteenth-century home, female employment was neither the ideal nor the norm in the eyes of most middle-class writers, so that even when the child-women being written about belong to the working classes, they represent an anomaly, a problem requiring a solution via a change (typically a more responsible attitude toward work) in their male protectors. But those authors who see male precocity as an unfortunate circumstance worthy of remark recognize a problem with the norm itself, given the prevalence of the use of paid labor as the chief socializing mechanism for masculinity. Precocious working girls are typically shown laboring on behalf of domesticity, striving to fill both the stereotypically masculine role of provider and the stereotypically feminine one of homemaker because the domestic ideal is so unquestionably good. Precocious working boys, more radically, operate not at the intersection of domesticity and paid employment but rather on the ground where these two principles battle, thus bringing the purported harmony of the separate spheres into question.

Conclusion:
The Adult Reader as Child

Propelled by rising literacy rates and ever-cheaper print technology, children's literature boomed, both in quantity and in quality, across the nineteenth century. Adapting to fit an evolving adult notion of what children's reading, and childhood itself, should be, such texts mixed an increasingly large proportion of delight into the inevitable instruction, so that children's literature became newly pleasurable for adult consumers. *Treasure Island*, for example, flopped in its first incarnation as a serial (1881–82) in *Young Folks*, some of whose youthful subscribers wrote to the editor to express their displeasure with the tale (D. Jackson 31), but garnered glowing reviews and popularity among adult readers, including W. E. Gladstone, when published in volume form in 1883. Such responses worried some Victorian critics, who considered that the phenomenon of adult fans of children's books signaled a regression to childhood that might go hand in hand with widespread social degeneration, much as the arrested child-man often figures a moral and/or evolutionary breakdown. As Andrew Lang commented in the 1880s, "The flutter in the dovecots of culture caused by three or four boys' books is amazing. Culture is saddened at discovering that not only boys and illiterate people, but even critics not wholly illiterate, can be moved by a tale of adventure" (qtd. in D. Jackson 28).[1]

But *culture* in this case seems to refer not to British society in general but to the faction that was just starting, at the time of Lang's remark, to be described as "highbrow" and that Lang clearly views here with some derision. It is important here to consider the critical context of this moment. In "Children's Literature: Theory and Practice," Felicity Hughes suggests that until the 1880s the English novel was always "at least potentially *family* reading" (543) and that efforts by such figures as Henry James and George Moore to raise the status of the form depended on uncoupling it from its association with the young reader. She quotes James decrying what he sees as fiction's excessive awareness "of the presence of the ladies and children—by whom I mean, in other words, the reader irreflective and uncritical," and Moore pleading for the renunciation of "the effort to reconcile these two irreconcilable things—art and young girls" (Hughes 547). Lang's reference to a "flutter in the dovecots of culture," then, takes note of a territorial battle, an effort to expand the boundaries of high culture by insisting on the incompatibility of adult and child readers.

As James lamented in an essay of 1899, however, even by the end of the century the novel had not become sufficiently elitist to suit him, as "the diffusion of the rudiments, the multiplication of the common schools, has more and more had the effect of making readers of women and of the very young" (qtd. in Hughes 546). And before the attempt to redefine the novel in the 1880s, the dominance of the middlebrow was untroubled. Thus in the mid-Victorian years, a time marked (as I noted in the introduction) by a plethora of advice manuals advertising the connection between the embrace of dominant adult gender roles and the improvement of society, it is on the level of the middlebrow that we find a contrasting set of texts: not only children's books circulating for the pleasure of adult readers but also adult works employing strategies more usually associated with children's fiction, a form that Lynne Rosenthal has dubbed the "children's book for adults." This phenomenon is far reaching, extending from sentimental fiction, romance, and adventure to inspirational nonfiction, humor, poetry, and stage plays such as *Peter Pan*, which played to packed adult houses in 1904. The children's book for adults is often, but by no means always, about childhood and (as the examples of *Kidnapped* and *Vice Versâ*, both discussed in chapter 5, suggest) embraces both the realistic and the fantastic. Its purpose wavers between offering readers a vacation from the burdens of the mundane world of adulthood and improving them, particularly by inculcating sympathy with childhood's more difficult aspects or by privileging a childlike mind-set conducive to absorbing practical or moral instruction. For a crucial characteristic of such works is that they see their readers as imperfect or incomplete, acutely in need of a kind of resocializing that is to be accomplished by means of regression.

Accordingly, while in the preceding chapters I have focused primarily on the world of the text, on representations of age inversion and the uses to which individual authors may be putting them, here I will take a slightly different direction by considering also what narrative theorists call the "implied reader," namely, the implicit and generalized vision of the reader's needs, wishes, emotions, and values that becomes apparent from the narrative. I am concerned here not with actual readers' responses, to the extent that they may be preserved in book reviews, memoirs, letters, and the like, but with what the narrative strategies of particular authors reveal about these authors' understanding of how their texts will ideally function to improve their audience. Specifically, I propose that despite the anxiety manifest in many textual representations of arrested child-men and child-women, the authors discussed in this conclusion evidently see a benefit in encouraging a kind of temporary age inversion, coterminous at least with the duration of the reading experience and directed toward permanently changing the way the implied reader enacts adulthood. In contrast, then, to the old-fashioned and precocious children examined elsewhere in this study, who typically emerge in response to some kind of adult failure or absence, the age-inverted implied adult reader introduced in this conclusion is a phenomenon consciously sought and induced by benevolent action on the part of another adult, an author who focuses on the positive aspects of age inversion rather than on its unnatural side.

To date, few scholars have explored the possible influence of children's fiction on Victorian literature for adults, save for the occasional discussion of fairy-tale imagery in works by authors such as Charlotte Brontë, Charles Dickens, and Elizabeth Gaskell. Even here, investigators sometimes perceive this imagery as differing in meaning and emotional weight from its counterpart in children's texts. Carole Silver, for instance, argues in *Strange and Secret Peoples* that nineteenth-century faëry was initially an adult mode, an expression of interest in folklore and the paranormal rendered jejune after the 1860s by a flood of children's titles that drove "the elfin peoples" out of the sophisticated texts they had once populated (187). In Silver's construct, Dickens's use of changeling figures, say, such as *The Old Curiosity Shop*'s Quilp, derives less from childhood reading than from a self-consciously adult Victorian tradition of medical and anthropological inquiry (Silver 73–80). Evidently, where Victorian literature is concerned, crabbed age and youth cannot live together.[2] Even if we grant that assumption, however, a shared interest in the supernatural is not the only possible commonality between children's literature and adult literature. Yet scholarly investigation into overlaps in outlook and authorial strategy has not progressed substantially beyond Rosenthal's early article on one of the most popular novels of 1869, Florence Montgomery's *Misunderstood*.

Sentiment as Regression in *Misunderstood*

The preface to *Misunderstood* opens with the line, "The following is not a child's story." Montgomery goes on to note that nonetheless her work is intended to teach: "It has been thought that the lives of children, as known by themselves from their own little point of view, are not always sufficiently realised, that they are sometimes overlooked or misunderstood; and to throw some light, however faint, upon the subject, is one of the objects of this little story" (7). This "light," of course, is for the benefit of adults; as Rosenthal observes, "Montgomery hoped to change the behavior of parents rather than of children" (94). Because *Misunderstood* posits a family made up of two boys and their widowed father and indicates that the lost mother's parenting skills needed no amendment, Montgomery plainly shares the perennial Victorian suspicion that social dominance and authority might be shutting out adult men, in particular, from something important.

The title *Misunderstood* thus refers ultimately to an apparently large number of real children, represented in the fiction by seven-year-old Humphrey Duncombe. Humphrey is what the mid-Victorians called a "pickle," a good-hearted and attractive child who is constantly in trouble because of his inability to be guided by authority. His father, Sir Everard, prefers the delicate and biddable younger son, Miles, who looks like the boys' dead mother. He interprets Miles's submissiveness as affection and, in an echo of some of the precocious child-woman novels discussed in chapter 4, uses him as an emotional substitute for his wife. Lady Duncombe, however, was especially attached to Humphrey, and one of Montgomery's objectives is to demonstrate that inside the noisy, active, and apparently hypermasculine "pickle" may lurk a sensitive, deeply emotional, and feminized true self. Sir Everard, whose public duties as a member of Parliament have often kept him away from home, comprehends that self only when Humphrey is paralyzed in a fall and is joyfully reunited with his mother in death. The adult male realm of politics, self-discipline, and deference to authority is thus explicitly identified as incomplete, and readers are urged to expand their world-views to embrace a different sensibility.

Rosenthal has observed that, in focusing on "the polarities of restraint and spontaneity" (96), *Misunderstood* recalls a number of eighteenth- and nineteenth-century children's books that seek to influence children to make "the rational or virtuous choice" (97). The novel, however, is not a cautionary tale about Humphrey's foolhardiness and disobedience, even though these traits lead to his fatal accident when a rotten branch, upon which he has been forbidden to climb, breaks under his weight. Rather, it is a cautionary tale about the dire consequences of Sir Everard's lack of perception, which ultimately leaves him not only contrite but also deeply powerless. Much of the pathos of the death-bed scene depends upon this powerlessness, which mirrors Humphrey's sudden physical immobility:

> "Humphrey, my darling," [Sir Everard] exclaimed, in his longing to do something, be it ever so little, to soothe his boy's dying hour, "what is it? What can I do for you?"
>
> Nothing! With all his love and all his yearning, nothing! . . .
>
> Vain is the father's endeavour to reach a trouble of this kind [Humphrey's religious anxieties]; vainly, bending over him, does he seek to discover its cause, in his longing to remove or alleviate it. (284–85)

Unlike Sir Everard, we adult readers understand the cause of Humphrey's distress, since the narrator has spelled it out for us. Nevertheless, because we are an audience rather than actors in the drama, we share both Sir Everard's "longing to remove or alleviate it" and his impotence.

We might thus ask *why* Montgomery imposed this particular sensation on her audience. Rosenthal suggests that she "hoped to shock her adult readers into an awareness of the paralysis of their own lives; to make them conscious of the degree to which they had become alienated, not only from their children, but from the sources of their own inner vitality" (101–2). The obvious source of this alienation is Victorian society's emphasis on economic advancement, which required middle-class men to direct their attention to business in preference to their family relationships. I would, however, add two further purposes here. First, Montgomery dramatizes through an adult sensibility a point that she has elsewhere made via a focus on the child: adults and children sometimes fail to grasp each other's feelings and concerns, and this mutual misunderstanding can cause pain to parents as much as to their offspring. Second, the scene is plainly intended to be deeply pathetic; our enforced helplessness should result in tears. Unlike those shed in earlier didactic texts for children, however, these tears are not a punitive stick designed to cause us to make a moral choice in future. Rather, they *are* a moral choice.

For earlier in the novel, the narrator has implied that Humphrey's boisterous behavior, which has caused his father to condemn him as unfeeling, is in part a mechanism for coping with his grief at the loss of his mother. The text notes that this response has its counterpart in adult consumerism: "Children of a larger growth, but children in understanding still, do not many of us wrestle with this undefined feeling in the same way? This mysterious thing, which we, with our maturer experience, call sorrow, is not our first thought when it assails us, 'How shall we drive it away?' . . . Does it not drive the rich to society, travelling, or excitement, and the poor to the public-house?" (166–67). Montgomery continues, however, by suggesting that rather than evading sorrow, one should move through it toward God—as Humphrey models for us in his fortunate fall, which leads him to heaven.

Adult readers, then, made conscious of their inadequacy by their pain at Humphrey's situation, are presented immediately with a religious resolution, whose joyfulness we can feel only if we have experienced the grief toward which Montgomery directs us. Significantly, however, while Sir Everard is a necessary player throughout, our attention is always focused primarily on the child, to whom the narrator repeatedly compares us. And significantly, too, our simulacrum is specifically a "*stricken* child," a "child, crushed and despairing" (170, emphasis added). If "one of the objects" of *Misunderstood*, as Montgomery notes in her preface, is to further adult empathy with children so that childish sorrow may be reduced, another would seem to be to transfer that sorrow to adults, on the grounds that woe will improve their chances of salvation. A favorite Victorian scripture, Matthew 18:3, advises, "Except ye be converted, and become as little children, ye shall not enter into the kingdom of Heaven." Montgomery's strategy in *Misunderstood* implies that becoming "as little children" involves the reacquisition, not of Romantic innocence, but rather of a condign sense of inadequacy, loss, and helplessness.

The gender composition of *Misunderstood*'s audience is also relevant. The novel's dominant subject is the adult male's emotional inadequacy, which apparently matters only in the absence of his idealized wife. Men and women are thus likely to respond to this fiction differently, women taking it as a validation of their domestic irreplaceability and comparative emotional expertise, men asking themselves nervously to what extent Sir Everard's faults are also theirs. The static quality that is so often associated with the arrested child-woman is here assigned to the fictional paterfamilias and to those readers, perhaps especially men, who identify with him. In effect, *Misunderstood* is not only a children's book for adults but also a woman's domestic novel about men. It translates into an all-male world the plot that Nina Baym has identified as central to the woman's novel in mid-nineteenth-century America, in which a "poor and friendless [female] child" (35) must cope with "mistreatment, unfairness, disadvantage, and powerlessness" (17), ultimately triumphing over them by developing "a strong conviction of her own worth" and altering "the world's attitude toward her" (19). Thus, while Montgomery's novel identifies mothers as superior to fathers in their insight and empathy, it simultaneously seeks to diminish "misunderstand[ing]" between women and men as well as between adults and children. Women are to see that men and boys too may feel undervalued and powerless, while male readers, by identifying with male characters of this type, are to project themselves into an emotional situation already familiar to many women. The favorable reviews and wide sales that *Misunderstood* enjoyed suggest that adult readers of the day got the point.

Learning Manliness from *Self-Help*

Misunderstood was participating in a commitment to moral uplift that was widespread in the nineteenth century. Influenced by modernism's aesthetic dictates, however, we tend to define the didactic urge as a hallmark of the marginalized or second-rate writer. Thus when Dinah Mulock takes exception to *The Mill on the Floss* in an 1861 *Macmillan's* article, instructing the reader to ask, "What good will it do? [Will it] lighten any burdened heart, help any perplexed spirit, comfort the sorrowful, succour the tempted, or bring back the erring into the way of peace[?]" (444), we may see the question as itself somewhat juvenile, a sign that Mulock does not understand how George Eliot's masterpiece "should" be read. By the standards of the day, however, perhaps it was Eliot who was missing the point. As Sally Mitchell notes, Mulock's name "was frequently paired with Eliot's during these [mid-century] years in a context which implies 'good literature' as opposed to the other sort" (*Craik* 114). Advice manuals and novels designed to inculcate principles of upward mobility in both a moral and a practical sense proliferated; didacticism was not confined to works for children. Yet because literature for the young was considered to have a particular responsibility to be didactic, writers who wanted to preach to adult readers might take children's works as their models.

This observation brings us to the central text of Victorian "success literature," Samuel Smiles's *Self-Help*, which seeks to teach ambitious working-class men the character traits that will turn them into gentlemen—in effect, to mass market a particular brand of masculinity. Published in November 1859, *Self-Help* had sold 20,000 copies by year's end (it required three reprintings in November alone) and some 250,000 by the time of the author's death in 1904.[3] The book's appeal has been traced to various sources, including Smiles's ability to express his era's optimism and energy while simultaneously addressing its anxiety about social class, his "muscular and succinct" prose style, and his habit of drawing his illustrations from all levels of society (K. Joseph 7–8). But an additional reason for *Self-Help*'s perceived effectiveness, I suggest, is its shrewd adaptation of the techniques of the children's literature of Smiles's youth, which similarly focuses on the consumer's replication of characteristics that authors have identified as desirable.

Like many Victorian texts for children and adults alike, *Self-Help* focuses on the honing of the male character, one trait at a time. In a characteristic chapter, "Men of Business," Smiles offers his audience—originally, young artisans belonging to a mutual-improvement society in Leeds in 1845—a taxonomy of masculine energy, which he subdivides into accuracy, method, and dispatch, among other qualities. In order to illustrate the benefits of these virtues, he tells anecdotes dealing with the lives of great men, advising the reader to rise by cultivating in himself, for example, Napoleon's mastery of detail and the Duke of Wellington's punctuality. In other words, Smiles sees character as flexible. Far from being fixed at one social level by heritage, upbringing, or innate talent, Smiles's readers, though nominally adult, are presumed to be *tabulae rasae* who may effectively become their own preceptors, recognizing weaknesses and acquiring attributes that they may hitherto have lacked. Middle-class status becomes in this formulation equivalent to adulthood; moreover, like chronological adulthood, it is potentially available to all. One needs only a set of blueprints, which this text provides through a host of mini-biographies.

Smiles's narrative style is not universally admired. As Christopher Clausen puts it, in his lack of organization and tendency to pad his chapters "Smiles resembled nothing so much as a vacuum cleaner that rolled from room to room of a large dusty house filling up its bag" (407–8). Yet as Clausen also indicates, the book's unsophisticated structure, a result of its emphasis on anecdote and its refusal to subordinate one anecdote to another, was a major source of its appeal for the working-class men who constituted its original audience (407). As far as its reading level is concerned, *Self-Help* makes few demands upon its consumers. It both permits and expects readers to be intellectually unformed, although, to recapitulate a distinction made in chapter 2, it also assumes that they are childlike rather than childish. They do not suffer the distracting claims of illicit sexual desire; moreover, they are prepared to relinquish the pleasures of selfishness even if—and here the resemblance to chapter 2's child-men is less acute—doing so means accepting the necessity of change. As in the children's books that it resembles, the sketches it contains are simple, clearly written, and short, their points readily apparent even to inexperienced readers. It is a book made to be dipped into by those who have limited leisure for reading, and if the reader has forgotten where he left off last time, no harm is done, as each moral is repeated again and again.

Here, for example, is an extract from Smiles's account of the surgeon and scientist John Hunter:

> He received little or no education until he was about twenty years of age, and it
> was with difficulty that he acquired the arts of reading and writing. He worked for
> some years as a common carpenter at Glasgow, after which he joined his brother
> William, who had settled in London as a lecturer and anatomical demonstrator.
> John entered his dissecting-room as an assistant, but soon shot ahead of his
> brother, partly by virtue of his great natural ability, but mainly by reason of his
> patient application and indefatigable industry. (97–98)

To readers familiar with the rational-moralist writers who flourished at the turn of the nineteenth century—and Smiles, who was born in 1812, would have grown up on their works—this sketch should have a familiar ring. In its emphasis on the cause-and-effect relationship of character trait and personal success, its assumption that personality may be described in terms of a concentrated quality consistently displayed, and especially its implication that the point of writing about admirable individuals is that readers may be inspired to emulation, the passage adopts strategies associated with children's authors such as Thomas Day, Maria Edgeworth, and the anonymous producer of an 1804 work resoundingly titled *The Renowned History of Primrose Prettyface, Who by Her Sweetness of Temper and Love of Learning Was Raised from Being the*

Daughter of a Poor Cottager to Great Riches and to the Dignity of the Lady of the Manor, Set Forth for the Benefit and Imitation of Those Pretty Little Boys and Girls Who by Learning Their Books and Obliging Mankind, Would to Beauty of Body Add Beauty of Mind.

According to Patricia Demers and Gordon Moyles, rational moralism—essentially, the principle that good sense and virtue are equivalent—continued to animate children's literature as late as 1850 (121). Its heyday began in the 1780s, with the appearance (over a six-year span) of Thomas Day's *The History of Sandford and Merton.* A wealthy eccentric, Day believed so fervently in the theories of Jean-Jacques Rousseau that he adopted two orphan girls in order to rear them according to his idol's precepts, planning to marry whichever of his charges turned out better. In other words, Day took seriously the idea that character is malleable. Thus, like the anecdotes contained in *Self-Help*, the various episodes of *Sandford and Merton* provide a laundry list of desirable character traits, from kindness to animals to diligence at learning to read, which are, of course, being recommended to the reader as well as acquired by little Tommy Merton. And although Day's upper-class status might seem to have won out in his own life, in that he ultimately married an heiress instead of either of his working-class wards, the ideology on display is essentially a leveling one; the novel decries its culture's tendency to emphasize class differences.

The same is true of Smiles, who assures his readers that social mobility is possible, that the gulf between them and dukes and emperors may be lessened by taking the latter as inspirations and models. Like Day, Smiles implies that members of different classes can interact as equals; he communicates this idea by juxtaposing anecdotes of the well-born with accounts of the plebeian and refusing to distinguish between the two. But my point here is not only that Smiles's message resembles those of certain rational-moralist children's authors popular in his youth, since similar messages may be found in many texts for adults that might equally well have shaped his outlook. The strategies of Smiles and the rational moralists are strikingly similar as well.

Take the techniques on display in Edgeworth's 1801 story "The Purple Jar," published in her *Early Lessons.* On one level, "The Purple Jar" is a cautionary tale about the foolishness of impulse buying, in which little Rosamond prefers what she takes to be an attractive *objet d'art* to a useful pair of shoes and lives to regret it. Not only do Rosamond's increasingly shabby old shoes inhibit her activities and pleasure but, in addition, when she looks more closely at what she has purchased, the jar turns out to be a plain white container whose purple color derived from its former (and now discarded) contents. Rosamond cannot benefit from her mother's advice; she is the kind of child who can only learn by experience. Yet the story is clearly written from the assumption that other children need not settle for her laborious trial-and-error approach, but can profit vicariously from her mistakes.

What drives the point home for the reader is less Edgeworth's evident faith in the utility of the lessons than how she embeds them in story and personality, which, as in Smiles's work, gives them emotional weight. Whereas many protagonists of pre-Victorian children's works tend to be generic, Edgeworth individualizes Rosamond enough to make her stand out from a somewhat featureless crowd. The intended reader is likely to identify with Rosamond both because they share an age and class status and because she is described in enough detail to come to life. Although the story is brief, Rosamond herself is unexpectedly complex. If some authors of cautionary tales focus on a single disastrous trait, Edgeworth suggests that character consists of chains of interlocking and sometimes contrasting qualities. Just as Tommy Merton's unfortunate upbringing has led not only to laziness but also to timidity, discourtesy, smugness, and incompetence, Rosamond's impulsiveness is linked to her love of beauty and her desire to assert herself, balanced by a willingness to acknowledge that she is in the wrong. Similarly, Smiles's model men rarely embody only the virtue under immediate scrutiny. Industry, say, will be shown to coexist with a network of additional traits, such as (in the case of the artist and blacksmith James Sharples) thoroughness, good sense, "genuine rightheartedness," and uxoriousness (135). Like Rosamond, Smiles's exemplary characters are distinct from the mob. Paradoxically, however, this individuality is offered to consumers as something to imitate.[4]

Anne Baltz Rodrick observes the rhetorical importance to the ethic of self-improvement of what we might term the "unimproved Other," members of the working class who failed to embrace the culture of improvement and were consequently viewed with hostility by their aspiring brothers. She identifies as Smiles's chief innovation "his articulation of the links between individual self-help and the overall improvement of a larger civic body," so that those who rejected personal ambition were also demonstrating selfishness by implicitly rejecting their duties as citizens (40). Yet in the context of rational moralism, this contribution too has an extensive pedigree. Rational-moralist works focus in roughly equal numbers on good examples and bad, often in the same text, with readers being invited to follow the one and despise the other. For instance,

Tommy Merton is contrasted to Harry Sandford, Rosamond's foolish behavior in "The Purple Jar" to her sensible behavior in "The Marble Pear," and the six children who make up the "Bad Family" in Mrs. Fenwick's *Lessons for Children* (1809) to the six who make up the "Good Family." The larger purpose of these works is clearly to use individual cases to construct a kind of corporate child-hood identity among readers—to improve in bulk, as it were, as a means of shaping a particular model of future citizen. The composite recommendation of an individual who is sensible, industrious, kind, responsible, detail-oriented, and obedient to authority is designed to further national stability; even while rational moralists may espouse democratic or class-blind attitudes, they eschew the hot-headed, romantic impulses that may be leading to revolution elsewhere. As Smiles's work implies, what is being engineered in such texts is essentially the improvement of an existing society, not its wholesale replacement.

Critics have noted that *Self-Help* influenced subsequent children's works. For example, Clausen cites the fiction of Horatio Alger (407); Richards, the novels of G. A. Henty; and Elleke Boehmer, Robert Baden-Powell's *Scouting for Boys* (xiv). But what are the implications of viewing *Self-Help*, or for that matter *Misunderstood*, in the context of earlier works for children? I would ar-gue that at stake here is more than a simple mapping of sources. For one thing, that Day, Edgeworth, and their colleagues wrote for a primary audience of prepubescent middle-class children, while Smiles addressed young men who were by Victorian standards adult and by our standards at least adolescent, tells us something about nineteenth-century understandings of both children and the working classes. The latter were frequently represented as bestial, dirty, poorly educated, and unrestrained in their appetites—in short, as arrested child-men, childish in the most negative sense of the word.[5] Yet in Smiles's work, the textual infantilizing of the working classes is intended as a precondi-tion for their empowerment, just as in Montgomery's novel the adult male reader is forced into powerlessness as a means of inculcating broader sympa-thies and new forms of sensibility. By reading exemplary lives, with their sim-ple diction, straightforward sentence structure, and strategic similarities to rational-moralist writings for small children, Smiles's ambitious audience can learn how to become respected adult citizens. By reading a cautionary tale, Montgomery's can learn how to understand the limitations of privilege. Both *Misunderstood* and *Self-Help* thus suggest the extent to which performing the role of the child could bestow cultural authority upon the Victorian adult.

Approaching Faith through the "Childlike" in MacDonald's Fiction

Smiles originally wrote for an audience made up primarily of young men, some perhaps still in their teens, most in their twenties, and all presumably self-supporting. Montgomery wrote for an audience of well-to-do adults, although her novel was readily accessible to children as well. In contrast, their near contemporary George MacDonald addressed a readership that he imagined as simultaneously insightful and uncontaminated, emotionally mature without being intellectually jaded, on the order of such figures as Mulock's child-woman Olive Rothesay, who combines virtuous precocity in youth with virtuous childlikeness in adulthood. He describes his ideal reader as "childlike," explaining in his 1893 essay "The Fantastic Imagination" that such a person might be "five, or fifty, or seventy-five" (25). In adapting the conventions of children's literature to the sophistication of the adult world, then, MacDonald rejects the convention that an author writes for a particular age group rather than for a set of ageless character traits. Or as Amy Sonheim puts it, "MacDonald refuses to polarize the world of adults from the world of children" (1). The intersection of these two worlds, of course, is the realm of age inversion.

Sonheim discusses MacDonald's fairy tale "The Light Princess," which today is classified as a children's story because of its genre, brevity, and twentieth-century illustrator, the Caldecott Medal winner Maurice Sendak. And indeed, Sonheim notes, the tale was originally created for MacDonald's own children. It was not, however, offered to the Victorian public as a juvenile fantasy. Perhaps influenced by John Ruskin's advice that the story was inappropriate for the young,[6] MacDonald incorporated it into the episodic structure of his adult novel *Adela Cathcart* (1864), within which, Sonheim argues, it offers a disguised commentary upon the events, setting, and concerns of its frame. Thus, as Sonheim notes, Adela lives in a house known as "The Swanspond," the Light Princess in a lakeside castle. Adela suffers from excessive melancholy, the bewitched Light Princess from insufficient gravity in both a literal and a metaphorical sense. Above all, the Light Princess is saved by a man's self-sacrifice when the hero demonstrates his willingness to immolate himself for her sake, while Adela is saved by a man's recognition that women must be granted spiritual and intellectual stimulation, conventional gender roles notwithstanding (Sonheim 5–6). In short, in "The Light Princess" MacDonald plays with questions of audience. He not only redirects toward adult readers a tale first told to children but also constructs the adult-oriented frame tale in a way that simultaneously illuminates the themes of the fairy tale and is illuminated by them. Together, Adela and the Light Princess provide both direct and indirect discussion of the fraught issue of women's social place and intellectual needs, a subject that might normally be considered adult but that in MacDonald's hands is represented as transcending age.

This approach is characteristic of MacDonald's authorial strategy, which frequently juxtaposes realism and fantasy, stories that seem adult-oriented and stories that seem child-oriented. Apparent opposites are ultimately revealed to be complements, the underlying similarity of their messages revealed by proximity. As "The Fantastic Imagination" makes clear, MacDonald saw the reader's interpretive task as the ultimate creative act in literature, trumping the author's attempt to inculcate a message:

> Everyone . . . who feels [a] story, will read its meaning after his own nature and development: one man will read one meaning in it, another will read another.
>
> "If so, how am I to assure myself that I am not reading my own meaning into it, but yours out of it?"
>
> Why should you be so assured? It may be better that you should read your meaning into it. That may be a higher operation of your intellect than the mere reading of mine out of it: your meaning may be superior to mine. (25)

The author, then, should endeavor to provide opportunities for independent thought on the reader's part, and the unexpected chiming of apparently unlike genres and modes of address will enhance such opportunities.

Consider the seemingly disparate plot threads in MacDonald's "The Gifts of the Child Christ" (1882). The tale concerns a neglected five-year-old, Phosy Greatorex, who, haunted by the saying "Whom the Lord loveth, he chasteneth," has been praying that God might chasten her (32). On Christmas Day, she wakes to discover in the guest room what she at first takes to be "the most exquisite of dolls," "the gift of the child Jesus," and subsequently identifies as "baby Jesus himself." Holding the infant (her newborn half-brother) tenderly, she becomes a Mary figure, "at once the mother and the slave of the Lord Jesus," but gradually realizes that the object of her worship is not an artificial child but a dead one (54–56). The household discovers the strange sight, and when Phosy sees her father, she wails out her anguish. For the first time, she becomes real to him; in a sense, she makes in his eyes the same transition from symbolic object to individual that the baby has just made in hers. The father's subsequent behavior suggests that MacDonald is urging his audience to reconfigure its own conception of childhood. Picking up his daughter, Greatorex comforts her, laying the groundwork for a relationship in which he will learn to respect her spiritual gifts. Like Montgomery's Humphrey, Phosy will no longer be "misunderstood"; father and child, as well as husband and wife, will draw closer together, making the hitherto unhappy household a place of joy. Meanwhile, Phosy's nursemaid, Alice, is likewise "chastened" when she learns first that a newly deceased uncle has left a substantial sum to his legal next of kin and later that she and her brother cannot inherit it because, it turns out, their parents were not married. The revelation is intensely humiliating to a woman who has prided herself on her respectability and has begun to develop grandiose fantasies about spending her new wealth. Nevertheless, the loss of the money is fortunate, as it preserves Alice's future with the modestly situated man who loves her.

"The Gifts of the Christ Child" may initially seem to lack unity. While both Alice and Greatorex are flawed, at first their situations do not appear parallel. Alice is a servant whose anticipated legacy has gone to her head, so that she speaks disrespectfully to her employers and breaks her engagement. Greatorex is a merchant who tends to value those around him only to the extent that their minds resemble his own, so that neither of his marriages has been emotionally successful. To a conventional middle-class Victorian reader, Alice's crime is her transgression against the behavioral standards required of female domestic servants: humility, deference, and the responsible performance of her duties (for example, she is somewhat neglectful and fierce toward Phosy). Greatorex, in contrast, appears to be hewing only too closely to the stereotype of the successful businessman as laid down in novels such as *Vice Versâ* and *Dombey and Son*. Like Dombey, if to a lesser extent, Greatorex is honest but also proud, insensitive, and cold—and desperately in need of redemption at his daughter's hands.

Because these unlike strands are juxtaposed, however, the reader recognizes the need to discover their underlying commonalities. Both plot lines, of course, illustrate that divine "chastening" ultimately increases happiness. Both, as Rolland Hein observes, demonstrate "that true conversion is a change of heart that issues in reconciled or renewed personal relationships" (342), a theme that runs throughout much of MacDonald's fiction, whether marketed primarily to adults or to children. And the parallel between Alice and Greatorex encourages us to see him, too, as an impertinent servant in God's household, a man who needs to learn obedience and to jettison his arrogance. Various words and phrases in the narrator's uncomplimentary early description of Greatorex, including "meanness," "presumptuous[ness]," "cramped . . . development," and "vainest hopes" (33–35), strengthen this parallel.

But works such as "The Gifts of the Child Christ" may be classified as children's stories for adults for reasons beyond their didacticism; the mind-set into which they urge adult readers is also relevant. Like virtuous arrested children of the Joe Gargery or Mr. Dick type, readers are to be open, humble, self-doubting, eager to seek the author's meaning by profiting from the clues he drops. MacDonald held that "it is God's things, his embodied thoughts, which alone a man has to use, modified and adapted to his own purposes, for the expression of his thoughts" ("Imagination" 27). In this context, it is possible to see a connection between the story's focus on God's chastening of his beloved children and the way in which the narrator both challenges his readers intellectually and warns them of the dangers of presumption. Although Mac-Donald believed in empowering readers, he simultaneously established his own position as their teacher, and therefore as their superior in understanding. Like Montgomery and Smiles, that is, MacDonald considered that the child-like adult reader, especially when taking direction from the adult author, is most amenable to improvement.

In the introduction I quote an assortment of nineteenth-century uses of the phrase *second childhood* that indicate the inferiority of old age to youth. But in their different ways, Montgomery, Smiles, and MacDonald all illustrate the not uncommon conviction, developed in the Romantic period but experiencing a resurgence especially toward the middle and end of Victoria's reign, that far from being a mere apprenticeship to adulthood, childhood might be the superior state to the "prime of life" as well. Precocity, as we have seen, is typically figured as a condition forced upon children by adult absence, inadequacy, or desire and thus as perhaps a necessity but not a source of pleasure for the children involved. Conversely, arrested development is commonly presented either as a deliberate choice on the part of individuals focused on their own gratification or as an abnormal but nonetheless natural circumstance. Either way, both Mr. Hyde and Mr. Dick appear happy in themselves in a way that Paul Dombey and even Sara Crewe do not.

Certainly, many of the texts examined in this study—*Dracula*, for one—are anxious about the uses to which prolonged or empowered childhood may be put. But simultaneously, others suggest, for instance through virtuous precocious child-women such as the young Olive Rothesay, that the child may be the mainstay of a family endangered by adult irresponsibility, so that in effect the child is better equipped to be an adult than the adults are. Still others, taking a more positive view of arrested adults than do authors such as Bram Stoker or H. G. Wells, accept the Romantic position that childhood is wasted on the young. For example, a comment published in *Blackwood's* in 1822 aptly summarizes the mind-set shared in particular by Montgomery and MacDonald:

> The frequent recurrence of [childlike] feelings is beneficial to the human heart, [in] that it helps to purify, to refine, and spiritualize its worldly and corrupt affections, restoring a sort of youthful elasticity to its nobler powers, and at the same time a meek and childlike sense of entire dependence no longer indeed on the tender earthly guardians of our helpless infancy, but on our Father which is in Heaven, *their* Father and ours, in whose sight we are all alike helpless, alike children. ("Childhood" 139, emphasis in original)

Children's literature for adults seeks to induce such a "recurrence of [childlike] feelings." Authorial strategies for accomplishing this end varied, as did the uses (e.g., sacred versus secular) to which the state of adult childhood was put and, in a larger sense, both the negative and the positive attitudes taken toward age inversion in both adults and children. Nevertheless, the extent of this phenomenon in Victorian literature illuminates the cultural position assigned to childhood—childhood as a construct if not childhood as actually experienced.

Over the course of this study, I have sought to catalog and analyze, and thus to illuminate, how and to what extent the idea of age as a construct, something separable from biological condition, was accepted by writers from the mid-nineteenth century up to the Great War. Moreover, these writers were aware that particular age constructs could be induced by particular circumstances, such as poverty, motherlessness, or (for more temporary purposes) the kind of authorial address used in the texts explored in this conclusion. If the idea of femininity—and masculinity—as masquerade is seen today as a twentieth-century insight, associated with theorists from Joan Rivière to more recent figures such as Judith Halberstam and Eve Sedgwick, the idea that childhood as a psychological condition could be ended, prolonged, or restored, deliberately or inadvertently, via outside human agency is clearly one that circulated widely in the nineteenth century. Recognizing this point and its implications may require us to revise some commonly held assumptions about Victorian approaches to childhood, maturity, and individuality more generally.

Above all, nonbiological constructs of age during this period were by no means stable. Even within the works of a single author, such as Dickens, age inversion may have radically different valences inflected by factors that include gender, social class, and the larger themes of the surrounding text. If it is possible to see the phenomenon of age inversion in part as a metaphorical exploration of the tension between the Victorian respect for history and heritage on the one hand and for innovation, progress, vitality, and newness on the other, it is not always possible to identify which term in this dialectic has dominance. And when we move from the mid-Victorian years (the moment of the works discussed in this conclusion) to the end of the century, we see representations of age inversion change under the pressure of trends in science or social science, revisions to domestic structures or attitudes toward child labor, politicized phenomena such as the rise of the New Woman, and more. Like our own day, the period that this study discusses was no more univocal in its approach to age than it was in its approach to gender, sexuality, family, or any other major area of life. Recognizing both the multivocality and the fluidity of age in Victorian and post-Victorian texts establishes the existence of complexities often overlooked, thereby making available new insights into a culture that continues to wield a profound influence over our own.

Notes

Introduction

1. "Towards the latter part of life he knew his own infirmities, and suffered himself to be in pupilage to his house-keeper; for he considered that, at a certain time of life, the second childhood of age demanded its wonted protection." *Encyclopaedia Britannica*, 6th ed., s.v. "Young, Dr. Edward."

2. David Lee Miller traces back to Virgil "the impulse to cherish precocious adulthood" ("Witness" 115), while the Romantic period saw what Judith Plotz terms an obsessive interest in "preserving childhood" (xvi)—in some cases, into adulthood, as exemplified in her study by Thomas De Quincey's and Hartley Coleridge's approaches to their own lives. Plotz observes, however, that the latter two figures "belong as much to Victorian as to Romantic culture" (xvi).

3. For example, the precocity of penury is taken for granted in the following passage from Mary Clementina Hibbert Ware's 1868 novel *Dr. Harcourt's Assistant*: "Blanche . . . looked down at the pale, anxious face of her little companion, a child in years, but a woman in her way of talking, and in her manner. No wonder, when she had been reared in poverty" (3:9).

4. The United States notoriously took a relaxed approach to foreign copyrights, which may help to explain why no British firm appears to have capitalized on the project of this series. Known collectively as "Dickens' Little Folks," the abridgements included, among other titles, *The Child-Wife*, based on *David Copperfield*; *Little Paul*, based on *Dombey and Son*; *Dame Durden*, based on *Bleak House*; and *Smike*, based on *Nicholas Nickleby*. The 1855 editions were advertised in J. S. Redfield's publisher's list as "books for children, of a vigorous, manly tone," but the entry continues by suggesting that "the well-known excellence of [Dickens's] portrayal of children, and the interests connected with children," are the "qualities which have given his volumes their strongest hold on the hearts of parents." By 1878 the series seems to have been marketed to a general audience, surely an acknowledgment of the abridgements' appeal to adults.

5. Nettie Adler and R. H. Tawney's 1909 pamphlet *Boy and Girl Labour*, urging the raising of the minimum school-leaving age from fourteen to fifteen and the abolition of the half-time system under which work and schooling might be combined, was packaged with advertisements for books on how London boys and girls might enter trades and with a plea to "help crippled boys" by patronizing the Depot of Cripples' Industries, which made brushes, repaired shoes, and knitted stockings. Clearly child labor was alive and well in the Edwardian period.

one: The Old-Fashioned Child and the Uncanny Double

1. The piece was reprinted in the American magazine *The Living Age* the following month, one of a number of demonstrations that the concept of the old-fashioned child circulated on both sides of the Atlantic.

2. Since in the present chapter I examine only children labeled *old-fashioned* within the texts that contain them, I reject some of Adye's assignments of this term, notably to Ewing's Jackanapes and Carroll's Alice; in their cases, the quality that Adye identifies as old-fashioned is closer to what today's critics call Romantic, although Alice is arguably Romantic only in the frame narrative's nostalgic attitude toward her. The most signal omission from this chapter is a child created after the publication of Adye's article, Little Father Time in Thomas Hardy's *Jude the Obscure* (1894–95). As Hardy's narrator never refers to him as old-fashioned, Jude's son and namesake appears in my chapter on the precocious child-man. He nonetheless shares important qualities with the old-fashioned children discussed here.

3. Nearly half a century later, Adye recalls a friend of his mother's running out to greet her spouse, "exclaiming with tears in her eyes and grief as for a real child in her voice, 'Oh, William, have you heard? Little Paul Dombey is dead!'" (287). This reader's response may have been heightened by her situation as a newly married woman "beguiling the tedium of her husband's absence" (287) with a novel that explores the conflicts between domesticity and business.

4. The adjective *major* permits the omission of children's texts, among others; for instance, Marah Gubar cites William Howitt's *The Boy's Country-Book: Being the Real Life of a Country Boy, Written by Himself* (1839) as an early example of a tale that out-innovates *Dombey and Son* by using a child narrator (*Dodgers* 217n11).

5. Dickens does not represent himself as an old-fashioned child in this fragment of autobiography, but he qualifies as a precocious child-man in a more general sense, given the enforced independence of his economic status and living arrangements, in combination with his report of his parents' response to this situation: "My father and mother were quite satisfied. They could hardly have been more so if I had been twenty years of age, distinguished at a grammar-school, and going to Cambridge" (qtd. in Forster 51).

6. For example, "Heine's Jupiter [in a work cited in "The 'Uncanny'"] . . . fills the roles of both the Urgent Child and the Archaic Father simultaneously. He is the impotent, declining patriarch who has been exiled from the active world and from his own past. He is also the dependent child relying on his nurse once again. . . . But Freud makes no mention of any of the details of Heine's text, rich as it is in explicit examples of the uncanny, and his omission of the monumental figure of Jupiter, monumentally inverted, constitutes a striking erasure" (McCaffrey 378–79).

7. Gerhard Joseph makes a similar point regarding the Dombeys, tying little Paul's oddness theoretically, not to Freud, but to the Swiss psychoanalyst Alice Miller and her study of the narcissism of parents who treat their offspring "as extensions of themselves, as objects whose attentive admiration and strict responsiveness are intended to provide the parent with a perpetually self-flattering 'mirror.'" Joseph sees "the death-seeking docility of young Paul Dombey" as a "pathological response" engendered by the pathology of the father (191–92).

8. Freud holds that the literary uncanny requires a setting of "material reality," since if the characters within the story accept ghosts, say, as a commonplace, the subsequent appearance of a ghost will not involve the return of the repressed (641). Thus M. E. Braddon's story "The Shadow in the Corner" (1879), in which sleeping in a room in which a man hanged himself drives a young maidservant with a "pale and somewhat old-fashioned face" to suicide (263), identifies the materialism of the adult occupants of the house as a contributing cause of the tragedy: just as the girl is out of place socially, having been educated above her station, she is forced into the wrong room because others will not acknowledge the possibility of revenants.

9. One online medical source lists "problems with walking, impaired bladder control leading to urinary frequency and/or incontinence, and progressive mental impairment and dementia" as symptoms of normal pressure hydrocephalus, a condition that worsens with age. See www.medicinenet.com/hydrocephalus/page3.htm (accessed 22 Sept. 2009).

10. *Elf*'s author continued to publish under her maiden name after her 1875 marriage to the sculptor John Adams-Acton. Hering was the name of the parents who had adopted her at age four; she was born Marion Hamilton in 1846, the illegitimate daughter of the Duke of Hamilton. *Elf* invokes this history in its dedication, "with all the Loyalty and Affection found by those born in Arran for the Ancient House of Hamilton," to the "baby princess of Arran," the three-year-old daughter of Hering's legitimate half-brother, the twelfth duke.

11. Corelli's use of *old-fashioned* here works to heighten the unnaturalness of the term in its other sense, as applied to Lionel. His tragedy is that unlike Lucy and the other working-class figures in the novel, he does not represent traditional values. As in many anti–New Woman novels, Ibsenism has intervened.

12. U. C. Knoepflmacher observes that the names Emily, Lottie (or Charlotte), and Anne indicate Burnett's covert construction of yet another identity for Sara as part of a Brontëan system (Introduction xvi–xvii).

13. Here I intend *always* to refer only to the 1905 version of the novel. See Nelson, *Strangers* 73–79, for a discussion of differences between the Sara of *A Little Princess* and her predecessor in "Sara Crewe"; if we set the two texts alongside each other, Sara's identity is considerably less stable.

14. Stables's Rupert, a maker of "odd remarks" (10) and a dreamer of "strange" dreams that he communicates to his brother (11), nonetheless embodies an authorial unease that might, for another writer, blossom into full-fledged uncanniness. As an admirable invalid, he represents an alternative to the muscular Christianity that Stables otherwise embraced in both his fiction and his medical-advice column in the *Boy's Own Paper*.

15. I thank Anne Morey for this insight.

16. In *Dombey and Son*, for instance, Polly's husband may work on the railroad, but he does so for economic rather than ideological reasons; figuratively as well as literally, the Toodle family is not driving the train. The couple's social subordination is demonstrated especially through their son Rob, who is shunted onto the track of delinquency by Dombey's decision to make him a Charitable Grinder.

two: The Arrested Child-Man and Social Threat

1. And it would remain a keynote of Hartley Coleridge's image as well. The poem was cited throughout the Victorian period (and beyond) as providing biographical insight at once efficient and effective. See, e.g., Bagehot 29; Sir Nathaniel 125; Stoddard 199; and Francis. For a more recent discussion of Hartley Coleridge's relationship to childhood over the course of his life, see Plotz ch. 5.

2. I discuss this phenomenon at length in *Boys Will Be Girls*.

3. The misery that can attend childhood is encapsulated in a brief episode in which the young Paul meets his "first chum," a boy who promptly commits suicide (while Paul looks on) in order to escape abuse (53).

4. The phrase *bread and cheese and kisses*, initially Jonathan Swift's definition of "bachelor's fare," was picked up in the nineteenth century in more than one comic song and as the title of a Christmas story by Benjamin Farjeon, among other occurrences. It typically connoted a kind of no-frills, sexually emphatic romance that has little attraction for Paul, who seems happiest loving from a distance.

5. While readers will understand Skimpole's enactment of childlike behavior as fraudulent, an essay in role-playing that enables him to evade duty, this evasion itself marks him as less than a man. He is indeed a child-man, but not in the innocent sense of the term. The inability to interpret Skimpole correctly establishes Jarndyce's naïve reluctance to understand that *child* encompasses the childish as well as the childlike. A thoroughgoing Romantic in this area, Jarndyce has too strongly repressed the Puritan vision of the unredeemed or ego-driven child.

6. Nordau's critics included the novelist Vernon Lee (writing in the *Fortnightly Review* in 1896) and the playwright George Bernard Shaw, who titled his 1895 riposte in *Liberty* "A Degenerate's View of Nordau." Mackenzie Bartlett adds, "Other critics who attacked Nordau included A. E. Hake, whose *Regeneration* (1895) primarily criticises Nordau for lacking a sense of humour, and Dr. William Hirsch, who argues in his psychological study *Genius and Degeneration* (1897) that Nordau consistently misuses the term degeneration (a term which, he argues, belongs only to the study of mental disorders)" (n. 3). *Degeneration* was one of a number of works by Nordau in which he sought to expose what he saw as the flaws and corruption of his era. Thus other Nordau titles include, for example, *Conventional Lies of Our Civilization* (1883, trans. 1895) and *The Malady of the Century* (1887, trans. 1895).

7. As we shall see in chapter 3, some writers saw New Women as arrested child-women; here, however, Grand unambiguously ascribes adulthood to her salvific figure. Cartoonists responded to such images of female power with magazine images featuring horrifyingly oversized women dominating helpless men. See, e.g., an American example from *Harper's Weekly*, 2 Nov. 1901, entitled "Sarah Grand and 'Mere Man,'" showing a tiny man skewered and wriggling in an undignified way on the end of Grand's pen, reprinted in Mangum, *Grand* 194 and cover; or Scott Rankin's illustration "People I Have Never Met: Grant Allen," in the *Idler*, July 1894, 153, which depicts a harridan looming over Allen, the latter appearing in the guise of an unwilling small schoolboy.

8. Ellis's position here is inconsistent. Two years later, in 1894, he argues that "simply because she is nearer to the child," woman "represents more nearly than man the human type to which man is approximating. This is true of physical characters: the

large-headed, delicate-faced, small-boned man of urban civilisation is much nearer to the typical woman than is the savage" (*Man* 447). Children, in other words, are here more highly evolved than the normal adult man, not less. In part this volte-face, an effective illustration of the plasticity of childhood as a concept even within the mind of a single Victorian individual, seems determined by context. In a discussion of masculine imperfection, children can be likened to criminals, while in a discussion of feminine delicacy, they look like angels. In both cases they represent a heightened version of the characteristics of the adults under discussion.

9. "There's all the past as well as all the future in a man's mind," Marlow muses in a passage crossed out in the manuscript (38n4). In contrast, the Russian child-man whom Marlow encounters, with his "beardless boyish face" and childlike eyes and nose (53), represents a better sort of arrested development because of his egolessness: "If the absolutely pure, uncalculating, unpractical spirit of adventure had ever ruled a human being, it ruled this be-patched youth. I almost envied him the possession of this modest and clear flame. It seemed to have consumed all thought of self so completely that even while he was talking to you, you forgot that it was he—the man before your eyes—who had gone through these things" (55).

10. See Taylor 93–102 for a discussion of how "Sully's work highlights the connections and tensions between mid-nineteenth-century theories of the unconscious and concepts of childhood and evolution" (93), including Sully's take on the atavistic aspects of childhood and how they might resurface in the adult.

11. The pattern of twinning in Wilde's novel, particularly as regards age, is of course stressed through the trope of the portrait, which bears the physical signs of Dorian's aging for him but, like a child, is kept locked in his old nursery. I thank Sara Day for her interesting remarks to me on this subject.

three: Women as Girls

1. I owe the term *infantuation* to Dennis Denisoff, who coined it to describe the theme of the 2005 conference of the Nineteenth Century Studies Association. This book grows out of that meeting.

2. A brief discussion of the series in which *The Child-Wife* was published appears in the introduction to the present volume.

3. Robson identifies stasis as among the characteristics of the ideal Victorian girl; see, e.g., her consideration of Dickens's Little Nell, esp. 87–90.

4. Somewhat similarly, Christine Roth details the "cult of the little girl" between 1860 and 1911, which was characterized by an obsessive mixture of eroticism and purity-worship and which in its most famous manifestations—John Ruskin and Rose La Touche, Charles Lutwidge Dodgson and "child-friends" such as Alice Liddell—tended to substitute for matrimony rather than to participate in it. While Roth's interest is in the interaction between adult men and young girls, the arrested child-woman also speaks to this phenomenon, insofar as men may see her as simultaneously pure and sexually available.

5. See Shields for a discussion of *Olive*'s treatment of nationality and ethnicity.

6. To invoke the actress is also to invoke the audience: for whom is Lady Audley performing, and at whose behest? Lynette Felber suggests that "while Braddon reveals

[through her description of Robert's and George's viewing of the portrait] the power-lessness of Victorian women subordinated by the male gaze, she also exposes the dis-simulation of those Victorian men who create empty fantasies, unable to confront the real objects of their desires and the true nature of their fears" (477).

7. This contrast has long been a focus for critical discussion of *Adam Bede*; see, e.g., Higdon, whose 1972 exploration of the iconography of the chapter (mirrors versus window, comb versus Bible) remains useful.

8. Contrast Hetty and Lady Audley's resistance to development with the altruistic Miss Mowcher's situation: she is surrounded by physically normal people who, in per-ceiving her as an insensate object, deny her ability to experience life at all. The contrast between Miss Mowcher's bitter self-revelation to David and her usual mode of self-presentation, which is comic, affiliates her with the figure of the tragic clown, amusing an audience despite a breaking heart. In other words, while the embracing of stasis is identified as a problem within texts about flawed child-women, the presumption that she cannot experience or feel in meaningful ways is imposed upon the virtuous child-woman from outside by a public invested in her stasis. Either way, stasis seems hard to escape.

9. Similarly, as we shall see in chapter 5, arrested child-men may be paired with their precocious counterparts, Dick Bultitude with his father or Alan Breck Stewart with David Balfour.

10. Recent examples of this approach include Lisa Hopkins's *Giants of the Past: Pop-ular Fictions and the Idea of Evolution* (2004).

11. Iveta Jusová comments that for some Victorian readers Egerton's remarks would "have simply reasserted the predominant placement of women on a lower level of the evolutionary ladder" (60), and certainly the tendency to see women's supposed "childlike" qualities as positive was not universal. Darwin writes in *The Descent of Man* (1871) that "some, at least, of [women's] faculties are characteristic of the lower races, and therefore of a past and lower state of civilisation" (470). Similarly, Carole Silver reports that in "dissecting a Bushwoman, anatomists Sir William Flower and James Murie were first struck with the 'remarkable agreement between [her proportions] and those of the European child between four and six. It would indeed appear as if the proportions of a child of that age had been permanently retained'" (133); their obser-vations do not imply that they perceived Bushwomen as somehow superior to the Western male.

12. Consider, for instance, Stevenson's Edward Hyde and Quilp in Dickens's *The Old Curiosity Shop*, who, while not a child-man because he is never described as child-like, is made the more repellent by his evident sexual attraction to child-women, his wife and Little Nell.

13. According to Sally Ledger, "It is now generally accepted that the fall of Oscar Wilde led to a general decline in the fortunes of writers in the 'new' literary schools of the *fin de siècle*. . . . *Punch* proudly announced, 'THE END OF THE NEW WOMAN.—The Crash Has Come at Last' in December 1895" (xi).

14. See Ledger xii–xiii for a discussion of nineteenth-century responses to these works. In the first year of its publication, *Keynotes* sold approximately six thousand copies, an impressive number for an unknown writer.

four: Girls as Women

1. Before 1875, the age of consent was twelve, but with the legal distinction that carnal knowledge of a girl under ten was a felony, but a misdemeanor when the girl was aged ten through twelve. The age of consent for girls became sixteen in 1885. Boys were not included in age-of-consent legislation until 1880, but Louise Jackson notes that in their case "the age of criminal responsibility—14—functioned for much of the century as an age of consent" because sexual contact between males was a criminal offense (14); thus the boy under fourteen would not be prosecuted for having consensual sex, while his older male partner would.

2. The census for 1851 puts the city's total population at approximately 2.65 million. Carolyn Steedman contends that in Victorian discussions of street traders, "girls were depicted out of proportion to their numbers" because they were more readily sentimentalized than boys (114).

3. See, e.g., Susan Egenolf's discussion of John Raphael Smith's 1780 mezzotint of a portrait by the painter Johann Zoffany of a nubile watercress vendor (82).

4. Some editions of Mayhew's *London Labour and the London Poor* contain an engraving of a coster girl selling apples; however, this illustration does not face the interview, and the text makes clear that the young woman in the picture is not the young woman whose remarks Mayhew quotes.

5. Since membership in the workforce was by no means unusual for thirteen-year-olds in the 1860s, the "most children" of the author's invoking are clearly middle-class.

6. Elsewhere in the piece she is denominated "convex" (see, e.g., 329).

7. For a discussion of a different aspect of this novel, see chapter 1. I examine Burnett's handling of the father-daughter bond in the context of American adoption novels in Nelson, "Wealth."

8. Reflecting on how happy her own situation might have been "if [Edward] had only loved her," Olivia seems particularly angered by what she considers Mary's inferiority to her adult self; she thinks of Edward's beloved as "a pale-faced child [who] had come between her and this redemption" (150).

9. Among other responses, we may well choose to read *The Child Wife* in the context of Vladimir Nabokov's *Lolita*, and Nabokov scholars have made clear that Lolita's resemblance to Blanche is no accident. See, for instance, Don Barton Johnson's exploration of the Russian-born writer's debt to Reid, a boyhood idol. A later article (and subsequent book chapter) by Elizabeth Freeman discusses *The Child Wife* in the context of the American "pedophiliac picaresque" and identifies the tale as "the novel that most directly influenced *Lolita*" (868).

10. Even in 2012 it was possible to send "To Olivia"—which addresses Olivia as "White flake of childhood, clinging so / To my soiled raiment, thy shy snow / At tenderest touch will shrink and go," and explains, "Because thy arrows, not yet dire, / Are still unbarbed with destined fire, / I fear thee more than hadst thou stood / Full-panoplied in womanhood" (lines 3–5, 11–14)—as part of a commercial e-card to a beloved. See www.poemhunter.com/poem/to-olivia/ (accessed 8 January 2012).

11. "Fifteen years" in this line evidently refers to the publication date of *Sister-Songs*; however, Thompson's preface to the first edition of his work notes, "This poem . . . was written some four years ago, about the same date as the *Hound of Heaven*" (n. pag.). Monica Meynell would have been eleven at that time.

five: Boys as Men

1. I do not mean to suggest here that Victorian and Edwardian boys were never represented as sexual objects or sexual actors, but rather that such representations do not typically entail age inversion—even though, as we have seen, the case is otherwise with eroticized representations of girls. A partial explanation may lie in social responses to adult attraction to the young. Men could marry girls in their mid-teens, as Mayne Reid did, as soon as they could persuade the girls' guardians that the girls in question were ready for marriage, in effect were older than their years. But men whose sexual interests were directed toward boys gained nothing from contending that the boys should be deemed consenting adults, since all male homosexual acts were criminal offenses. If anything, such men gained advantage (intellectually though not legally) from invoking the model of ancient Greece and its institutionalized pederasty, as John Addington Symonds does in *A Problem in Greek Ethics* (written 1873, privately published 1883), which stresses the moral benefits the Greeks claimed for the practice. In this model, the boy is envisioned not as a fellow, if younger, adult but as a beloved distinguished from the lover by his youth, which substitutes for gender difference and thus is emphasized rather than erased.

2. For a discussion of Bart as changeling, see Silver 78, 80. Some of the medical authorities cited in Silver's chapter associate the changeling myth with the syndrome more recently known as "failure to thrive," which is characterized, notes Joyce Munro, by "voracious and strange appetites, hyperactivity and disturbed interpersonal relationships" (qtd. in Silver 75–76), qualities that could be said to apply, at least metaphorically, to all the Smallweeds.

3. Age inversions occur throughout *Bleak House*, to sinister effect. Even an apparently benevolent instance, Mr. Jarndyce's nicknaming of Esther in a way that assigns her to the category of the elderly, is disturbing in its erasure of her identity, although he intends the epithets as a playful tribute to her virtue: "[I was] called Old Woman, and Little Old Woman, and Cobweb, and Mrs. Shipton, and Mother Hubbard, and Dame Durden, and so many names of that sort, that my own name soon became quite lost among them" (148). Yet elsewhere Dickens occasionally implies that age inversion may be the means for restoring morality. In her report on the manuscript of the present book, Teresa Mangum suggested of *A Christmas Carol* (1843) that Scrooge may be "an unusually complex case—revisiting his childhood and becoming a child in order to bond with a child now that he's a properly childlike adult." As Chase notes, it is "with the happy squeal that 'I'm quite a baby'" that this "old man embraces his recovered humanity" (13).

4. Tom's upbringing is closer to Bart's than to the Dodger's inasmuch as he too has been permitted no acquaintance with fancy, but it is the Dodger who is brought to mind by a description of Tom hiding in Sleary's circus after robbing Bounderby's bank, disguised "in a preposterous coat, like a beadle's, with cuffs and flaps exaggerated to an unspeakable extent; in an immense waistcoat, knee-breeches, buckled shoes, and a mad cocked hat; with nothing fitting him, and everything of coarse material, moth-eaten and full of holes" (208). While Tom is a young adult at the time, the garb visually identifies him as what he has been from his earliest years, a child uncomfortably trapped in a man's role. Louisa too has had precocity forced upon her, but her affection for Tom (which he is incapable of reciprocating to any meaningful extent until he is on his deathbed) makes her a far more sympathetic character than he is.

5. As the narrator points out, this bereavement has made domestic happiness harder for the Bultitudes, since "no doubt the loss of a mother's loving tact, which can check the heedless merriment before it becomes intolerable, and interpret and soften the most peevish and unreasonable of rebukes, had done much to make the relations between parent and children more strained than they might otherwise have been" (4–5). From Paul's perspective, however, the loss of his wife may primarily mean that he now has fewer distractions from the business world. As his response to Dulcie suggests, Paul is consistently against romance throughout the novel.

6. Stableford notes that Guthrie wrote only one work specifically intended for children, the 1902 fantasy *Only Toys*, which "counsels children against being too eager to emerge from the nursery into the adult world" (72).

7. See Nelson, *Boys* 128–31.

8. As I have argued in earlier chapters, the "ideal" was far from being the only association made with childhood during the period under discussion; however, Dickens, Guthrie, and Stevenson all adopt Romantic perspectives in works examined in this chapter.

9. For many productive discussions of *The Heavenly Twins*, my thanks to Martha Vicinus and my fellow participants in the NEH summer seminar hosted by the University of Michigan in 1992.

10. Elaine Showalter quotes Charles F. Marshall, a former assistant surgeon at the Hospital for Diseases of the Skin at Blackfriars, London, who in 1906 recorded a description of the syphilitic infant in terms similar to those that Grand uses. Marshall describes such a child as a "small, wizened, atrophied, weakly, sickly creature," like a "monkey or a little old man" (Showalter, "Syphilis" 95; Marshall 328). Even so, Marshall also provides a detailed list of symptoms of infantile syphilis that is essentially identical to its twenty-first-century counterparts (333). Observing that some of Grand's contemporaries were able to publish works that give much more frank and elaborate descriptions of syphilitic symptoms than may be found in *The Heavenly Twins*, Meegan Kennedy points out that "it is remarkable that a novel designed to shock Victorian readers out of their complacency regarding the horror of syphilis . . . contents itself with infrequent euphemisms like 'ghastly' for the sores and suppurating flesh of end-stage syphilis" (269). That Grand evidently considered the invoking of age inversion a satisfactory substitute for more literal descriptions suggests the late nineteenth-century power of age inversion's associations with the unnatural and with the damaged family.

Conclusion: The Adult Reader as Child

1. Some critics conveyed their praise for *Treasure Island* by suggesting that Stevenson's talents were worthy of a better field. The unsigned *Pall Mall* review of 15 December 1883, for instance, remarks, "It is clear that fiction is a field in which Mr. Stevenson is even stronger than in essay and in humorous and sentimental journeying. After this romance for boys he must give us a novel for men and women" (qtd. in N. Wood 78).

2. To be sure, not all investigators draw a firm line between childhood experience and adult literary output. Studies such as Michael Kotzin's *Dickens and the Fairy Tale* (1972) and Harry Stone's *Dickens and the Invisible World* (1979) have traced the influence of a childhood spent with Aesop, the brothers Grimm, Charles Perrault, and the *Arabian Nights* upon Dickens's fiction. Useful as investigations of this type are, however,

they address a somewhat different phenomenon than the one that forms the subject of this concluding chapter.

3. For publishing information, see Houghton 191; Richards 52; and K. Joseph 7.

4. This strategy would remain popular in later texts for self-improvement. Anne Morey, for instance, notes of a Hollywood correspondence school for aspiring screenwriters in the 1910s and 1920s that "while standardization was the key to turning students into successful screenwriters, the apparent promotion of individuality was the key to recruitment of students in the first place" (72).

5. Samuel Garratt's "The Irish in London," in *Motives for Missions* (1852), can afford to be particularly forthright because its subject is a despised minority. "For the most part, the native Irish of London know nothing," he notes, adding, "You must speak to them as if they were children" (qtd. in Garwood 263).

6. "It is too amorous throughout. . . . You are too pure-minded yourself to feel this—but I assure you the swimming scenes and love scenes would be to many children seriously harmful," Ruskin wrote in a letter of 22 July 1863 (qtd. in Knoepflmacher, *Ventures* 138).

Works Cited

Primary Works

Acton, William. "Extent of Prostitution." In *Prostitution, Considered in Its Moral, Social and Sanitary Aspects*, 15–19. London: John Churchill, 1857.

Adler, Nettie, and R. H. Tawney. *Boy and Girl Labour*. London: Women's Industrial Council, 1909.

Adye, Frederic. "Old-Fashioned Children." *Macmillan's* 68 (Aug. 1893): 286–92.

Anstey, F. [Thomas Anstey Guthrie]. *Vice Versâ: A Lesson to Fathers*. 4th ed. London: Smith, Elder, 1882.

Ashford, Faith. *Child-Man in Britain*. London: G. G. Harrap, 1913. www.archive.org /details/childmaninbritaiooashfiala. Accessed 15 May 2008.

Bagehot, Walter. "Hartley Coleridge." 1852. In *Estimations in Criticism*, vol. 1, *Poets and Poetry*, ed. Cuthbert Lennox, 1–39. London: Andrew Melrose, 1908.

"Belles Lettres." *Westminster Review* 130 (July–Dec. 1888): 112–18.

Bennett, Arnold. *Clayhanger*. New York: Dutton, 1910.

Braddon, Mary Elizabeth. *John Marchmont's Legacy*. 1862–64. Ed. Toru Sasaki and Norman Page. New York: Oxford University Press, 1999.

———. *Lady Audley's Secret*. 1861–62. Ed. David Skilton. New York: Oxford University Press, 1987.

———. "The Shadow in the Corner." 1879. In *Flower and Weed; and Other Tales*, 259–77. London: Simpkin, Marshall, Hamilton, Kent, 1891.

Brontë, Charlotte. *Villette*. 1853. New York: Dutton, 1978.

[Brown, Samuel]. "Ghosts and Ghost-Seers." *North British Review* 9.18 (Aug. 1848): 393–416.

Buckman, S. S. "Babies and Monkeys." *Nineteenth Century* 36 (Nov. 1894): 727–43.

Bulwer-Lytton, Edward. *The Coming Race*. Edinburgh: William Blackwood and Sons, 1871.

Burnett, Frances Hodgson. *A Little Princess*. 1905. New York: Dell, 1979.

Carlyle, Thomas. "The Hero as Poet: Dante; Shakspeare." In *On Heroes and Hero Worship and the Heroic in History*, 94–135. Whitefish, MT: Kessinger, 2003.

———. *The Life of Friedrich Schiller, Comprehending an Examination of His Works*. New York: George Dearborn, 1837.

———. *Past and Present*. 1843. London: Chapman & Hall, 1870.

———. *Pen Portraits by Thomas Carlyle: Found in His Works and Correspondence by R. Brimley Johnson*. London: George Allen, 1896.

Chamberlain, Alexander F. "The Child Type." *Pedagogical Seminary* 6 (1898–99): 471–84.

"Childhood." *Blackwood's Magazine* 12.67 (1822): 139–45.

"The Child Wife: A Tale of the Two Worlds; By Captain Mayne Reid." Book review. *American Quarterly Church Review* 21 (Apr. 1869): 154.

Clyde, Alton. "Effie's Trial." *Quiver*, 3rd ser., 2 (1 June 1867): 577–80.

Coates, Thomas F. G., and R. S. Warren Bell. *Marie Corelli: The Writer and the Woman.* London: Hutchinson, 1903.

Coleridge, Hartley. "Sonnet IX." In *Poems*, 1:9. Leeds: F. E. Bingley, 1833.

Coleridge, S. T. "Essay 1." In *The Friend: A Series of Essays, in Three Volumes, to Aid in the Formation of Fixed Principles in Politics, Morals, and Religion, with Literary Amusements Interspersed*, 3:67–92. New ed. London: Printed for Rest Fenner, 1818.

Collins, Wilkie. *The Woman in White.* 1859–60. New York: Penguin, 1974.

Conrad, Joseph. *Heart of Darkness.* Ed. Robert Kimbrough. 3rd ed. New York: Norton, 1988.

"Contemporary Literature." *Ladies' Repository* 29 (Feb. 1869): 155–58.

Corelli, Marie [Mary Mackay]. *The Mighty Atom.* London: Hutchinson, 1896.

"Current Literature." *Overland Monthly* 2.3 (Mar. 1869): 289–96.

Darwin, Charles. *The Descent of Man.* 2nd ed. 1874. www.forgottenbooks.org/info /9781605062815. Accessed 1 Feb. 2010.

Dickens, Charles. *Bleak House.* 1852–53. New York: Penguin, 1981.

———. *The Child Wife from the David Copperfield of Charles Dickens.* New York: John W. Anderson, 1878.

———. *David Copperfield.* 1849–50. New York: Bantam, 1981.

———. *Dombey and Son.* 1846–48. New York: Oxford University Press, 1982.

———. *Hard Times.* 1854. New York: Norton, 1990.

———. *Nicholas Nickleby.* 1838–39. Ed. Michael Slater. New York: Penguin, 1978.

———. *The Old Curiosity Shop.* 1840–41. New York: Oxford University Press, 1999.

———. *Oliver Twist.* 1837–39. New York: Penguin, 1986.

———. *Our Mutual Friend.* 1864–65. New York: Penguin, 1997.

———. Speech of 9 February 1858, given at the Anniversary Festival of the Hospital for Sick Children. In *Speeches: Literary and Social*, transcribed from the 1880 Chatto and Windus edition by David Price, 46–49. Project Gutenberg, www.readeasily. com/charles-dickens/00117/001170049.php.

Doyle, Arthur Conan. *The Sign of Four.* 1890. In *The Complete Sherlock Holmes*, 89–173. Garden City, NY: Garden City, 1938.

Du Maurier, George. *Trilby.* New York: Harper & Brothers, 1894.

Ecker, Alexander. "On a Characteristic Peculiarity in the Form of the Female Skull, and Its Significance for Comparative Anthropology." *Anthropological Review* 6 (Oct. 1868): 350–56.

Egerton, George [Mary Chavelita Dunne]. *Symphonies.* London: John Lane, 1897.

Eliot, George [Mary Ann Evans]. *Adam Bede.* 1859. New York: Penguin, 1985.

Ellis, Havelock. *The Criminal.* London: Walter Scott, 1892.

———. *Man and Woman: A Study of Human Secondary Sexual Characters.* 1894. 4th ed. London: Walter Scott, 1904.

Ewing, Juliana Horatia. *Mary's Meadow.* 1883–84. In *Mary's Meadow, Snap-Dragons, Dandelion Clocks, and Other Stories*, 1–93. Boston: Little, Brown, 1900.

———. *The Story of a Short Life.* 1872. In *The Story of a Short Life, Jackanapes, and Daddy Darwin's Dovecot*, 1–138. New York: A. L. Burt, n.d.

Forster, John. *The Life of Charles Dickens.* Vol. 1, *1812–1842.* Philadelphia: Lippincott, 1874.

Francis, J. "Hartley Coleridge." *New York Times,* 8 Dec. 1900, BR54.

Freud, Sigmund. *Civilization and Its Discontents.* 1930. Trans., ed., and intro. James Strachey. New York: Norton, 1961.

———. "The 'Uncanny.'" *New Literary History* 7.3 (Spring 1976): 619–45. First published in *The Standard Edition of the Complete Psychological Works of Sigmund Freud,* trans., ed., and rev. James Strachey, vol. 17 (London: Hogarth, 1955).

Garwood, John. *The Million-Peopled City; or, One-Half of the People of London Made Known to the Other Half.* London: Wertheim & Macintosh, 1853. www.victorianlondon.org/publications4/peopled.htm. Accessed 24 July 2004.

Geddes, Patrick, and J. Arthur Thomson. *The Evolution of Sex.* 1889. New York: Scribner & Welford, 1890.

Graham, Jeffrey. "Cui Bono? Or, the Story of Chloe Tenterden." *Belgravia Annual* 34 (Christmas 1877): 45–70.

Grand, Sarah [Frances Clarke McFall]. *The Heavenly Twins.* 1893. Ann Arbor: University of Michigan Press, 1993.

———. "The New Aspect of the Woman Question." *North American Review* 158 (Mar. 1894): 270–76.

"A Group of Story-Tellers: George Egerton." *Literary World,* n.s., 56 (23 July 1897): 67–68.

Haggard, H. Rider. *Ayesha: The Return of She.* 1905. New York: Ballantine, 1978.

———. *King Solomon's Mines.* 1885. New York: Puffin, 1985.

———. *She.* 1886–87. New York: Oxford University Press, 1998.

Hardy, Thomas. *Jude the Obscure.* 1894–95. New York: Oxford University Press, 1985.

Harper, Charles G. Preface to *Revolted Woman: Past, Present, and to Come,* ix–xi. London: Elkin Mathews, 1894.

Hering, Jeanie [Marion Adams-Acton]. *Elf.* London: George Routledge & Sons, 1887.

Hibbert Ware, Mary Clementina. *Dr. Harcourt's Assistant: A Tale of the Present Day.* 3 vols. London: T. Cautley Newby, 1868.

Holyoake, Maltus Questell. "Captain Mayne Reid: Soldier and Novelist." *Strand* 2 (July–Dec. 1891): 93–102.

[Jacox, Francis]. *Cues from All Quarters; Or, Literary Musings of a Clerical Recluse.* London: Hodder & Stoughton, 1871.

Jerome, Jerome K. *Paul Kelver.* New York: Dodd, Mead, 1902.

Kavanagh, Julia. *Daisy Burns: A Tale.* New York: D. Appleton, 1853.

Knight, George. *Sapphira of the Stage.* London: Jarrold & Sons, 1896.

"Literary Notices." *Congregational Review* 9.45 (Jan. 1869): 104–14.

MacDonald, George. "The Fantastic Imagination." 1893. In *The Gifts of the Child Christ: Fairy Tales and Stories for the Childlike,* ed. Glenn Edward Sadler, 1:23–28. Grand Rapids, MI: Eerdmans, 1973.

———. "The Gifts of the Child Christ." 1882. In *The Gifts of the Child Christ: Fairy Tales and Stories for the Childlike,* ed. Glenn Edward Sadler, 1:31–60. Grand Rapids, MI: Eerdmans, 1973.

Marshall, C. F. *Syphilology and Venereal Disease.* 2nd ed. New York: William Wood, 1912.

Maudsley, Henry. "The Genesis of Mind." Pt. 2. *Journal of Mental Science* 8 (1862): 61–102.

Mayhew, Henry. *London Labour and the London Poor: The Condition and Earnings of Those that Will Work, Cannot Work, and Will Not Work.* Vol. 1, *London Street-Folk.* 1851. London: Charles Griffin, n.d.

Milnes, Richard Monckton. "Second Childhood." In *Poems: A Selection from the Works of Lord Houghton*, 89–91. London: Edward Moxon, 1868.

Montgomery, Florence. *Misunderstood.* 1869. Leipzig: Tauchnitz, n.d.

Müller, F. Max. "The Story of an Indian Child-Wife." *Contemporary Review* 60 (Aug. 1891): 183–87.

Mulock [Craik], Dinah. *Olive: A Young Girl's Triumph over Prejudice.* 1850. New York: Oxford University Press, 1996.

———. "To Novelists—and a Novelist." *Macmillan's* 3 (1861): 441–48.

Nordau, Max. *Degeneration.* Translated from the Second Edition of the German Work. 4th ed. New York: D. Appleton, 1895.

O'Reilly, Rev. Bernard. *The Mirror of True Womanhood: A Book of Instruction for Women in the World.* 16th ed. New York: P. J. Kenedy, Excelsior Catholic Publishing House, 1886.

Ouida [Marie Louise de la Ramée]. "The New Woman." *North American Review* 158 (May 1894): 610–19.

Reid, Elizabeth Hyde. *Captain Mayne Reid: His Life and Adventures.* Assisted by Charles H. Coe. London: Greening, 1900.

Reid, Mayne. *The Child Wife.* 1868. London: Routledge, 1905.

"The Reviews Reviewed." *Review of Reviews* 4.19 (July 1891): 171–80.

Sala, George Augustus. "Strollers at Dumbledowndeary." In *Gaslight and Daylight, With Some London Scenes They Shine Upon*, 315–30. London: Chapman & Hall, 1859.

Saleeby, Monica. "Retrospect." In *Eyes of Youth: A Book of Verse*, by Padraic Colum et al., 81–82. 1910. London: Burns & Oates, 1912.

Sir Nathaniel. "Scissors-and-Paste-Work: Select Letters of Robert Southey." *New Monthly Magazine* 107 (1856): 116–26.

Smiles, Samuel. *Self-Help: With Illustrations of Conduct and Perseverance.* 1859. Abr. ed., Harmondsworth, UK: Penguin, 1986.

Stables, Gordon. *From Squire to Squatter: A Tale of the Old Land and the New.* London: John F. Shaw, 1888.

[Stead, W. T.]. *The Maiden Tribute of Modern Babylon: The Report of the "Pall Mall Gazette's" Secret Commission.* 1885. London: Richard Lambert, n.d.

Stevenson, Robert Louis. *Kidnapped: Being Memoirs of the Adventures of David Balfour in the Year 1751.* 1886. New York: Scribner's, 1941.

———. *The Strange Case of Dr. Jekyll and Mr. Hyde.* 1886. Ed. Susan J. Wolfson and Barry V. Qualls. Acton, MA: Copley, 2000.

Stoddard, Richard Henry. "Hartley Coleridge." In *Under the Evening Lamp*, 182–99. New York: Charles Scribner's Sons, 1892.

Stoker, Bram. *Dracula.* 1897. Ed. Nina Auerbach and David J. Skal. New York: Norton, 1997.

Thackeray, William Makepeace. *Vanity Fair: A Novel Without a Hero.* 1847–48. Ed. Geoffrey Tillotson and Kathleen Tillotson. Boston: Houghton Mifflin, 1963.

Thompson, Francis. *Sister-Songs: An Offering to Two Sisters.* London: John Lane, 1895.

Travels in the East. 1884. In *One Dinner a Week and Travels in the East*, 32–141. High Wycombe, Bucks.: Marcan, 1987.

[Vernon, John Richard]. "Dog-Violet and Mignonette." *Tinsleys' Magazine*, Jan. 1876, 45–64.

Wells, H. G. *The Time Machine*. 1895. In *The Time Machine and The Invisible Man*, ed. Alfred Mac Adam. New York: Barnes & Noble, 2003.

Wood, L. S., ed. *A Book of English Verse on Infancy and Childhood*. London: Macmillan, 1923.

Woolf, Virginia. "Professions for Women." www.sfu.ca/~scheel/english338/Professions.htm. Accessed 19 Mar. 2009.

Secondary Works

Adrian, Arthur. "Dickens and Inverted Parenthood." *Dickensian* 67 (1971): 3–11.

———. *Dickens and the Parent-Child Relationship*. Athens: Ohio University Press, 1984.

Andrews, Malcolm. *Dickens and the Grown-Up Child*. Iowa City: University of Iowa Press, 1994.

Ariès, Philippe. *Centuries of Childhood*. Trans. Robert Baldick. New York: Vintage, 1962.

Banfield, Marie. "Darwinism, Doxology, and Energy Physics: The New Sciences, the Poetry and the Poetics of Gerard Manley Hopkins." *Victorian Poetry* 45.2 (Summer 2007): 175–94.

Bartlett, Mackenzie. "'The pleasure of fiends': Degenerate Laughter in Stoker's *Dracula*." In "Evolutions," special issue, *Forum: The University of Edinburgh Postgraduate Journal of Culture and the Arts*, Apr. 2007. forum.llc.ed.ac.uk/si1/bartlett.html#ref3. Accessed 18 Mar. 2009.

Baym, Nina. *Woman's Fiction: A Guide to Novels by and about Women in America, 1820–1870*. 1978. Ithaca, NY: Cornell University Press, 1980.

Berman, Jeffrey. "Infanticide and Object Loss in *Jude the Obscure*." In *Compromise Formations: Current Directions in Psychoanalytic Criticism*, ed. Vera J. Camden, 155–81. Kent, OH: Kent State University Press, 1989.

Berry, Laura. *The Child, the State, and the Victorian Novel*. Charlottesville: University of Virginia Press, 1999.

Blake, Kathleen. "Sue Bridehead, 'The Woman of the Feminist Movement.'" *Studies in English Literature, 1500–1900* 18.4 (Autumn 1978): 703–26.

Block, Ed, Jr. "James Sully, Evolutionist Psychology, and Late Victorian Gothic Fiction." *Victorian Studies* 25.4 (Summer 1982): 443–67.

Boehmer, Elleke. Introduction to *Scouting for Boys: A Handbook for Instruction in Good Citizenship*, by Robert Baden-Powell, xi–xxxix. Oxford: Oxford University Press, 2004.

Bubel, Katharine. "Knowing God 'Other-wise': The Wise Old Woman Archetype in George MacDonald's *The Princess and the Goblin*, *The Princess and Curdie* and 'The Golden Key.'" *North Wind* 25 (2006): 1–17.

Buckton, Oliver. "'Mr. Betwixt-and-Between': The Politics of Narrative Indeterminacy in Stevenson's *Kidnapped* and *David Balfour*." In *Narrative Beginnings: Theories and Practices*, ed. Brian Richardson, 228–45. Omaha: University of Nebraska Press, 2008.

Casey, Janet Galligani. "Marie Corelli and Fin-de-Siècle Feminism." *English Language in Transition* 35.2 (1992): 163–78.

Chase, Karen. *The Victorians and Old Age*. Oxford: Oxford University Press, 2009.

Clausen, Christopher. "How to Join the Middle Classes: With the Help of Dr. Smiles and Mrs. Beeton." *American Scholar* 62.3 (1993): 403–18.

Colley, Ann C. "'Writing Towards Home': The Landscape of *A Child's Garden of Verses*." In *Robert Louis Stevenson Reconsidered: New Critical Perspectives*, ed. William B. Jones Jr., 174–91. Jefferson, NC: McFarland, 2003.

Craft, Christopher. "'Kiss Me with Those Red Lips': Gender and Inversion in Bram Stoker's *Dracula*." *Representations* 8 (Fall 1984): 107–33.

Darby, Margaret Flanders. "Dora and Doady." *Dickens Studies Annual* 22 (1993): 155–69.

Deane, Bradley. "Mummy Fiction and the Occupation of Egypt: Imperial Striptease." *English Literature in Transition, 1880–1920* 51.4 (2008): 381–410.

Demers, Patricia, and Gordon Moyles, eds. *From Instruction to Delight: An Anthology of Children's Literature to 1850*. Toronto: Oxford University Press, 1982.

Denisoff, Dennis. "'Men of My Own Sex': Genius, Sexuality, and George Du Maurier's Artists." In *Victorian Sexual Dissidence*, ed. Richard Dellamora, 147–69. Chicago: University of Chicago Press, 1995.

Dickson, Donald R. "'In a mirror that mirrors the soul': Masks and Mirrors in Dorian Gray." *English Literature in Transition, 1880–1920* 26.1 (1983): 5–15.

Driscoll, William. "The Metaphor of Syphilis in Grand's *Heavenly Twins*." *Nineteenth-Century Gender Studies* 5.1 (Spring 2009). www.ncgsjournal.com/issue51/driscoll.htm. Accessed 18 July 2010.

Dutta, Shanta. *Ambivalence in Hardy: A Study of His Attitude to Women*. 2000. London: Anthem, 2010.

Egenolf, Susan B. *The Art of Political Fiction in Hamilton, Edgeworth, and Owenson*. Burlington, VT: Ashgate, 2009.

Etherington, Norman. Introduction to *The Annotated "She": A Critical Edition of H. Rider Haggard's Victorian Romance*, ed. Norman Etherington, xv–xliv. Bloomington: Indiana University Press, 1991.

Farrell, Kirby. *Post-Traumatic Culture: Injury and Interpretation in the Nineties*. Baltimore: Johns Hopkins University Press, 1998.

Federico, Annette. *Idol of Suburbia: Marie Corelli and Late-Victorian Literary Culture*. Charlottesville: University Press of Virginia, 2000.

Felber, Lynette. "The Literary Portrait as Centerfold: Fetishism in Mary Elizabeth Braddon's *Lady Audley's Secret*." *Victorian Literature and Culture* 35.2 (2007): 471–88.

Flegel, Monica. *Conceptualizing Cruelty to Children in Nineteenth-Century England: Literature, Representation, and the NSPCC*. Burlington, VT: Ashgate, 2009.

———. "'Masquerading Work': Class Transvestism in Victorian Texts for and about Children." *Children's Literature* 37 (2009): 61–83.

Freeman, Elizabeth. "Honeymoon with a Stranger: Pedophiliac Picaresques from Poe to Nabokov." *American Literature* 70.4 (Dec. 1998): 863–97.

Gannon, Susan R. "The Illustrator as Interpreter: N. C. Wyeth's Illustrations for the Adventure Novels of Robert Louis Stevenson." *Children's Literature* 19 (1991): 90–106.

Glover, David. "'Our Enemy Is Not Merely Spiritual': Degeneration and Modernity in Bram Stoker's *Dracula*." *Victorian Literature and Culture* 22 (1994): 249–65.

Goetsch, Paul. "Old-Fashioned Children: From Dickens to Hardy and James." *Anglini Zeitschrift für Englische Philologie* 123.1 (2005): 45–69.

Gottfried, Barbara. "Household Arrangements and the Patriarchal Order in *Bleak House*." *Journal of Narrative Technique* 24.1 (1994): 1–17.

Grylls, David. *Guardians and Angels: Parents and Children in Nineteenth-Century Literature*. London: Faber & Faber, 1978.

Gubar, Marah. *Artful Dodgers: Reconceiving the Golden Age of Children's Literature*. New York: Oxford University Press, 2009.

———. "The Drama of Precocity: Child Performers on the Victorian Stage." In *The Nineteenth-Century Child and Consumer Culture*, ed. Dennis Denisoff, 63–78. Burlington, VT: Ashgate, 2008.

Hacking, Ian. *Rewriting the Soul: Multiple Personality and the Sciences of Memory*. Princeton, NJ: Princeton University Press, 1995.

Hall, Donald E. " 'We and the World': Juliana Horatia Ewing and Victorian Colonialism for Children." *Children's Literature Association Quarterly* 16.2 (Summer 1991): 51–55.

Hartnell, Elaine. "Morals and Metaphysics: Marie Corelli, Religion and the Gothic." *Women's Writing* 13.2 (June 2006): 284–303.

Hein, Rolland. *George MacDonald: Victorian Mythmaker*. Nashville: Star Song, 1993.

Hemmings, Robert. "A Taste of Nostalgia: Children's Books from the Golden Age—Carroll, Grahame, and Milne." *Children's Literature* 35 (2007): 54–79.

Higdon, David Leon. "The Iconographic Backgrounds of *Adam Bede*, Chapter 15." *Nineteenth-Century Fiction* 27.2 (Sept. 1972): 155–70.

Hockey, Jenny, and Allison James. "Back to Our Futures: Imaging Second Childhood." In *Images of Aging: Cultural Representations of Later Life*, ed. Mike Featherstone and Andrew Wernick, 135–48. New York: Routledge, 1995.

Hoddinott, Alison. "Reading Books and Looking at Pictures in the Novels of Charlotte Brontë." *Brontë Studies* 32.1 (Mar. 2007): 1–10.

Houghton, Walter E. *The Victorian Frame of Mind, 1830–1870*. New Haven, CT: Yale University Press, 1957.

Hughes, Felicity A. "Children's Literature: Theory and Practice." *ELH* 45.3 (Autumn 1978): 542–61.

Jackson, David H. "*Treasure Island* as a Late-Victorian Adults' Novel." *Victorian Newsletter* 72 (1987): 28–32.

Jackson, Louise A. *Child Sexual Abuse in Victorian England*. New York: Routledge, 2000.

Johnson, Don Barton. "Vladimir Nabokov and Captain Mayne Reid." *Cycnos* 10.1 (Jan. 1993). //revel.unice.fr/cycnos/index.html?id=1303. Accessed 3 May 2010.

Joseph, Gerhard. "Change and the Changeling in *Dombey and Son*." *Dickens Studies Annual* 18 (1989): 179–95.

Joseph, Keith. Introduction to *Self-Help: With Illustrations of Conduct and Perseverance*, by Samuel Smiles, 7–16. Abr. ed. Harmondsworth, UK: Penguin, 1986.

Jusová, Iveta. "George Egerton: Nietzschean Feminism." In *The New Woman and the Empire*, 49–88. Columbus: Ohio State University Press, 2005.

Kennedy, Meegan. "Syphilis and the Hysterical Female: The Limits of Realism in Sarah Grand's *The Heavenly Twins*." *Women's Writing* 11.2 (2004): 259–80.

Kershner, R. B. "Modernism's Mirror: The Sorrows of Marie Corelli." In *Transforming Genres: New Approaches to British Fiction of the 1890s*, ed. Nikki Lee Manos and Meri-Jane Rochelson, 67–86. New York: St. Martin's, 1994.

Kidd, Kenneth. *Making American Boys: The Science of Boyology and the Feral Tale*. Minneapolis: University of Minnesota Press, 2004.

Kincaid, James R. *Annoying the Victorians*. New York: Routledge, 1995.

———. *Child-Loving: The Erotic Child and Victorian Culture*. New York: Routledge, 1992.

Knoepflmacher, U. C. "Hardy's Subterranean Child." In *Thomas Hardy Reappraised: Essays in Honour of Michael Millgate*, ed. Keith Wilson, 78–95. Toronto: University of Toronto Press, 2006.

———. Introduction to *A Little Princess*, by Frances Hodgson Burnett, vii–xxiii. New York: Penguin, 2002.

———. *Ventures into Childland: Victorians, Fairy Tales, and Femininity*. Chicago: University of Chicago Press, 1998.

Kucich, John. *Imperial Masochism: British Fiction, Fantasy, and Social Class*. Princeton, NJ: Princeton University Press, 2007.

Leblanc, André. "The Origins of the Concept of Dissociation: Paul Janet, His Nephew Pierre, and the Problem of Post-hypnotic Suggestion." *History of Science* 39 (2001): 57–69. articles.adsabs.harvard.edu//full/2001HiSc..39 . . . 57L/0000057.000.html. Accessed 19 Mar. 2009.

Ledger, Sally. Introduction to *Keynotes and Discords*, by George Egerton, ed. Sally Ledger, ix–xxvi. 2003. London: Continuum, 2006.

Lesnik-Oberstein, Karín. "*Oliver Twist*: The Narrator's Tale." *Textual Practice* 15.1 (2001): 87–100.

Levy, Anita. "Public Spaces, Private Eyes: Gender and the Social Work of Aesthetics in Charlotte Brontë's *Villette*." *Nineteenth-Century Contexts* 22.3 (Dec. 2000): 391–416.

Mangum, Teresa. "Little Women: The Aging Female Character in Nineteenth-Century British Children's Literature." In *Figuring Age: Women, Bodies, Generations*, ed. Kathleen Woodward, 59–87. Bloomington: Indiana University Press, 1999.

———. *Married, Middlebrow, and Militant: Sarah Grand and the New Woman Novel*. Ann Arbor: University of Michigan Press, 1998.

McCaffrey, Phillip. "Erasing the Body: Freud's Uncanny Father-Child." *American Imago* 49.4 (1992): 371–89.

Mighall, Robert. *A Geography of Victorian Gothic Fiction: Mapping History's Nightmares*. New York: Oxford University Press, 1999.

Miller, David Lee. "Charles Dickens: A Dead Hand at a Baby." In *Dreams of the Burning Child: Sacrificial Sons and the Father's Witness*, 130–59. Ithaca, NY: Cornell University Press, 2003.

———. "The Father's Witness: Patriarchal Images of Boys." *Representations* 70 (Spring 2000): 115–41.

Mitchell, Sally. *Daily Life in Victorian England*. Westport, CT: Greenwood, 1996.

———. *Dinah Mulock Craik*. Boston: Twayne, 1983. www.victorianweb.org/authors /craik/mitchell. Accessed 7 Jan. 2007.

———. *The Fallen Angel: Chastity, Class and Women's Reading, 1835–1880*. Bowling Green, OH: Bowling Green University Popular Press, 1981.

Moody, Nickianne. "Moral Uncertainty and the Afterlife: Explaining the Popularity of Marie Corelli's Early Novels." *Women's Writing* 13.2 (June 2006): 188–205.

Morey, Anne. *Hollywood Outsiders: The Adaptation of the Film Industry, 1913–1934*. Minneapolis: University of Minnesota Press, 2003.

Mulvey, Laura. "Afterthoughts on 'Visual Pleasure and Narrative Cinema' Inspired by *Duel in the Sun*." *Framework* 15/16/17 (Summer 1981): 12–15.

Murphy, Patricia. "The Gendering of History in *She*." *SEL Studies in English Literature 1500–1900* 39.4 (1999): 747–72.

———. *Time Is of the Essence: Temporality, Gender, and the New Woman*. Albany: SUNY Press, 2001.

Nelson, Claudia. *Boys Will Be Girls: The Feminine Ethic and British Children's Fiction, 1857–1917*. New Brunswick, NJ: Rutgers University Press, 1991.

———. *Invisible Men: Fatherhood in Victorian Periodicals, 1850–1910*. Athens: University of Georgia Press, 1995.

———. *Little Strangers: Portrayals of Adoption and Foster Care in America, 1850–1929*. Bloomington: Indiana University Press, 2003.

———. "A Wealth of Fatherhood: Paternal Roles in American Adoption Texts." In *Gender and Fatherhood in the Nineteenth Century*, ed. Trev Lynn Broughton and Helen Rogers, 165–77. Basingstoke: Palgrave, 2007.

Newsom, Robert. "Fictions of Childhood." In *The Cambridge Companion to Charles Dickens*, ed. John O. Jordan, 92–105. New York: Cambridge University Press, 2001.

Odden, Karen M. " 'Reading Coolly' in *John Marchmont's Legacy*: Reconsidering M. E. Braddon's Legacy." *Studies in the Novel* 36.1 (Mar. 2004): 21–41.

Plotz, Judith. *Romanticism and the Vocation of Childhood*. New York: Palgrave, 2001.

Polhemus, Robert M. *Lot's Daughters: Sex, Redemption, and Women's Quest for Authority*. Stanford, CA: Stanford University Press, 2005.

Potkay, Adam. "Beckford's Heaven of Boys." *Raritan* 13.1 (Summer 1993): 73–86.

Reimer, Mavis. "Making Princesses, Re-making *A Little Princess*." In *Voices of the Other: Children's Literature and the Postcolonial Context*, ed. Roderick McGillis, 111–34. New York: Garland, 2000.

Richards, Jeffrey. "Spreading the Gospel of Self-Help: G. A. Henty and Samuel Smiles." *Journal of Popular Culture* 16.2 (1982): 52–65.

Richardson, Angelique. "Allopathic Pills? Health, Fitness and New Woman Fictions." *Women: A Cultural Review* 10.1 (1999): 1–21.

Robson, Catherine. *Men in Wonderland: The Lost Girlhood of the Victorian Gentleman*. Princeton, NJ: Princeton University Press, 2001.

Rodrick, Anne Baltz. "The Importance of Being an Earnest Improver: Class, Caste, and *Self-Help* in Mid-Victorian England." *Victorian Literature and Culture* 29.1 (2001): 39–50.

Rosenthal, Lynne. "*Misunderstood*: A Victorian Children's Book for Adults." *Children's Literature* 1 (1974): 94–102.

Roth, Christine. "Cherry Ripe: Cult-of-the-Little-Girl Narratives in Late-Victorian Britain." Book manuscript.

Russett, Cynthia Eagle. *Sexual Science: The Victorian Construction of Womanhood*. Cambridge, MA: Harvard University Press, 1989.

Schotland, Sara D. "Who's That in Charge? It's Jenny Wren, 'The Person of the House.' " *Disability Studies Quarterly* 29.3 (2009). www.dsq-sds.org/article/view/933/1109. Accessed 5 Nov. 2009.

Shields, Juliet. "The Races of Women: Gender, Hybridity, and National Identity in Dinah Craik's *Olive*." *Studies in the Novel* 39.3 (Fall 2007): 284–300.

Showalter, Elaine. "Dinah Mulock Craik and the Tactics of Sentiment: A Case Study in Victorian Female Authorship." *Feminist Studies* 2.2–3 (1975): 5–23.

———. "Syphilis, Sexuality, and the Fiction of the Fin de Siècle." In *Sex, Politics, and Science in the Nineteenth-Century Novel*, ed. Ruth Bernard Yeazell, 88–115. Baltimore: Johns Hopkins University Press, 1985.

Shuttleworth, Sally. "'Done because we are too menny': Little Father Time and Child Suicide in Late-Victorian Culture." In *Thomas Hardy: Texts and Contexts*, ed. Phillip Mallett, 133–55. Basingstoke: Palgrave Macmillan, 2002.

Silver, Carole G. *Strange and Secret Peoples: Fairies and Victorian Consciousness.* New York: Oxford University Press, 1999.

Small, Helen. *The Long Life.* Oxford: Oxford University Press, 2007.

Sonheim, Amy L. "The Unbearable Lightness of Childhood: George MacDonald Takes Seriously *The Light Princess*." Paper presented at the annual meeting of the Nineteenth Century Studies Association, Augusta, GA, 12 Mar. 2005.

Squillace, Robert. *Modernism, Modernity, and Arnold Bennett.* Cranbury, NJ: Associated University Presses, 1997.

Stableford, Brian M. "*Vice Versa*." In *Yesterday's Bestsellers: A Journey through Literary History*, 67–74. 1998. N.p.: Wildside, 2006.

Steedman, Carolyn. *Strange Dislocations: Childhood and the Idea of Human Interiority, 1780–1930.* Cambridge, MA: Harvard University Press, 1995.

Steiner, John. "Revenge and Resentment in the 'Oedipus Situation.'" *International Journal of Psycho-Analysis* 77.3 (1996): 433–43.

Stockton, Kathryn Bond. "Growing Sideways, or Versions of the Queer Child: The Ghost, the Homosexual, the Freudian, the Innocent, and the Interval of Animal." In *Curiouser: On the Queerness of Children*, ed. Steven Bruhm and Natasha Hurley, 277–315. Minneapolis: University of Minnesota Press, 2004.

Studlar, Gaylyn. *In the Realm of Pleasure: Von Sternberg, Dietrich, and the Masochistic Aesthetic.* 1988. New York: Columbia University Press, 1993.

Taylor, Jenny Bourne. "Between Atavism and Altruism: The Child on the Threshold in Victorian Psychology and Edwardian Children's Fiction." In *Children in Culture: Approaches to Childhood*, ed. Karín Lesnik-Oberstein, 89–121. Houndmills, Basingstoke: Palgrave, 1998.

Thwaite, Ann. *Waiting for the Party: The Life of Frances Hodgson Burnett, 1849–1924.* 1974. Boston: Godine, 1991.

Titus, Mary. "Cather's Creative Women and DuMaurier's Cozy Men: *The Song of the Lark* and *Trilby*." *Modern Language Studies* 24.2 (Spring 1994): 27–37.

Tosh, John. *Manliness and Masculinities in Nineteenth-Century Britain: Essays on Gender, Family and Empire.* Harlow, UK: Pearson, 2005.

———. *A Man's Place: Masculinity and the Middle-Class Home in Victorian England.* New Haven, CT: Yale University Press, 1999.

Tucker, Nicholas. "*Vice Versa*: The First Subversive Novel for Children." *Children's Literature in Education* 18.3 (1987): 139–47.

Welsh, Alexander. *Dickens Redressed: The Art of "Bleak House" and "Hard Times."* New Haven: Yale University Press, 2000.

Wolff, Larry. "'The Boys are Pickpockets, and the Girl is a Prostitute': Gender and Juvenile Criminality in Early Victorian England from *Oliver Twist* to *London Labour*." *New Literary History* 27.2 (Spring 1996): 227–49.

Wood, Naomi J. "Gold Standards and Silver Subversions: *Treasure Island* and the Romance of Money." *Children's Literature* 26 (1998): 61–85.

Woodward, Kathleen. "Instant Repulsion: Decrepitude, the Mirror Stage, and the Literary Imagination." *Kenyon Review* 5.4 (1983): 43–66.

Index